# 41 D
## Man of Valor

# 41 D
# Man of Valor

*The Story of SWAT Officer Randy Simmons*

## Lisa Simmons

iUniverse, Inc.
Bloomington

41 D — Man of Valor
The Story of SWAT Officer Randy Simmons

Copyright © 2012 Lisa Simmons

All rights reserved. No part of this book may be used or reproduced by any means, graphic, electronic, or mechanical, including photocopying, recording, taping or by any information storage retrieval system without the written permission of the publisher except in the case of brief quotations embodied in critical articles and reviews.

"I have tried to recreate events, locales and conversations from my memories of them. In order to maintain their anonymity in some instances I have changed the names of individuals and places, I may have changed some identifying characteristics and details such as physical properties, occupations and places of residence."

iUniverse books may be ordered through booksellers or by contacting:

iUniverse
1663 Liberty Drive
Bloomington, IN 47403
www.iuniverse.com
1-800-Authors (1-800-288-4677)

Because of the dynamic nature of the Internet, any Web addresses or links contained in this book may have changed since publication and may no longer be valid. The views expressed in this work are solely those of the author and do not necessarily reflect the views of the publisher, and the publisher hereby disclaims any responsibility for them.

Certain images purchased from The Associated Press.

ISBN: 9781-4759-3705-3 (sc)
ISBN: 978-1-4759-3706-0 (hc)
ISBN: 978-1-4759-3707-7 (e)

Library of Congress Control Number: 2012912197

Printed in the United States of America

iUniverse rev. date: 7/20/2012

To my beloved children, Matthew Excel Simmons and Gabrielle Randi Simmons, who both paid the ultimate sacrifice when they lost their dearly loved father in the line of duty. Matthew and Gabrielle, you have been through the fire and the storm, yet you have come through with more courage and grace than anyone could have thought possible. Your strength and faithfulness to God inspires me, and I am so proud to call myself your mother. I want to thank you both for being my greatest encouragement, strength, and support—and to thank you for your unconditional love. You are my greatest joy, and my love for you is endless!

"Okay, boys and girls, we're going to learn a new scripture verse. Are you ready?" Randy asked.

*Let your light so shine before men, that they may see your good works, and glorify your Father which is in heaven.*
—Matthew 5:16

To all the Glory Kids:

For every child who sat on the tarp and listened to Randy as he preached the word of God and mentored you, remember Randy's smile, remember his laugh, remember his teachings and scripture verses, and don't ever forget to pray. Always remember how much he loved you and wanted the best for you. But most of all, remember what he would say to you over and over again: "Jesus loves you more than you could ever imagine."

Go out in the world and show God's glory! And sometimes, when you think of Randy, look to the heavens and shout, *"Glory Kids are in the house!"*

# Contents

Acknowledgments . . . . . . . . . . . . . . . . . . . . . . xi
Introduction . . . . . . . . . . . . . . . . . . . . . . . . . . xv
Prologue . . . . . . . . . . . . . . . . . . . . . . . . . . . . xxi
1. Saying Good-Bye to New York . . . . . . . . . . . . 1
2. Welcome to California . . . . . . . . . . . . . . . . . . 9
3. From Fairfax to Washington State . . . . . . . . . 14
4. Far from Home . . . . . . . . . . . . . . . . . . . . . . 24
5. An Unexpected Journey . . . . . . . . . . . . . . . . 35
6. A Badge for Officer Simmons . . . . . . . . . . . . 41
7. SWAT . . . . . . . . . . . . . . . . . . . . . . . . . . . . . 46
8. T.G.I. Friday's . . . . . . . . . . . . . . . . . . . . . . . 50
9. Dating "Baby Girl" . . . . . . . . . . . . . . . . . . . . 56
10. Tying the Knot . . . . . . . . . . . . . . . . . . . . . . 67
11. And the Two Shall Become One . . . . . . . . . . 75
12. Family + SWAT + Church = A Busy Lifestyle . . . 89
13. The Balancing Act . . . . . . . . . . . . . . . . . . . . 98
14. Committing to a Vigorous and Rigorous Life . . . 111
15. Call to Duty . . . . . . . . . . . . . . . . . . . . . . . . 118
16. Church, Family, and Glory Kids . . . . . . . . . . 127
17. Sacrifices . . . . . . . . . . . . . . . . . . . . . . . . . . 137
18. Time Is a Silent Thief . . . . . . . . . . . . . . . . . 149
19. Welby Way . . . . . . . . . . . . . . . . . . . . . . . . 163
20. Press B, Please . . . . . . . . . . . . . . . . . . . . . . 168

| | | |
|---|---|---|
| 21. | Breaking News | 176 |
| 22. | Planning the Funeral | 185 |
| 23. | The Outpouring of Love | 202 |
| 24. | 41D—End of Watch | 216 |
| 25. | The Aftermath | 233 |
| 26. | The Unsubstantiated Investigation | 247 |
| 27. | Mixed Emotions | 259 |
| 28. | A Twist in the Maze | 272 |
| 29. | Honors and Dedications | 284 |
| 30. | My New Normal | 291 |
| 31. | Grace for a New Season | 300 |
| | Epilogue | 313 |

# Acknowledgments

As I started to write these acknowledgments, I realized that few words can genuinely express my gratitude, my appreciation, and my love for all those who have been with me on this special journey. I thank you all from the bottom of my heart.

Everyone knows that nothing of great importance is ever achieved without the love and support of family, friends, and special people who cross our paths, and I have been so blessed with countless individuals who have supported me through the entire process of writing this important book. I want every one of you to know how I feel.

To William: I want to first thank God for bringing you into my life during my darkest hour. I thank Him for loving me so much that He gave me a companion so that I wouldn't have to continue on this journey alone. I also want to extend a special thank-you for your love, patience, strength, support, and most of all for showing me that love can truly develop out of a great friendship. God has given you a special gift of compassion and a powerful sense of self-confidence that makes your eyes and heart see beyond what most people see. I thank you for walking beside me, for lifting me up and understanding my need to write this book. You are a beautiful person with a big heart. Our life together is a living testimony and inspiration to anyone who may have experienced a great loss, as I want them to see exactly how God's blessings are endless. With love and admiration.

To my wonderful mother, Veronica: I especially want to thank you for the countless times you have supported me in all my endeavors, even the crazy ones. You always believed in me and in my dreams. You are my greatest inspiration and my forever cheerleader. I am so blessed to have you as my mother. I love you dearly.

To my sisters, Sharon "Cookie" and Melinda "Packa": I thank you both for encouraging me repeatedly to *write a book!* Most of all, I thank you for believing that Randy's life is an inspiring story that should be told to the world. Your support shows how much you love both him and me. I also thank you for the numerous hours you spent reading and critiquing my writing. You are both amazing, and I love you.

To my brother-in-law Wilfred: I thank you for loving Randy so much and for demonstrating it through your creative talent of photography. You will forever be connected to him in a brotherly way.

To Officer James Hart, Officer Floyd Curry, Officer Steve Scallon, retired Officer Todd Rheingold, and all the officers of the Los Angeles Police Department: I thank you for your love and support as well as the sacrifices you have made to keep our streets safe on a daily basis. You are all mighty men and women of valor.

To Charlene Rashkow, Barry Cooper, and Cynthia Manker: I thank each of you for believing in my ability to write Randy's life story. You have encouraged me to bring to life the essence of an extraordinary man. I appreciate your talent and knowledge in the fascinating creative field of writing.

To photographer Glenn Grossman: Thank you for always being there to capture memories for surviving families to cherish forever.

To website designer Chalise "Lisa" Greene: I am so impressed by your awesome talent, and I thank you for pulling it together as you always do. You are truly a gifted individual.

To my office staff members - Tina, Geri, Samira and Deonna : Thank you for your leadership, loyalty, love and continuous support.

To The Randal D. Simmons Outreach Foundation board members:

Active: William L. Jones, Jr., Sharon Sumlin, Wilfred Sumlin, Amia Sumlin, Melinda Harleaux, Alberta Brinson-Moore, Dayna Dorris,

Richard Cornell, Simone Clinton, Hasani Lefall, Ralph Mansion, Shaune Lacy-Ortiz, and Yolanda Womack

Honorary: Matthew Simmons, Gabrielle Simmons, Gina Davis, Veronica L. Hunter, Harold Jackson, Dwayne Harleaux, Denise Beaudoin, James Hart, Suzette Gauthier, Floyd Curry, Jessica Meraz, Christopher Meraz, and Dominic Sumlin

Mere words cannot express how thankful I am to have you as my board members. Your faithfulness and dedication to the countless hours you spend volunteering your time and mentoring children in the inner city speaks volumes to the world. Your efforts and selfless support exemplifies your labor of love. May the blessing of God be upon your lives always.

## Introduction

When telling a story, it's usually more effective to wait until the end before revealing the outcome. Unfortunately, everyone already knows how this story ends. But the outcome isn't the end of the story; it's merely the beginning of an even deeper and more profound episode of one man's extraordinary life.

That life belonged to my husband, Randy Simmons. You may or may not have heard about Randy, but he proudly served for twenty-seven years in an admirable career with the Los Angeles Police Department. Without question, he was blessed with many important things in his life, including a devoted wife, two beautiful children, family, tons of friends, and a career that he loved. Sadly, he was gunned down at the hands of a mentally deranged man while attempting to rescue victims in an eleven-hour hostage standoff.

On a fateful night four years ago, a dark cloud fell upon our home, bringing with it a tragic storm, a storm so intense that it would unquestionably test my faith. Randy, my devoted husband of seventeen years, was killed while on duty as a special weapons and tactics team (SWAT) officer. He and his partner, Johnny Verman, were both shot in the face and immediately taken to Northridge Hospital, where Randy was pronounced dead at 12:55 the next morning. Johnny survived the shooting but was critically injured, both emotionally and physically. The tragedy not only shattered my home, but it also left the entire police force distraught and devastated over the loss of their fallen brother.

In the blink of an eye, the remarkable man that I adored was gone, and I was left to somehow pick up the pieces and try to carry on. It was truly a tragedy and a devastating experience, especially because Randy was so loved. But there is far more to this story than just the sadness of Randy's death; there is the joy of a legacy left by a magnificent human being. In many ways, although he is not here in the flesh, he lives on: through his children, through his work, through his faith, through his service, and through the many people whose lives he touched. While Randy's life took many twists and turns, it was a life well lived.

Despite my attempts at resolving the pain and conflict of losing someone so dear to me, I am still working through an enduring journey that I could never have foreseen. As a result, I have experienced many unusual things since his death. I am still attempting to understand many things surrounding his death and have only just begun the process of accepting what happened.

There were events I experienced before, during, and after Randy's death that I now believe were messages the Holy Spirit sent to me. As a Christian, I totally and wholeheartedly trust in God and in His word, but unfortunately, like so many Christians, I failed to hear God's voice. A revelation regarding these events came to me much later.

One of those messages occurred in my life through a letter my great-aunt Juanita wrote me. Included with the letter was a beautiful string of rosary beads in a small rosary purse; inside the purse she had placed a prayer for me to read. The prayer was partly taken from a scripture in the book of Numbers, and even after many years, I can hold the rosary beads and read the prayer in silence, yet I still hear Aunt Juanita's voice saying the prayer aloud, resonating deeply within my mind:

> *Lisa, may the Lord bless you and keep you.*
>
> *May the Lord make his face to shine upon you and be gracious unto you.*
>
> *May the Lord give you His peace in your going out and in your coming in, in your lying down and in your rising up, in your labor and in your leisure, in your laughter and in your tears until that day when you come to stand before Jesus when there is no sunset and no dawning. Amen.*

The letter went on to read:

> *Lisa, may it bring you peace someday in your time of sorrow. My prayers are with you.*
>
> *Love, Aunt Juanita*

That letter was written prior to Randy's death and just before my aunt passed away, and today I can't help but wonder if something in her spirit told her I would one day face a life-altering tragedy. It's almost as if she knew I would need this lovely prayer for reassurance and comfort, for in fact, it happened that I definitely needed God to keep me, to be gracious to me, and to give me a peace and acceptance about things I couldn't understand, expect, or change.

Randy lost his life when he was only fifty-one years of age, but even at such a young age, he was a man of valor, one who worked hard all his life, providing well for his family and at the same time finding ways to help many others in need. What he did, he did well, for he believed that his role in life was to be of service.

Randy had been planning his retirement a short time before he died, as his hope was living out the rest of his life in service through community outreach, but he never got the chance to fulfill his dream. Some would say his life was cut short, and in truth it was, but from my vantage point, Randy had lived and contributed more to life in his fifty-one years than someone who might have lived well over one hundred years. He was a devoted husband, father, mentor, minister, football coach, and police officer. Not only was he loved and respected by all, and vice versa, but he also loved everything he did with a passion.

Randy's death did not go unnoticed. It made headline news and was covered by several media stations nationally and internationally. And in recognition of his standing in life and his achievements as a loved and respected officer, over ten thousand people from all over the country and even the world attended his funeral, including high-ranking dignitaries. It was one of the most unprecedented funerals in Los Angeles history.

After we laid him to rest, the honors continued, and dozens of well-respected organizations presented us with acknowledgments. Recognition for his heroism and humanitarian efforts was also demonstrated at many different memorials. In addition, the members of the Los Angeles Police Department showed their support and love for Randy through their numerous dedications and memorial ceremonies. As a family, my children and I went from memorial to memorial, accompanied by SWAT team members as we attended events on a weekly basis, all to receive awards for Randy's life of service.

Attending the countless events became a full-time job, and my schedule was overwhelming. I wanted to be present at all the events, and I did so with pride and gratitude, but one thing stayed at the forefront of my mind, and I couldn't shake it. No matter how busy I was, how active my days were, one thing consumed me. I was baffled by the tactical procedures that were deployed during the hostage rescue operation. And although I tried desperately and delicately to obtain answers about the planning, preparation, policy, and tactics of that fateful night that made Randy the first LAPD SWAT officer killed in the line of duty, my inquisition was in vain. I couldn't get anyone to give me a detailed written report of the incident. As a result, I relied heavily on sympathetic officers who were so kind to give me their version of what happened. Unfortunately, there were too many different and conflicting stories surrounding the incident, which left me even more perplexed about my husband's death.

I sensed that my pursuit for obtaining information was viewed by some as being accusatory; however, that was never the case. Being a SWAT officer's wife for seventeen years and hearing almost all of Randy's successful SWAT stories simply led me to want a more definitive explanation. I needed to understand what happened, mostly so that I could have closure. Regrettably, after requesting permission several times to attend the formal investigations and debriefing hearing, I was denied attendance at the hearings due to policy and procedure. I didn't understand or agree with this decision. I felt that if the suspect had lived, the case would have gone to trial, and I would have been able to hear all the facts surrounding the case. Ultimately, internal procedures took precedence over a widow's request to receive detailed information about the death of her husband.

I want to emphasize that my disappointment in the investigation has absolutely no reflection on the tremendous support that my family and I have received from the Los Angeles Police Department. They were extremely compassionate toward my children and me during such a difficult time. Their support and protection surpassed anything I could have ever imagined. I believe it would have exceeded Randy's expectations as well.

After several years passed, my obsession with obtaining much-needed information settled down to a whisper. I reached a point where I had to take solace in knowing that Randy, being a man of valor, wouldn't have hesitated to put himself in harm's way to save the life of another human being. I also did not want my dissatisfaction at being left out of the investigation process to affect the great and enduring relationship I had developed with so many of the officers, sergeants, lieutenants, captains, and the chief. It was simply time for me to move on and start a new life without Randy.

Thus my children and I began to find a new "normal" one, with the memory of Randy etched in our hearts forever. We realized that the best way to honor Randy's memory was to continue trusting God, moving forward, and living a life that would have made him proud. I knew without any doubt that it was what Randy would have wanted for us, so I tried with every fiber of my being to put it behind me.

It is from that place that I write this story. Based on my persistent efforts to survive this horrendous ordeal, I believe the story needs to be told, as all too often when people pass on, we forget about the amazing things they brought to life. I don't ever want anyone to forget Randy.

I also want to share this story because one day when my children, and hopefully my grandchildren, are older, they will want to know more about their father and grandfather, about all the details about his life. The multifaceted aspects of Randy's life, his experiences from childhood, his trials and tribulations, and his ability to use his faith to achieve victory over every situation, even up to the moment of his premature death, all add to the quality of his life and to this story. The pages that follow are about this unique, humble, and beautiful man, a man who lived his life with such commitment, dignity, and grace that it made us all extremely proud.

As you read the pages of this book, my wish for you is that you find comfort in knowing Randy, for he cared deeply about people and about life. As an extraordinary human being, he used himself fully every day to better humankind. I hope you can draw inspiration from this special person who left a huge legacy to his wife, to his children, to his community and to the world. Ultimately, my hope is that as you get to know Randy, he will serve as a catalyst to open your heart, your mind, and your eyes to your own God-given abilities.

## *Prologue*

"Lisa, Lisa wake up!" William's voice is shouting at me.

I hear his words calling me as I awaken from a troubled sleep. His hands are shaking me abruptly, and his voice is forceful yet tender as he speaks in my ear. It was my panicked state of hyperventilating and the intense sweating and moaning that prompted him to awaken me. Hearing me cry in my sleep once again was painful to William, and he wanted to comfort me somehow. I sat up in bed as he rubbed my back and neck, gently attempting to hold me down, saying repeatedly, "It's okay … It's okay, Lisa." With a concerned voice, he turns and asks me as he has so many times in the past, "Are you having another one of those dreams?"

"More like a nightmare," I say reluctantly.

I actually don't even want to respond to his question because I am frustrated and embarrassed by my subconscious behavior. I am also concerned that William will finally start to think I'm going crazy, since the dreams are becoming more frequent and increasingly real.

As I look up at William and see the expression of worry on his face, I feel such a deep sense of love for him, as he is without a doubt the most compassionate man in the world—truly heaven sent as far as I'm concerned. My heart goes out to him for his sweet concern, especially since I realize that not too many men would put up with or endure the aftermath of my previous life. Yet William's faith, confidence, and maturity have enabled him not only to walk this walk with me but also to support me through a storm that is taking longer to pass than I thought.

Taking on the therapist role, William tries in vain to help me analyze my dream. "You want to talk about it?" he asks me compassionately.

In my frustration, I begin to share the dream that I've had many times. I tell him as sweetly as I can, "William, my dream always has the same concept, but the scenes are different. It's as if Randy has been away for a while, but now he is returning from some unknown place and is lost in time."

"Is he happy, sad, or what?" William asks with curiosity.

"He's more confused than anything," I reply. "He never speaks in words, but I get the distinct feeling that he's trying to ask me what happened or why it happened. As always, the dream ends with intense emotion, and I feel myself expressing my thoughts to Randy about how sorry I am about what happened to him."

I know that William can see the stress on my face and the bewilderment that haunts my conscious mind. "Lisa, you know it's okay to go talk to someone. A therapist might be able to help clarify the dreams you're having."

"I'm not crazy, William," I say in an agitated voice.

"No, no, no … At least I hope you're not," he jokes, trying to lighten the mood.

We both laugh, and William continues lovingly. "I'm not saying you're crazy, but you, Matt, and Gabby have been through so much. It's okay to talk out your feelings and to examine what you're experiencing. It might help."

"I'll think on it," I respond, grabbing the covers and throwing them back over my body.

William lies down next to me, giving me a big hug and kissing my forehead. He assures me that everything is going to be okay and tells me that whatever I am experiencing is normal. As I lay there in my bed, looking up at the ceiling, I think about our conversation. I can't help but wonder whether these dreams are normal, but regardless, I do know that after I wake from them, I am left with a heartache that words cannot describe. These dreams take me to places that are painful, yet I am forced to experience them.

The hardest part about the aftermath of the dreams is that they make me wonder again about what happened on that dreadful night when Randy was killed—and why it happened. Sometimes in my mind, I reenact the events, trying to piece together what could have possibly taken place on Welby Way. Again giving some thought and attention to what actually transpired, I clearly see the SWAT team entering the house, hear the shots being fired by the deranged Edwin Rivera, and Randy going down—with Johnny Verman shot right after him. I visualize Randy in the ambulance while paramedics work so hard to save his life. Mostly I think about what his spirit might have been thinking as he fought for his life. I cannot help but wonder what his last thoughts might have been as he transitioned into heaven.

Knowing him as well as I do, I envision him having an out-of-body experience and saying to himself, "Please don't let me die, because my wife is going to kill me!" That's exactly the type of humor and sarcasm Randy displayed. His next words would have been, "Please, God, Matthew and Gabrielle, my babies, still need me. But if it be Thy will God, I'm ready."

I begin to think again about when the bizarre dreams started. I can't put my finger on exactly when or why I began having them, but I can tell you that the first time I dreamed about Randy was the most amazing experience I'd ever had. In that first dream, two men were escorting me into our downstairs bedroom just to see Randy. (We called our bedroom the "prayer room," a room Randy and I had converted into a study when we purchased our home. We called it that because Randy spent so much time studying the word of God and praying in that room.) I saw Randy in a long white gown trimmed in gold. There was a belt tied around his waist, and it looked like a pure gold rope. His hair was white as snow and styled in rolls almost like President George Washington's, but he looked young, vibrant, and peaceful. Opened before him was a book that appeared to be the Bible. The room was dark, but a light totally illuminated him.

The vision was startling to me and upon seeing him, my legs went weak and I fell to the floor on my knees. Looking up at him in total shock, I was mystified by his presence, but I was not afraid. I knew that in my natural state of being, I would have run to him and hugged him, but something in my spirit told me to respect his space and not touch him. In that precious moment, we just stared at each other in silence.

When I awoke from that first dream, my eyes were bugging out of my head and my breathing was labored. I slowly pulled the covers back up my body, clenching them to my chest. I lay back down in my bed and remained motionless. Never in all my life had I ever experienced such a spiritual dream. I felt that God had shown me that Randy had arrived at his new home … in heaven.

And now, four years later, I'm sad to say that my dreams are no longer beautiful and spiritual but heartrending, crazy, and confusing. I am beginning to consider taking William's advice by seeing a shrink, one who can help me analyze my dreams and assist me in uncovering or maybe discovering what could possibly be causing me to continue having these crazy dreams.

I'm not against therapy, especially for others, as I know it helps, but I must admit that I don't feel I need therapy. I have always been in control of my emotions and thoughts, so I rationalize. I think to myself that maybe this is a process of grieving and the dreams will eventually stop. But every month, sometimes twice a month, I have the same type of sad dream, along with an anxiety attack. As I did earlier, I often find myself awakening from these dreams breathing hard, sweating profusely, and pleading for God to help me.

I think back to when my father died, after being married to my mother for thirty-three years, and I remember my grandmother telling my mother, "You can't live with the dead. You must go on." I feel as if I have heeded my grandmother's advice and taken several steps in an attempt to continue my journey through life.

I should interject here that it's not as if I walk around in my conscious state consumed by the tragedy. I actually appear fine to everyone, and I sense that I'm okay. Naturally, I have my moments, like anyone who's suffered a great loss, but I have tried and succeeded at many levels to move on with my life.

Therefore, I have to ask myself why I am still having these crazy dreams. Are they trying to show me something … or perhaps trying to tell me something? Could it be that I haven't truly accepted Randy's sudden death? Am I still plagued by what happened? Maybe it's that I still have so many unanswered questions, like *Why Randy? Why, at the pinnacle of his life, did this happen?*

I don't think even Sigmund Freud would have been equipped to answer these questions, and based on my strong Christian faith, I realize that only God knows the answer. Someday, if He sees fit, perhaps He'll share it with me. But for now, I have to keep telling myself to trust my faith and to remember that Randy is in God's hands. I have to consider that while I may have had other plans, God had something else in mind for Randy.

Perhaps Randy fulfilled his role and his life of service. Perhaps I have something important to learn because of this experience and one day it will be revealed. In either case, as I take you on this adventure and share the details about this wonderful man and the contribution he made to life, I pray for guidance, acceptance, and peace of mind. Most of all, I pray that I remain grateful and aware of the time we spent together and for the life we shared in Christ.

# CHAPTER 1

# Saying Good-Bye to New York

Walking out onto the streets in Brooklyn, New York, the smell of warm baking bread coming from one of the nearby pizzerias was wafting through the air, while at the other end of the block lots of activity was going on. However, the congregant members of the Deliverance Evangelistic Center, Pentecostal Church, were oblivious to the aromas and busy streets that defined the district, as they were all more concerned about what was going on in their own lives and in their church.

Outside the church on the hot, humid day in August of 1970, several men were strutting about in their Sunday best, shaking hands with the reverend and others who were attending church. The men looked fancy in their three-piece suits with matching ties. Some even added character to their apparel by wearing shiny Stacy Adam shoes and Stetson top hats adorned with feathers placed aptly on the side. The women were also a sight to see as they paraded around in their finest apparel, complete with beautiful big hats and pointy three-inch heels, accessorized with matching purses. Those who were really into fashion and style topped off their smart-looking outfits with summery white gloves and wore strong flowery perfume. Looking fastidious yet lovely in their finery, they greeted each other with high-pitched voices, giving out hugs and kisses to friends as their children yelled, played, and ran in between them while holding tightly to their Sunday school projects.

The congregant members appeared to be happy and inspired by

the sermon of the day. However, fourteen-year-old Randy Simmons felt quite the opposite; He felt that life was crashing down on him. An unexpected and unwanted turn of events was about to happen, and Randy was struggling with emotion that could not be voiced.

Standing in the doorway of the church, Randy sadly watched his parents, Dallas and Constance Simmons, as they stood on the steps of the church, kissing congregants as they said their final good-byes. They were leaving Brooklyn and their friends behind because of a calling on Dallas's life, leading him to the West Coast, where he planned to attend Fuller Seminary College in Pasadena, California.

Randy's religious father, Matthew Dallas Simmons, known to friends and congregants as Dallas, stood tall, slender, and handsome. As he was an African American man with a very light complexion, some questioned his nationality. His straight black hair and high cheekbones reflected his Indian heritage, completing his sharp, keen features. He was a good-looking man with the qualities of a striking movie star.

Randy's mother, Constance Simmons, known as Connie, was also attractive. She was a dark-complexioned African American woman of average height and size. She took great pride in her appearance and looked sophisticated all the time, with a style that was nothing short of elegant.

It was an exciting time for Dallas, as he was optimistic about receiving a master's degree in divinity and one day being the pastor of his own church. Reverend Skinner, an older African American man and pastor to Dallas, proudly gave Dallas his blessing. Ultimately, Reverend Skinner would be the catalyst that connected Dallas to some very prominent men of the cloth in California.

As Dallas said his good-byes to Reverend Skinner, he took him aside and carefully chose his words. "I want to thank you for your teachings," he said. "I truly appreciate you and will never forget all that you have done for me and my family."

Reverend Skinner responded by saying, "We'll be praying for you, Connie, and the kids, and if there is anything you need from us, please don't hesitate to call." He extended his hand and then gave Dallas a big hug.

Randy with Mother and Father.

Dallas and Connie Simmons in the early years.

Young Randy, the skinny little child of Dallas and Connie, had other plans and dreams, so he was not enthused about the move to California. Quite frankly, he was furious. The thought of being pulled away from his friends was too much for him to bear, but he was a humble and obedient young man, so he said nothing. Generally quiet around people he didn't know, Randy only let his hair down when he was with his friends, and only then would he allow himself to be loud and crazy. Most people characterized him as a good kid who was respectful of others and didn't like trouble. He was a good boy across the board.

As Randy walked back and sat inside on the pew of the now-emptied church, he looked around at the familiar view, tears filling his eyes and streaming down his face. He felt hopeless and started praying, asking God for help. He had often heard the adult members of the church praying, screaming, and shouting for a blessing from above. Maybe, just maybe, if he did the same, the Holy Ghost would miraculously change his father's heart and mind about this move to California.

Exiting the church, Randy's heart was broken because he knew that his world was going to change forever. As far as Randy was concerned, his father's timing couldn't be worse, as things were starting to look up for Randy. Recently, he and his friends had been on the practice field at Hofstra University Stadium and met the handsome and popular quarterback Joe Namath of the New York Jets. Realizing that the boys dreamed of one day playing football, Mr. Namath gave them some advice on working out and building muscles so that they could be strong enough to play one day.

"You boys do well in school," he said. "Eat right and exercise every day."

"We will, Mr. Namath," replied the boys enthusiastically.

As Joe Namath walked away tossing a football, Randy and his friends watched with awe.

As a group, Randy and his friends had been as close as the Rat Pack. They had been friends for quite a while, and they made a promise to each other that they would work out together and play football every day so that one day they would be drafted into the NFL. But now a drastic move to California was about to interrupt Randy's plans and his workout routine. His father was taking him thousands of miles away from his friends, and it would probably be years before he'd see them again.

Randy's mind was working overtime, trying hard to come up with all sorts of reasons to give his father about why they should not move to California. However, he dared not question his father about any decision, nor could he show any signs of displeasure or discord, since his father was as a strict disciplinarian. Consequently, any opposition might be misconstrued as disobedience. It was therefore in Randy's best interest not to speak about what he felt, but instead to keep his feelings to himself and simply go along with his father's wishes.

Perhaps Dallas's upbringing was responsible for his firm disposition. He was the youngest of eight children, and his mother died shortly after he was born, leaving him to be raised by his handsome playboy father, a man who had abandoned his family and spent most of his time in the streets chasing women.

Given that most of Dallas's siblings were older and already living on their own, only a few younger children were at home and in need of their father's attention. However, his lifestyle conflicted with his parenting role, and he refused to be weighed down with the responsibility of raising baby Dallas or the other young children. As a result, Dallas and his siblings were split up and sent to foster care, where Dallas spent his younger years being neglected and mistreated.

Dallas's older siblings tried earnestly to save their little brother by taking him out of foster care whenever their finances would permit, but shortly thereafter, when their money ran out, they would lose him back to the foster care system.

In contrast, Connie, Randy's mother, came from a much different childhood. As the youngest of nine children, Connie was from a humble upbringing, living in a religious house where prayer was as common as eating. Connie's mother, who was affectionately known as "Big Mama," courageously chose to leave Norfolk, Virginia, in her attempt to get away from an abusive and alcoholic husband. She secretly saved up enough money and toted her kids by train to New York. Big Mama was poor and at times struggled desperately to keep her family healthy and together, but her faith led her to persevere, no matter how difficult or how tough things became. Even through poverty, she managed, as a single parent, to raise her children in a happy and healthy environment.

Unfortunately, Dallas's lack of parental love and a difficult upbringing accounted for his inability to connect with Randy in the traditional ways that most dads connected with their sons. He had his own way of expressing love, and the interactive activities that he had with Randy normally stayed within the realm of religion. Consequently, there was never any real father-son activity outside of church and the Christian community outreach for the poor.

A father and son bond of tossing a football, fishing at a lake, or making a trip to a baseball game were activities that were far and few. In fact, Dallas would often interrupt Randy's activity time with church activity or prayer. He would often call Randy in from playing football with his friends to have prayer time with the family. Initially, Randy would be frustrated at his father's prayer request, but the moment he knelt down to pray, he would adjust his attitude and give reverence to God. For at a young age, Randy knew and understood that nothing, including football, superseded worshipping God.

Even though Randy thought his father's religious rituals were a little outlandish at times, he took it all in stride. He actually admired and respected many things about his father. He admired his compassion for the poor and his empathy for mankind, and after church services, he would sometimes accompany his father into poverty-stricken housing project sites in New York so Dallas could share the gospel. Randy would be there right beside him, handing out pamphlets to the homeless, the sick, the poor, and the brokenhearted, as well as those who lived in underserved areas. He would watch and listen to his father preach to them about salvation and the kingdom of God, and the sermons fascinated him. He was amazed by his father's knowledge and wisdom about the Bible. And even though this wasn't a traditional father and son outing, it was what his father knew Randy needed to hear, as the word of God would carry him through life. It was Dallas's own special and unique way of spending time with his son and expressing his love for him.

Connie, Randy's mother, was religious as well and lived her life as a faithful Christian woman, devoted wife, and loving mother. In fact, she was an anchor and pillar of strength for the entire family. Besides providing a sense of comfort to Randy and his two sisters, she was perceived as the endearing mommy, the one who often served as the buffer between her kids and her husband. She and Randy had a wonderful relationship, and Randy confided in her about everything. When he became a teenager, he used her as his sounding board to complain endlessly about his father's actions, behavior, and warped sense of thinking, which became more stringent over the years. In return, Connie listened with a compassionate heart and an open mind. She responded with words of encouragement, a biblical scripture, prayer, or the warmth of a hug. More often than not, she agreed with Randy's valid points, which made him feel better about the situation; however, she would never contradict her husband's actions or his way of handling things. Nevertheless, she did act on Randy's behalf every so often, bringing a petition to her husband to lessen a punishment or reverse a denied request.

Connie was totally committed to supporting her husband and his dreams, so she never wavered in her faithfulness or thought twice about going against decisions Dallas had made. Instead, she was always there by his side, ready to take on the consequences of his actions ... good, bad, or indifferent. She exemplified and defined what most would perceive as the good, faithful, and obedient wife. At times, and to her own detriment, she excused his wrongdoings and indiscretions by rationalizing his behavior.

She essentially had a hard time holding Dallas accountable for his actions because she loved him so much and because of his good looks and charisma. Dallas's behavior was easily forgiven. Through her forgiveness of his worldly ways, it was obvious that Connie worshipped the ground he walked on. And now she was taking her commitment to Dallas even further, as she was ready to support him 100 percent in his pursuit of becoming a reverend in California.

In the middle of August, the moving van arrived at the Simmons household. All their bags and belongings had been packed, and they said their good-byes to the Uniondale, Long Island, New York, address. They were as prepared as they could be for the far move, traveling from the East Coast to the West Coast.

Randy, the middle child, with about five-year age difference between each sister, traveled by plane with his younger sister, Gina, and his parents, while his older sister, Valjean, who was nineteen then, stayed behind in New York fulfilling employment obligations. Randy and his younger sister Gina, who was about nine years of age, sat together on the plane. They were excited about their first flight, which became even more exciting when they met the famous basketball star Wilt Chamberlain. Displaying feelings of excitement, they could barely sit still. To help pass the time, they played creative games that included analyzing clouds in the sky and relating their shapes to earthly objects. When Randy became bored with games, he spent a few hours sleeping, drawing, and thinking about football and his workout plan. He visualized his new school, wondering what life would be like in California.

As they flew farther away from New York, Randy began to feel the anticipation of his new life. In an attempt to feel better, he started rationalizing the move by thinking the transition would probably be easy for him since technically he was a true Californian. He would often brag to his New York buddies about how he was born in San Bernardino, California, when his father was in the military and stationed at Norton Air Force Base. But within minutes, he would quickly snap back to reality, faced with the fact that he knew nothing about California, since New York was really his home. It took approximately six and a half hours before their flight landed in California, and for most of the flight, Randy could not help but hope that leaving New York would ultimately be a decision his father would come to regret, and that they would be back to his real home within the year.

## CHAPTER 2

# Welcome to California

When Randy and his family arrived in California, they couldn't help but be impressed by the sunny weather, the gorgeous palm trees, the mountains that appeared to touch the sky, the beautiful beaches that outlined the city, and the beautiful girls the Beach Boys sang about. It wasn't too long before Randy's view about California started to change.

Randy's father and mother initially settled in a residence near Fuller Seminary College in Pasadena, California, mostly because it seemed more practical since Dallas would be attending college in Pasadena. Randy was enrolled in John Muir Junior High School, which was near the family home. Being a newcomer, Randy tried eagerly to make friends; however, a group of bullies greeted him every day, each one picking fights and stealing things from him regularly. The torturous behavior made him even more homesick for New York, and he was relentless in his complaints to his mother.

"Mommy, I hate it here!" he cried. "Someone stole my leather jacket! When are we going back to New York?"

"This is home now, Randy, but things will get better. I promise you." She hugged him. "Daddy and I are going to the school tomorrow to talk with the principal about those boys."

"I don't fit in here. I hate California! The kids here are mean. Can you just talk to Daddy about going back to New York? Please, Mommy," Randy begged.

Randy pleaded with his mom constantly, hoping she would ask his father to return home to New York, but it was too late for such a request. His parents had already settled in to new employment, with his father landing a job as a city bus driver for the Regional Transportation District, also known as RTD, and his mother finding employment doing accounting work for a retail store. Randy's hopes of returning to New York were getting slimmer as the days went by.

Since they were new to the California community, the Simmons family didn't have many acquaintances, but they did have a few connections that were associated with their church, thanks to their introduction by Reverend Skinner. The first family to welcome them into their new home was the wonderful Reverend Elliott Mason of Trinity Baptist Church in Los Angeles and his lovely wife, Geraldine. They kindly shared many different tidbits about California and familiarized them with the sights and scenery that surrounded them. Best of all, the Masons had four children who were relatively close in age to Randy and his sisters. Immediately, Randy felt a tremendous amount of respect for the Masons' sons, who were a few years older and already attended Fairfax High School on the Westside of Los Angeles, a good school known for teaching students of Hollywood celebrities. Not only was it ethnically diverse, but it was also situated in a good location. Randy would have loved to attend the school; however, he had one more year of junior high to complete before he could attend Fairfax High School.

Miraculously and quite unexpectedly, a pleasant change occurred. The Simmons family was moving again, but it wasn't back to New York; it was to the Westside of Los Angeles. Much to Randy's surprise, he was going to have the opportunity to try a new school. He was quickly transferred to Audubon Junior High School, where happily the school turned out to be a better environment and a much smoother transition for Randy. Not only did the kids at the school have more of an appreciation for newcomers, but they also made Randy feel welcome. He finished out the remainder of the school year at Audubon Junior High and began preparing for Fairfax High School.

After a partially tumultuous year in junior high, Randy was determined to have an awesome summer, and for him, living in California meant it was going to be the summer of physical transformation. He had already implemented a workout regimen that was going to prepare him physically and mentally for football. As far as he was concerned, nothing was going to stop him. He was also adamant about his family taking his program and his ambition to heart. So he sat his parents down and explained to them in as much detail as he could that although he tried to start his program in New York, no one took him seriously, especially his sisters. They would laugh at him as he struggled to walk around the house with ankle weights in an attempt to make his legs stronger. But the program was important to him, and he needed their support to make it work.

In his eagerness for everyone to be on his side this time around, he was going to make sure the entire family understood exactly what he was trying to accomplish. He was determined that it was no longer going to be just a young boy's fantasy or a joke to the family. This was the real deal. Thus he explained to them that in order to play football, a person's body must be bulked up so that it could take hard hits. He further explained that every muscle in his body needed to be strong, at which time he lifted his arms to show his parents his biceps.

He continued this lengthy conversation as he sat at the kitchen table while his mother was preparing dinner. Randy knew dinner was a good time to discuss the details of his program, especially since important foods played a major role in his success.

"I'm going to need to exercise my body nonstop," he said. "So, Mommy, I'm going to need you to cook things with lots of carbohydrates and protein."

"Carbohydrates and protein?" she replied.

"Yeah, foods like pasta and rice for my carbs and steaks and hamburgers for my protein," he responded.

His parents chuckled, as they knew that steak was a food meant only for the man of the house, but his parents could see how serious Randy was about his plan, and they wanted to help him achieve his goal. Much to Randy's delight, Dallas agreed to share his steaks, and collectively his parents and sisters promised to support his meal plan.

Randy spent the entire summer attending football practice at Fairfax High School, working out as much and as often as he could. He exercised his arms and stomach as well, doing leg reps along with football drills, plus he took long jogs to condition his body. He lifted weights with some of the other Fairfax football players in the gym, and they would spot each other while lifting heavy weights.

When Randy got home after a hard day of practice, his supportive mother would have dinner ready, with extra food for Randy. She also made sure that all the things she cooked were part of his meal plan. And to make sure he got all the nutrients he needed, Randy supplemented his meals with vitamins and lots of protein shakes. He was adamant about reaching his fitness goals, as he knew the program he'd adopted was finally going to allow him to play football for his high school.

On top of all the exercise and eating the best foods, Randy read as many fitness books as he could get his hands on, and soon he became a young health fanatic. Everything he did involved his effort of getting bigger and stronger and in shape. By the end of the summer, he'd reached his goal. Nothing could have made him happier than becoming well equipped to play football for Fairfax High School.

However, there was one more major transformation that needed to take place before school started. For this transformation, Randy would request the assistance of his younger sister, Gina, since he knew he needed an ally to attain their parents' permission. Both Gina and Randy often complained about the strict, conservative rules that were associated with their religious beliefs. In a hush-hush conversation, Randy and Gina agreed that somehow they needed to convince their parents that things were different in California. After all, the fashion style was a little more liberal, and rhythm and blues as well as rock and jazz were part of every teenager's life.

Randy wanted to be allowed to listen to secular music, and Gina wanted her parents to support her fashion sense by allowing her to wear pants instead of dresses to school every day. Together they approached their mother, since they needed her support first before they could ask their father. Pleading their case, they explained to her what they wanted as a way of fitting in, and quite surprisingly, she agreed. Even more shocking, once they presented their case to Dallas, unpredictably and quite astoundingly, he decided to be a little more flexible with the rules.

As you might imagine, Randy and Gina were terribly excited by this change of heart, as it was truly a great start to the newfound freedom they were experiencing in California. Randy, having an ear for music, found great joy in listening to all types of music, but he tended to gravitate more toward jazz while working out. Happily, Gina was finally able to toss some of her dresses and add some stylish pants to her wardrobe. To the kids in the Simmons household, California was definitely having a positive influence on their parents—and indeed, there was no doubt their father was changing in more ways than they could have ever imagined or expected.

## CHAPTER 3

# From Fairfax to Washington State

By his senior year at Fairfax High School, Randy had become known throughout the city as a great defensive back and running back, averaging 5.5 yards per carry. He received recognition as a Prep All-American and lettered in wrestling as well. With that kind of athletic talent, he was confident that he would receive a scholarship to college.

Tall, handsome, and statuesque, he could outlift most of the guys on the team, and although he was loud, crazy, and obnoxious among his peers, he always remained humble and respectful to his teachers and coaches. Because he was such a good athlete, his coaches loved him, but his teachers… well, they thought he was a typical jock doing just enough to remain on the football team. They would often tell him that he could be a better than average student if he just applied himself. But all effort went strictly toward football.

Randy was far from becoming the school's valedictorian, but he did his best and remained an average student. One day while at football practice, Coach Frank D'Allessandro, known as Coach D, yelled out to him, "Hey, Randy, I need to talk with you about your grades."

Randy hustled off the football field immediately to talk with him.

"Son, it looks like you're having a hard time with Hebrew."

"Yeah, Coach D," Randy replied, trying to catch his breath.

"Is there any reason that you're taking Hebrew?" asked the coach.

"Uh, yeah, a lot of my friends are Jewish. I just thought it would be cool to learn their culture and language."

"I see," Coach D said. "That's admirable, Randy, but if this grade doesn't come up by the next progress report, then I think you'll have to try Spanish. That language might work better for you. Remember, our goal is to keep your grades up so you can remain on the team, son."

"Okay, Coach," Randy said.

Randy was growing up. Not only was he maturing from a physical standpoint, but he was also growing as a young man. He was no longer that little boy from New York whose opinion didn't matter. In his maturity, he was also starting to turn away from some of his father's strict rules, which caused a lot of friction in the household. His father was firm with Randy about being home before nightfall mostly because he didn't want Randy to get caught up in the troubles that often occur among young men at night.

One night Randy missed curfew, arriving home a couple hours after dusk. As he entered the front door and greeted everyone, he started walking toward his bedroom. Dallas called out to him and asked him to come see him. Dallas was sitting in the den, looking at some bills on his desk. Keeping his eyes entirely off Randy and focusing solely on the bills, he said, "Randy, it's after nine. Where were you?"

"I was just lifting with some of the football players," Randy said.

"I want you in this house before dark, and this is the last time I'm going to tell you anything about your curfew," Dallas sternly replied, never looking up at Randy.

Randy didn't respond. He just looked over at his mother and sighed with his hands behind his father's back as if to say, *Come on now! Why is Dad being so unreasonable?*

Constance just shook her head and put her finger to her mouth as she silently mouthed, "Shush! Do not talk back." Constance didn't want Randy to get into trouble. But Randy was furious and went to his room.

Randy made it home by about eight o'clock the next night. It was a little after dusk, and Randy honestly thought that eight o'clock was an appropriate time to be home, especially for a high school senior.

Randy at Fairfax High School.

He ran into the house and greeted everyone again, not thinking his father was about to become extremely angry. After all, the spring season had just started, and the days were getting longer, so dusk came later. His father saw it differently. He saw it as a sign of disrespect and disobedience.

"Since you refuse to abide by my rules, I need you to pack your bags and get out!" Dallas said.

"What?" Randy exclaimed.

"You heard me. Get out!" Dallas shouted.

"But ... but ... Daddy, I—," Randy stuttered.

"I don't want to hear it! You like the streets—then you go live in the streets!" Dallas said firmly.

Randy, fed up with his father's strict rules, decided to call his bluff. He was sick of his finding fault with everything he did, so he wasn't going to try to reason with him or apologize. He felt as if his father had it in for him no matter what he did, so maybe he would be a lot happier living on the streets.

Constance pleaded and begged Dallas to give Randy another chance, but Randy was already in his room packing his clothes to leave.

Constance was upset as she approached Randy in his room. She began to cry as Randy kissed her on the cheek and told her not to worry. He then walked out of the house with a duffel bag over his shoulder and headed down the street. Although he put on a brave face, he was quite upset.

Constance rarely objected to any decisions that Dallas made when it came to disciplining the kids, and it was only on extraordinary occasions like this that she would step in and try to override Dallas's orders. She was caught in the middle of two stubborn men that she loved very much, but she didn't want her son to be thrown out of the house. She had to convince Dallas to let Randy stay. His sister cried hysterically as she watched from a window while her brother walked aimlessly down the street.

A few minutes later, Constance ran out of the house behind Randy, noticing him sitting at a bus stop a block away. She grabbed him and hugged him as he looked straight ahead, motionless, overcome with hurt and pain. She pleaded for him to return home, but Randy was upset and would not budge or talk. So Constance did the talking.

"Randy, Daddy said you could stay if you listen and follow the rules. Right after football practice, you must come home. If you want to stay out later, you must first come to us and ask," she said.

"But I'm not doing anything except hanging out with my friends. Nobody goes straight home from school! We're just hanging out having fun like normal teens." Randy was frustrated.

He then looked her in the eyes and continued to rant. "Why is he always on me? It's like … he looks for things to be mad at me about." Tears were falling down his cheeks. "Sometimes he acts like he hates me," Randy said with intense emotion.

"Randy, you know that's not true! Your father loves you very much, but you have to listen. I don't always agree with his decisions, but the Bible teaches us that obedience is better than sacrifice. When God sees your obedience, He will fight your battles for you. He will always work it out for you. You know that."

Holding his hand firmly, Constance went on to say, "All through life, you're going to have to follow rules. You might not like some of them … but rules are there for a reason. They are not meant to be broken, for when they are, there are consequences to pay, and they're usually not good. What your father is trying to instill in you and show you is that that there are penalties for not following rules."

Picking up his duffel bag and putting it over her shoulder, she explained compassionately, "Being obedient is what's going to keep you out of trouble. Your father is just afraid you're going to get in some kind of trouble. He saw many horrible things living in the streets when he was a foster child, so he, better than most, knows how rough the streets can be. He doesn't want anything bad to ever happen to you." She then touched Randy's shoulder right there at the bus stop and started to pray in a soft whisper. Eventually, she convinced him to come home. After all, he didn't have anywhere else to go.

Ironically, one month later, Randy was walking home from school in time to make his curfew when a police car drove by. The officers stopped and asked him to come to the car. Once he walked over to them, they asked him why he was in the neighborhood, at which time he politely told them that he was going home, and he pointed to where he lived, which happened to be right in front of where he was standing. The police officers pulled their patrol car over to the side of the road and got out of the car, walking Randy to the door. They wanted to verify that what Randy was saying was true. Randy wasn't afraid of what they were doing; he was more baffled.

Constance and Dallas answered the door and were shocked to see Randy standing there with the police officers. The officers were polite and informed Dallas and Constance that they were just making sure Randy was telling the truth about where he lived since there were a few incidents in the neighborhood and they wanted to use extra caution.

But Dallas was offended. "I assure you, my son is no criminal. He is a Christian boy who has never been in any kind of trouble," Dallas said in a perturbed tone.

"Can't you see that he's holding books in his hands?" Constance said emphatically. He goes to school and plays football for Fairfax High School. We are law-abiding citizens and Christians."

Dallas and Constance were upset, but Dallas could see why the police may have stopped Randy. In the 1970s, the Fairfax District was a Jewish community, and it wasn't very often that you saw a young buff black guy with a big Afro walking around the neighborhood. It confirmed and gave extra weight to Dallas's request for Randy to be home at a decent hour. This was a clear example of why Dallas didn't want Randy running the streets after dusk.

The police apologized after Randy's parents gave them a respectable sermon. They told Randy to do well in school and complimented and joked with him about his muscles, which helped ease the tension. When the police left, Randy's father had a talk with him about his huge Afro. He insisted that Randy clean up his appearance, starting immediately with a haircut.

After that incident, there were more quarrels over the length of Randy's hair. Big afros were in style, but his father wanted Randy to have a clean-cut look, so Dallas demanded that he keep his hair trim and neat at all times.

In his effort to stay in tune with the styles of the seventies, Randy refused to get a haircut. He let his Afro grow big, which made his father angry. He was not going to permit Randy to look like a thug. Dallas believed that a thuggish look always brought on negative attention and led one into trouble. He didn't want people to have the wrong impression of his son, and he surely didn't need the police knocking on his door again.

But no matter how many times he preached to Randy about getting a haircut, he wouldn't listen. Instead, to appease his father, he would cut off an inch of hair so Dallas would leave him alone.

Wanting to be in control, Dallas thought about how he could get his son to listen. Realizing the spanking method would no longer work, as Randy was too big for that type of punishment, plus he dared not try to go one-on-one with his hard-as-a-rock son, Dallas decided he had to make a point. Without even thinking twice about it, he resorted to harsh and unusual punishment by doing the unthinkable. Dallas picked up the phone and called Randy's football coach, Coach D'Allessandro, and told him that Randy could no longer participate in their football program. He literally took Randy off the football team.

As far as Randy was concerned, that was worse than any spanking he had received as a child. Randy couldn't believe his father would resort to such great lengths to punish him over a haircut.

Anger took on a new meaning for Randy, and he was convinced that his father was clinically crazy; he classified him as totally unreasonable. As usual, he complained to his mother about his father's bizarre behavior, and as always, she extended her hand in prayer. They prayed that his father would soften his heart and lift Randy's punishment. And once again, God heard their prayers.

After missing several practices and games, Randy got a haircut and was allowed to go back on the team. Because of that punishment, it was clear to Randy that his father's penalty definitely defined the consequences of his actions, in a manner Randy understood so convincingly that he would never forget. He knew his father was serious, and his rules were not intended to be broken. As a result, Randy tried his best to adhere to all his father's rules, at least during football season and until he went away to college. Randy knew another interruption like that could be detrimental to his football endeavor, possibly ruining his chances of receiving a football scholarship.

After football season, Randy focused more on keeping up with his grades. He then decided to take his coach's advice, dropping Hebrew and taking Spanish instead after receiving a D on the progress report. He continued to take all the subjects that were necessary for college admissions, for he was looking forward to attending college. He watched his father work hard to get his master's degree in divinity from Fuller Seminary College, and he thought that surely he could accomplish the same by playing football and getting a degree in criminal justice or sociology.

As far as Randy was concerned, graduation wasn't coming soon enough for him. Although, he'd enjoyed his school years at Fairfax High School, it was now time for him to move on. He had made many good friends, dated a few pretty girls, and learned from many great teachers and coaches, but now he wanted to take his football talent to the next level. His greatest concern was that he had missed so many opportunities to showcase his talent to scouts during his punishment phase that he wasn't sure someone from some college would notice his talent. He was praying that the effects of his punishment during his senior year had not screwed up his chances.

During the spring months of his senior year, Randy anxiously awaited to hear from colleges. Every day after school, he would rush home, hoping that something had arrived from one of the schools he had applied to, but nothing came. He had heard Coach D mention that a recruiter from Washington State was interested in him, but Randy hadn't received a scholarship letter.

As graduation drew nearer, Randy knew that other students were getting their acceptance letters from colleges all over the country. Now he began to worry because his phone was not ringing and the mailbox was empty.

Unfortunately and quite surprisingly, Randy did not get a scholarship during his freshman year; however, he did get accepted into Washington State in the autumn of 1974. Coach D knew Randy was disappointed that he had not gotten a scholarship, and he wanted to do everything possible to help him. Coach D believed in him, so he was instrumental in encouraging Washington State coaches to let Randy walk on and display his talent. He also helped Randy with the application process and provided him with all the information he needed so his family could apply for loans during his first semester.

But approaching his parents and telling them he didn't get a football scholarship was one of the hardest things Randy had to do. After all his hard work, he struggled with how to tell them the unfortunate news.

It was difficult, but he finally got up the nerve to tell them that he didn't get a scholarship. To ease the disappointment, he also told them that there was still hope. Apparently, the coaches at Washington State were still looking at him, but he would have to come as a walk-on and start on their junior varsity team. After that, he would have to earn his scholarship for the varsity team, which would take him through the remaining years in college.

He further explained that he would need their support financially, and that they would have to apply for a loan to pay for his freshman year in college. He truly thought it was going to be a big issue, as his parents didn't have the money or the means to support him. The last thing they needed was another bill to pay.

But much to Randy's surprise, Dallas and Constance didn't think twice about helping their son with college. In fact, they didn't hesitate to apply for the loan necessary to support their son in his endeavors to play football. Better than anyone, his parents recognized how hard Randy worked and what an unbelievable talent he possessed. They had seen him evolve into a great athlete over the years, so they agreed to the loan. As far as his parents were concerned, with continuous prayer, God was going to position Randy to reach his goals, and He would also help him earn a scholarship.

With an unrelenting and positive attitude, along with her optimistic approach about Randy's football future, Constance cooked one of Randy's favorite meals to celebrate his entrance into college: her signature enchiladas, a tossed salad, and Randy's favorite upside down pineapple cake. She knew he was terribly disappointed, so she wanted to encourage him in the best way she knew. She also wanted him to look forward to attending college, as she realized it would be a great experience. After all, football was only one activity, and she wanted him to appreciate the opportunity of being able to attend college.

Maintaining such a positive attitude got everyone excited and enthusiastic, plus it stirred up Randy's confidence level again. "I can't wait to get there and show them that I deserve to be on the varsity team," he said as he sat down at the kitchen table. "It's just a matter of time," he added with a bit of bravado.

"That's right, son. Get those papers to us and we'll complete the loan package," his father said, extending his hands to the family while blessing the table prior to eating.

After the blessing, there was lots of excitement among the family as they ate to their hearts' content. During dinner, Randy noticed his sister Gina looking a little perplexed as she pondered a serious thought.

"Excuse me ... Uh, Randy, where is Washington State?"

"It's in Pullman, Washington," Randy replied.

"Where's Pullman, Washington?" she asked, still looking rather bewildered.

"I'm not sure, but I know it's in Washington," Randy said, laughing and gobbling down his food.

It was a happy moment for the family as everyone laughed and enjoyed the celebration of Randy's acceptance into college. It was the beginning of a new chapter in his life—as well as in theirs.

# CHAPTER 4

# Far from Home

IN THE LATE SUMMER OF 1974, Randy's father took him to Washington State for the fall school semester. It took two days and two nights before Randy and his father arrived at Pullman, Washington, with Randy doing most of the driving. During the drive, his father talked to him about everything under the sun.

Randy didn't mind his long lectures, because he knew they involved things he needed to hear, all of which would help him with this new phase of his life and his new adult responsibilities. Unlike during his high school days, Randy had come to appreciate his father's wisdom and interest, as he now understood that Dallas was making sure Randy had what he needed spiritually. Randy was going to definitely need God's grace to help him prove that he could be on the varsity team while also getting acclimated to a newer, much smaller city such as Pullman, Washington.

Pullman, it turned out, was a beautiful, quaint, serene city filled with tall pine trees as far as the eye could see. The scent of pine overpowered the smell of the strong fertilizer that was used by most of the farmers. Unlike the smog that Randy had become accustomed to in Los Angeles, the air in Pullman was fresh and clean.

The majority of the city consisted of green plains and hills with farm animals grazing on the green grass. There was vegetation everywhere, with farmers working on their tractors as they tended to the crops. Farmland and barns separated every house.

The business district was just a few blocks long and mostly lined with old one-story buildings. As they drove through Pullman, trying to find the Washington State campus, Randy had a concerned look on his face. He was quiet and showed no sign of excitement. Pullman did not appear to be a city to him; rather, it felt like a little country bumpkin town that was in need of some activities. It was very different from Los Angeles, California.

"Are you sure we're in the right place?" Randy asked his father.

"Yes, son. I believe this is it," his father replied.

"Daddy, there's nothing here but land, cows, horses, barnyards, plains, and hills," he said in sheer frustration.

"That's good, son, that way there will be fewer distractions. This a good place to commune with God. Plus, you're here for education first and football second. Don't forget that," his father said with a stern voice.

Dallas's remarks sounded good in theory, but Randy was used to the social life that the big cities of New York and Los Angeles offered. He didn't know what to think about Washington. Never in his wildest dreams had he envisioned it being in the boonies.

For a moment, he contemplated asking his father if he could turn around and go back home with him. However, he knew this was potentially a free ticket for a college degree, a chance to play football, and ultimately a ticket to the NFL. Besides, quitting was not an option in the Simmons household. So Randy held on to the possibility that maybe there was another city nearby, with more buildings, cars, and people of diverse backgrounds.

As they drove onto the college campus, Randy was a little more relieved as he noticed hundreds of students walking around the campus. Some students were hauling luggage, and some were carrying books. They all appeared to be his age, and most had a hippy or disco type of style. Long hair, Afros, sideburns, bell-bottom pants, miniskirts, suede vests, psychedelic T-shirts, and moccasin shoes reflected the 1970s era.

There were also multilevel buildings throughout the campus and, more importantly, a football field. The college was notorious for being a veterinarian and agriculture school and seemed to be more of a city than the city itself. Randy decided immediately that he would give Washington State a chance before passing judgment.

With his father alongside him, Randy checked into the admissions office and received his freshman registration packet. As soon as that was completed, he and his father drove to an off-campus student housing site to find the apartment he would be sharing with an upperclassman during his freshman year. The apartment was less than a quarter of a mile from campus, a quick trip within walking distance. Randy was starting to get excited and nervous all at the same time.

When Randy and his father arrived at the apartment, they looked at each other simultaneously, and without words their expressions said, *This is it.* They got out of the car and walked up to the apartment door, turned the key, and slowly walked inside. They walked around the apartment, which was already furnished since his roommate had lived there for a few years and had decorated the apartment to his own liking. Randy located his bedroom and started unpacking his things with his father by his side.

"Daddy, I just want to thank you and Mommy for believing in me. Ahh-I know this loan is another bill for you, but I promise, when I make it to the NFL, I'm gonna take good care of you guys," Randy said with confidence and emotion.

"Well, let's just take care of first things first," his father replied. "Let's try and get you that scholarship so you can continue your education here; we'll worry about the NFL later."

After Randy was settled in his off-campus apartment, his father was ready to head home. "Well, I guess I'm not going to meet your roommate today. I have to get back home so I can work. You don't work and you don't eat," his father said loudly, patting Randy affectionately on the back as he recited his favorite cliché.

Together they walked out of the house and back to the car, his father's arm struggling to get around Randy's big shoulders in a sort of half hug. Before driving off, Dallas prayed with Randy, gave him a big hug, and then pulled away down the long dirt road. Randy stood there in the middle of the road and began to cry. Although he and his father had their differences, he loved his father and his family, and he knew he was going to miss their nearby support. Somehow his eagerness to leave his family quickly diminished as his father and the car vanished out of sight. It was his first day of college, and already Randy was homesick.

Randy walked back to his apartment, where his new roommate, Curtis, had just returned from grocery shopping. Curtis was African American, light brown–complexioned, of medium height, and sported a large Afro with long sideburns. At first glance, Randy was unsure about Curtis. He had a cool but weird demeanor and appeared to be older. He didn't even look at Randy when he walked into the room. To make matters worse, he walked over to turn on his stereo system and then sat in a low beanbag chair, closed his eyes, and started smoking a reefer, all the while blasting some traditional jazz.

Curtis then began a conversation that went something like this: "Hey, young brother, welcome to Wazzu," he said as he inhaled his joint.

"Thanks. I'm Randy." Randy extended his hand toward Curtis for a handshake as Curtis opened his eyes. He looked up at Randy, taking his hand to shake it.

"Damn, you're a big cat! How much iron you pumpin'?"

"I bench-press over four hundred and squat lift about four sixty-five," Randy replied.

"How tall are you and how much do you weigh?" Curtis asked.

Starting to get perturbed by his questioning and his smoking, Randy responded sharply, "What ... you writing a book?"

"Nah, man ... just askin'. Trying to get to know my new roommate, that's all. After all, we'll be living together at least for this year," Curtis said sarcastically.

"Five eleven, one eighty," Randy responded, turning his back and looking through some jazz albums that Curtis had in a crate.

"Hey, you want a hit? This is how the ball players do it on the first day," Curtis said.

"No, thanks. I'm cool. What position do you play?"

"Man, I used to play ball, but I don't play anymore. I'm on my way out of here. I'm a senior. You registered late for housing, which is how you got placed with me. Don't worry about it, though. I'mma take care of you."

Curtis got up and walked over to another crate full of albums. He put on a jazz album and asked Randy, "You like jazz?"

Randy, listening and grooving, to the sound replied, "Can't nobody blow like Coltrane!"

"Well, I'll be damned, Curtis said with a laugh. I have a connoisseur of music as my roommate! Give me five, bro."

They gave each other five, slapping each other's hand hard, and continued to listen to the sounds of jazz. They sat up all night long, eating beans and wieners that Curtis cooked and listening to different jazz albums, including John Coltrane, Billie Holiday, Charlie Bird, Sarah Vaughn, Dizzy Gillespie, Weather Report, Joe Sample, Nancy Wilson, and Miles Davis.

Curtis was impressed by Randy's appreciation and knowledge of jazz, and Randy, who'd initially thought Curtis was weird, was actually impressed with Curtis's unique and eccentric personality. In fact, Curtis was actually what some would consider ahead of his time. He was extremely intelligent, plus he was also philosophical, especially after smoking a joint. He was a deep thinker and loved to raise thought-provoking questions on issues involving politics, poverty, religion, and world issues. He was passionate and disciplined when it came to his studies, which ultimately became a behavior that Randy would come to emulate.

He and Randy became good friends with a mutual respect for one another. Curtis respected Randy as a student, a football player, roommate, and a jazz lover, while Randy respected Curtis as an ambitious student. He made Randy's freshman year away from home … home.

Randy adjusted well to Washington State, going to his classes and football practice while meeting new friends. He also found his way around the city thanks to Curtis, who had an old Cadillac that he let Randy borrow from time to time. Slowly but surely, Randy got used to the slow pace of Pullman, Washington, and gained an appreciation for a peaceful and serene environment.

And Randy did just as he promised his parents. He continued to work hard on the JV football team, which earned him a starting position as a defensive back. He did so well his freshman year that the coaches made him part of the varsity program and also gave him a scholarship. By sophomore year, he was placed on the varsity team, but he had to redshirt so he could develop his skills and extend his eligibility.

That was a hard pill for Randy to swallow, especially since he'd been a star player at Fairfax High School. However, there were no other options. Randy was just happy that he had finally made the team and was excited about his free ride to college. For him, this was a step closer to the NFL. When he informed his parents of the news, they were elated and showed their support by attending the games and cheering on Randy and the Cougars.

By sophomore year, Curtis had graduated, and Randy was now living in the dorms with most of the other football players. He had pretty much adjusted to Washington State, and he enjoyed staying on campus and hanging out with his football friends. He met some great Washington State football players, namely Dexter Tisby, Eason Ramson, Donald McCall, Cedric Watkins, Mike Washington, Wardell David, Mel Sanders, Jack Thompson, Mike Levenseller, Basil Kimbrew, Dean Pedigo, Ray Williams, Mike Wilson, Greg Hicks, Mark Hicks, Gavin Hedrick, Don Schwartz, Ken Greene, Rufus Cunningham, Greg Sykes, and Ray Kimball, to mention a few.

He was officially part of the Washington State Cougars football program. Things were really starting to change. During Randy's freshman year, he had been running home to Los Angeles every chance he could, catching rides during any and all school breaks to get out of Pullman, Washington, especially when it was cold, overcast, and snowing. In his first year, he longed for sunny California, his family, and the renowned Gold's Gym, which was always known as the most famous gym in Muscle Beach, located in Venice, California. However, sophomore year was different. He had somewhat adjusted to the four seasons and the slower, peaceful lifestyle that Pullman offered. Although Pullman was different, it turned out to be a fun and good change. Besides, Los Angeles wasn't as much fun as it once had been.

During Randy's sophomore year, his family moved to a suburban city thirty miles east of Los Angeles: Diamond Bar, California. It seemed to Randy that the move put some distance and strain on his parents' relationship because it appeared that they weren't as close as they had once been. They now spent more time fighting than praying, and the tension in the house was so thick that you could cut it with a knife. In addition, being home was sometimes boring, as Diamond Bar was in some ways similar to Washington State. It was a lovely city, with green hills and farm animals grazing on the green grass, but it did not offer much in the way of activity unless you drove to Los Angeles.

Many of Randy's Fairfax buddies were either away at college, married, or in the military. So the several days of driving in the snow from Pullman to Los Angeles became less appealing as time went on.

By his junior year, Randy and all the other Washington State athletes had become popular. Randy was an awesome football player, playing as their cornerback and recognized for tackling and for hard hits. But his rough tackles and hard falls put his college football career in jeopardy, especially because he had a knee injury that required constant attention.

Randy had become popular for other reasons as well. His years of working out had paid off, and he was so muscular that he would put any bodybuilder to shame. Everywhere he went, young men looked at him in awe and young women stared and flirted. He was not only muscular but also handsome and far from conceited. He was known on campus as being an extremely humble and nice guy. He was nice to all people and never missed an opportunity to speak to anyone, including the nerds, who would often break their necks to get close to this gentle giant. They were amazed that Randy would take the time to talk and joke around with them. They couldn't believe how humorous, kind, and thoughtful he was.

Besides classes, his life at Washington State consisted of workouts, football, and pretty women, who were always at his disposal. It was the late seventies, and R & B artists were at their peak. The incredible Stevie Wonder had defined a look that some of the black males on the football team were trying to imitate. Stevie Wonder's famous cornrows depicted his African heritage and were beautifully displayed on his *Talking Book* album.

It didn't take much effort for Randy to get lady friends to stop by the dorm to braid his hair. No longer having to adhere to his father's strict rules, he developed a unique style and look all his own. He alternated between braided cornrows and a huge Afro with a part on the side. His look would frighten any mother and would cause any father to pull out a Smith & Wesson .38 to protect his daughter. Nonetheless, the female students admired his look and found him to be very funny and handsome. He was the life of any party and often found himself in trouble for partying too much.

Randy played defensive back at Washington State, #17.
He enjoyed attending college there and being a cougar.

When it came to parties, Randy and his football buddies didn't hesitate to throw one, especially during off-season. Some of his wildest and craziest football teammates were from Oakland, Compton, and Los Angeles, and they all lived to party. Adjusting to the quiet and serene life of Pullman, they either found a party to attend or threw a party themselves just so they could liven up the place. His friends had a lot of street experience, something Randy didn't get under the watchful eye of his father, and at times, their wild and crazy ideas and pranks got them into trouble.

At age twenty-one, Randy was legally an adult. He was a good guy with a level head, and he was never influenced by peer pressure, not as a kid and not now. He'd never gotten into any trouble in the past, primarily because he feared the wrath of his father. Besides, his parents had taught him right from wrong through parental discipline and biblical teachings. Now he was responsible for his own actions. Consequently, any little illegal prank could be considered a misdemeanor offense and possibly a felony.

Boys being boys, one boring college weekend, Randy and his buddies decided to throw the party of the century. Everybody who was anybody was going to be there. They invited friends from as far away as Seattle, Washington, even inviting their football and basketball rivals, which happened to be the University of Washington Huskies. Additionally, they had some friends driving up from Los Angeles and Oakland. To top off the party, there were going to be beautiful girls coming from all parts of town. This was going to be a party that put Washington State on the map. But just as they were getting ready for the party scene, there was a loud bang on the door.

"Cougs, we got a problem," one of the teammates exclaimed.

Randy and the others listened with concern.

"My stereo system blew out. Nothing's working … and there's no sound coming from my speakers."

"You've got to be kidding!" one of the guys shouted.

"The party is in less than five hours!" Randy yelled.

"Man, what are we going to do?" one of the other teammates asked.

"I know that across campus in the music room is a loud sound system, and it could blow the roof off any apartment building," one of the guys said.

He had the outrageous idea of borrowing it for the night. Randy and the others, facing a desperate situation and dilemma, hesitated, as they knew it was wrong to take it. But because they were in a pinch, they all came to terms with the insane idea, rationalizing their decision, and together they agreed that borrowing was not stealing.

The plan was to use the sound system for the party and then return it the next day. Unfortunately, things did not go as planned. One of the teammates decided he was going to enjoy the stereo system a little longer since it sounded so good. Thus the borrowing went from one day to several days, until the police came to retrieve it, also arresting everyone who gave the party.

"Jesus, please," Randy uttered as he sat in a holding cell in jail trying to make a deal with Jesus. "If you deliver me from this, I promise I'll go to church every day and do things right!" he cried.

Randy was sick to his stomach. He had never been anywhere near a jail, let alone in one. He kept thinking about how disappointed his parents would be if they saw him in this situation. He shivered at the thought of what his coaches would say and do and wondered how many years he would spend in prison for this crime. His main concern was whether he would still be able to play football when he got out of jail.

He was angry with himself for agreeing with such a boneheaded decision. Nothing was worth this humiliating disgrace, not even the party of the century. If only he could wind back the hands of time. He prayed again that God would have mercy and lighten the consequences of his action.

A few hours later, God answered Randy's prayers. He had mercy on all of them, but there was still a consequence. The coaches had come to an agreement with the authorities on their punishment and decided that Randy and his teammates would have to spend every weekend in jail for a month. They were only allowed to attend football practice on the weekend.

The coaches, knowing how their parents would feel if they found out, were kind enough not to notify them. They felt that being in jail was a harsh enough punishment. Randy was embarrassed and ashamed of what he had done, and he kept the horrible experience a secret.

After Randy served his weekend jail time with his friends, he became more focused on his life, reevaluating his friendships. He started narrowing in on his dream and realized it was crunch time, which meant foolishness had no place in his life. The National Football League draft was happening soon, and he was not going to miss out on a once-in-a-lifetime opportunity just to have fun. He continued to work out and practice hard, and any free time he had was spent working out or dating.

In the spring of 1979, Randy graduated from Washington State with a degree in sociology. The draft came and went, but Randy's name was never called. Some attributed it to his knee injury, but Randy was humble enough to accept the fact that maybe he needed to kick it up a notch in terms of his performance.

He was not discouraged, for he had learned that the Seattle Seahawks and Dallas Cowboys expressed an interest in him. The Dallas Cowboys were popular, well recognized, and highly respected by the league, and he was soon invited to the Cowboys training camp in Thousand Oaks, California, to display his skills. He decided to walk on to their training camp as a free agent. But after weeks of training and endless drills, Randy's hard work and effort just weren't enough to earn him a position with the team. His dream of playing for the Dallas Cowboys was over.

## CHAPTER 5

# An Unexpected Journey

NATURALLY, RANDY WAS DEVASTATED WHEN he didn't make the team, especially since football meant everything to him. It was what he longed for since he was a little boy way back in New York. With this turn of events, Randy was consumed with what he was going to do next.

Wondering if it was his performance as a football athlete or the fact that he was considered a liability because of his injury, Randy couldn't help but wonder if this outcome might have been any different if he walked on with the Seahawks as a free agent. He even thought about his buddies in New York and wondered how their lives were going. What outcomes did they have all these years later? Even though he wondered, he realized that knowing what they were doing really didn't matter anymore.

Sad, disgusted, and frustrated, he packed his bags and headed home to Diamond Bar, where his family welcomed him home with open arms. Together they prayed and encouraged him with words of comfort. Randy, being a realist, knew that his chances of having a career in the NFL were slim to nothing, and things started looking particularly bleak. That's when he began to believe that maybe God had other plans for him and his life. He had no idea what those plans were, but he was on a mission to find out.

Being faithful to God, Randy prayed fervently, asking God for guidance. As He had in the past and in His time, God gradually began opening doors and showing Randy his future.

His next step was working as a substitute teacher at Los Altos High school in Hacienda Heights, California. He loved children, so teaching came naturally to him. However, it was only a part-time position, and he needed full-time employment and the income to match. On top of the money issue, there was another concern at hand: the high school's female students found themselves more interested in Randy then in their schoolbooks, as Randy's rugged good looks just continued to progress with age.

Without question, he defined good looks and a healthy body. At five feet eleven, with a handsome, brown smooth face coupled with sharp, keen features, the two-hundred-pound Randy was all muscle. He also had a chiseled six-pack, huge biceps, muscular thighs, and a high, firm butt. Men envied him, and the ladies adored him, with girls literally drooling at the mere sight of him. However, Randy didn't let his physical features dictate his character and personality. Instead, his spirit remained as humble as ever.

To Randy's way of thinking, he wasn't staying fit to seek the attention of others. He truly loved staying healthy, as it was a way of life for him. Nonetheless, a twenty-three-year-old handsome young man with a beautiful body only worked as a disadvantage in a high school filled with hormonally charged teenage girls. Randy used his sprinting talents and ran out of there as quickly as possible.

Besides the female problem, Randy had another issue that concerned him, as things were starting to bother him at home. He loved his family very much, but he missed the good old days of Washington State, where he had his space, privacy, and total independence. He didn't like depending on his parents for money, and the truth of the matter was that they had little to give him financially.

Randy had no choice but to find a good-paying full-time job with benefits. He knew he had to hit the pavement every day and seriously look for work, which in and of itself became a full-time job.

Consequently, Randy spent a great deal of time driving back to LA since Diamond Bar was so boring. There was simply no meaningful activity for young people. And with all his friends and acquaintances practically living at the gym in LA, Randy realized he felt best when lifting weights with the guys, who shared the same passion for fitness, plus he enjoyed all the parties and the beautiful women Los Angeles had to offer. It was obvious why Randy made Venice Beach and Gold's Gym his second home.

Randy wanted desperately to get back to the city life, so he spent a great deal of time pondering what it would take to return to Los Angeles. Marriage was definitely not an option, especially since he wasn't ready for the ball and chain. He had received several open invitations to live with different women friends; however, his Christian faith ruled out cohabitating with the opposite sex.

He desperately needed a job and money. Little did Randy know that God would arrange it so that a parking ticket and an unknown stranger would be the gatekeeper and the moving force that would lead him to a lifelong commitment of service.

Angry at having received a parking ticket, Randy headed to downtown Los Angeles to pay the ticket. He knew that the money he was going to spend paying a parking ticket could have been better spent on paying another bill; nevertheless, it was either paying the ticket with accumulated penalties and late fees or an unwanted warrant for his arrest. Based on his unpleasant jail experience in Pullman, Washington, he opted to pay the ticket.

On the way to the building to pay the ticket, Randy ran into a man who asked, "Sir, are you a police officer?"

Randy chuckled. "No, not all," he replied.

"As big as you are, you sure look like one. You should consider it," the man said.

Randy pondered the thought as he walked up and down the streets of downtown Los Angeles. He considered that becoming a police officer might be a good move. After all, he had majored in sociology with a minor in criminal justice. In addition, he'd always had an interest in doing social work in some form. As the thought went through his mind, he started talking to himself aloud, and a bunch of rambling thoughts came pouring out of his mouth: "Yeah ... I could ... No way ... Why not? You idiot, did you forget about that criminal activity at Washington State? Do you even know if you have a record? What do I have to lose? I've already faced the worst, since nothing could be as bad as getting cut from the NFL."

Randy walked back toward the LAPD Parker Center to apply for a job as a police officer. As he walked into the center, he was instructed to enter the recruiting office, where he met with a recruiting officer and was told to complete an application. While Randy filled out the application, he disclosed everything about his experience to the officer, including his lack of experience and his inappropriate behavior in Pullman, Washington. Again God's grace emerged and shined on Randy, for the recruiter ran his record and cleared him. Much to his surprise, Randy was in fact eligible to move forward with the process of becoming a Los Angeles police officer.

He exited the recruiting center with a feeling of exhilaration. Immediately, he envisioned himself as a police officer, and it filled him with great anticipation and exhilaration. The recruiter had shared with Randy all the different positions that he could eventually go into, including detective work, surveillance, undercover work with the CRASH unit, the Bomb Squad, the K-9 unit, and SWAT. He then added an extracurricular activity that he knew would sell Randy on being a police officer.

Once hearing about Randy's background in football, the recruiter shared with him the details about the awesome talent of the LAPD's football team, the Centurions. That was music to Randy's ears and the icing on the cake. For Randy, it meant having an opportunity to have a full-time job and also play football. No, it wasn't the NFL, but it was gainful employment, complete with a good salary and benefits. Finally, it seemed to Randy that things were turning around for him.

Randy drove home filled with excitement and thanking God for both forgiving him and for giving him another chance. He thanked Him for not casting him out of His good graces, for he knew he had strayed away from the things of God many times. He wouldn't have blamed God if he hadn't placed favor over his life, but as always, God was merciful, for He always extends His love by giving us unmerited favor.

When Randy arrived home, he was excited to tell his parents about the good news. And they were happy for him, except that the countenance on their faces said something different. It appeared that something was going on between his parents, and it made him uncomfortable; therefore, his good news was overshadowed by what looked to be earth-shattering.

Randy was perplexed by his parents' behavior, as they were sad, distant, and disconnected from each other.

"What's going on between you two?" Randy stated. "I sense that something's wrong."

Being gone all the time and inundated with his own problems, Randy hadn't noticed that his parents were having serious problems and drifting further apart. Baffled by their odd behavior, he demanded to know what was happening to his family.

Constance was the first to respond to Randy's insistence for some answers. The pain on her face was obvious as she divulged the news to Randy. "Randy, your father is leaving me for another woman."

Randy couldn't believe his ears. This man, the one who adamantly preached to him against sinful things and condemned lustful and adulterous behavior, was leaving his mother for another woman! Randy could hardly believe what he was hearing. "What?" he said in disbelief with his mouth opened wide, sensing it was true.

His heart was broken. He loved his parents and didn't want to see them split up. He certainly couldn't accept his father's defiant behavior. And he couldn't understand. As a family, they had always relied on prayer as their main source of healing and resolving family issues. He couldn't understand why his father was suddenly ignoring this method of healing. He thought that surely God could heal their marriage, but there was only one heart willing to work with God, and that was his mother's.

Randy thought that not only was his father losing his mind, but he also could possibly be losing his salvation. All Randy could think about was that Dallas had to do something to pull himself out of this insane fantasy, and he had to do it quickly.

Randy was extremely concerned about his mother, as the news of his father leaving had obviously left her devastated. It was as if her entire life had been stripped away, for it was all she knew. She had married Dallas when she was twenty years of age, and he was the only man she ever loved as well as the only one she knew intimately. Randy's father was everything to her, and she would have followed him to the ends of the earth. Unfortunately, the feeling was no longer mutual, and Dallas was making his exit.

Randy was furious with Dallas's selfish and self-centered ways. He always respected and tried to obey his father, but his irrational behavior was in need of some tough love. The man who had preached to them about salvation was now showing behavior that was contradictory to all the principals he ever taught, causing the family pain, anguish, fear, and frustration.

"You're not going anywhere!" he shouted in a serious act of violence toward his father, who was behind the closed bedroom door. Delirious with fear and anger, Randy busted down his parents' bedroom door, attempting to talk some sense into his father while he was packing his things to leave. Looking his father straight in the eye, he shouted, "You can't do this, Daddy! You have always taught us right from wrong, and this is wrong."

And although Randy used every intimidating feature to convince his father to stay, it was to no avail. His father wanted out. He wanted a divorce, and Connie had no choice but to grant him his wish. Sorrowfully, his leaving was the beginning of a twenty-five year estrangement between Randy's father and the family he once loved, a family who thought they knew the man that was the head of their house.

The next few years were filled with both tears of happiness and tears of pain. The family tried desperately to get Randy's father to return home, but the harder they tried, the more he sought to remove himself from their lives. Dallas had mentally cut his family out of his life. Eventually, there was no form of communication. No phone calls, no meetings, and no further discussions.

Randy's mom felt completely alone, whereas Randy felt angry and deceived. Dallas managed to justify his own hypocritical, wayward, eccentric behavior. He defied all the principals that he'd spent years indoctrinating in them. It was as if he simply gave himself a pass. In his rage and disappointment, Randy surmised that his father's gibberish preaching and praying was a facade. He classified his father as someone in desperate need of spiritual guidance and help.

# CHAPTER 6

# A Badge for Officer Simmons

Although the family was going through a difficult time, Randy moved on with his life, officially joining the Los Angeles Police Department on January 26, 1981, and proudly carrying identification number 22885 and badge number 8579.

Graduating from the police academy was one of the happiest days of his life yet also one of the most disappointing. Every member of his family was present to congratulate him in this great endeavor and to cheer him on, except for his father—the man who was partially responsible for raising such a fine, disciplined, humble, and obedient officer. His absence was like a knife in Randy's heart. He wanted his father to be present for the important day ... to witness his great accomplishment of becoming an LAPD officer.

Dallas's cold behavior and lack of support felt strange to Randy. His family didn't seem complete without his father, and it felt almost as if a death had occurred in the family. In spite of his father's stern manner, Randy still loved him, and he knew—or thought he knew—that his father loved him too.

Randy felt as if his father had literally peeled away from his family like a jet fighter leaving his unit to fend for themselves. It was becoming clear to Randy that contrary to what he and his family wanted to believe, his father's fantasy had become a reality. He was truly missing in action, and he wasn't coming back to the fold any time soon.

Randy was now the man of the family, a title that Randy detested and felt forced into. He didn't want to step into his father's shoes, and he certainly didn't want to take on a responsibility that his father selfishly relinquished. He was still trying to find his place in life, and he wasn't mentally prepared for this monumental role.

Nonetheless, the pressure was on. Randy was trying to become a top police officer while at the same time helping his mother adjust to a life she couldn't and didn't want to accept. He was so grateful that his younger sister, Gina, lived with his mother, as she was a steady support.

In between learning his police duties and working out, he tried to get to Diamond Bar to take care of family matters. And despite Constance's plea for him to remain in Diamond Bar, Randy refused. Since he was happy with his new career and his life in LA, he did not want to make Diamond Bar his home. He wanted to remove himself from the sad memories and emotional trauma his father had bestowed on his family. Besides, Diamond Bar was too far of a commute for Randy's job and his social life.

Randy and a recruit classmate named James Craig from Detroit, Michigan, rented an apartment together in LA. To Randy, this was the life! They worked hard and balanced it by partying at popular dance clubs. Initially, Randy worked patrol, and soon after, he got to work undercover in the Community Resources Against Street Hoodlums, better known as the CRASH unit.

Working CRASH in South Central Los Angeles was exciting, but working undercover as a street solicitor for dope and prostitution was risky. The details that surrounded these assignments often saddened Randy, as the street life was cruel, dangerous, and ruthless.

At times, it was like a war zone, and unfortunately, innocent neighborhood residents were caught in the middle of the madness simply because of where they lived. Randy often felt conflicted, especially when his job called for him to arrest a street hooker and she begged Randy to forgive her line of work. "It's the only means I have of putting food on the table for my children," one of them said to Randy. "Please don't arrest me; it will only make my life harder."

Randy was serious about police work, but he knew how to balance it with that million dollar smile he gave to people in the community.

Randy understood that some of the prostitute criminals were victims of a generation's curse or circumstances. He knew that some of these women didn't have many options for a better life based on their environments and upbringing. Because of his compassionate nature, he would often find himself counseling these girls while taking them to the station to be booked.

In his effort to help them, he would share the details about lawful employment opportunities and tell them about resource centers where they could get the help they needed. But Randy knew their chances of recovery were slim.

What Randy came to understand was that the majority of young prostitutes had pimps they feared, who also kept them in bondage, both physically and mentally. Only the strong could walk away from the street life, and if it happened occasionally, it was usually with the help of some spiritual intervention.

The CRASH unit kept Randy busy and often working overtime. It also put him in the hospital more than a few times. During one particular incident, a pimp shot him while he was soliciting a well-known prostitute called "Pus Face," a name she adopted because of her severe acne. While working undercover, Randy solicited Pus Face for services, and she agreed, asking him to meet her around the corner to assure her that no one was watching. Little did Randy suspect it was a setup, as her pimp was stashed around the corner, prepared to ambush Randy.

The pimp had seen Randy work the area and had gotten wind that he was an undercover cop who had arrested some of his other girls. Naturally, this infuriated the pimp because Randy was affecting his cash flow.

Just as Randy drove around the corner, he noticed that Pus Face was still walking the streets, and he could tell that she was apprehensive about getting into the car. Randy thought her nervousness was because of her suspicion about his being a cop, so he got out of his car to pursue her again. Just as Randy started to go after her, she started running away, and in a flash, her pimp revealed himself from a hidden location, immediately opening fire on Randy. Randy returned fire and ran to his Chevy Camaro, yelling for backup. He used his car door as a shield to protect himself from the flying bullets, and fortunately for Randy, the caper was not fatal. He was only shot in the ankle, and luckily the suspect was arrested and sentenced to life for attempting to kill a peace officer.

On another occasion, Randy was seriously injured when he was chasing down a dope dealer in the projects after a drug transaction took place. As Randy pursued the suspect, he attempted to jump a fence but barbed wire was caught in his mouth and knocked out almost all his teeth. He claimed that his injuries from that incident caused the most excruciating pain he had ever experienced in his life. His lips were severely severed, and his mouth was bloody and busted up.

Randy had to undergo several orthodontic surgeries for his mouth, and he had to get a whole new set of teeth as well. His mother always jokingly expressed how painful it was for her to see all her hard-earned money that went toward years of braces for Randy end up down the drain.

Nonetheless, he recovered both times and eagerly went back to work the streets of Los Angeles.

# CHAPTER 7

# SWAT

Randy used CRASH as a stepping-stone to a more specialized unit, one he had researched as soon as he came on board with LAPD. He had his eyes set on LAPD'S elite Special Weapons and Tactics team, also known as SWAT. It was a future goal he wanted to achieve, so he spent time preparing for SWAT long before applying, by first working in other units. Being a perfectionist by nature, he made sure that he worked hard, stayed in shape, and did things according to LAPD standards, which would assure that his job performance and conduct were exemplary.

He admired the guys on SWAT and was impressed with the tactics and details that this specialized unit performed. At the time, in the entire history of SWAT, only a few African American SWAT officers preceded him. Randy did everything in his power to make sure he would become added to that list of African American SWAT officers, based solely on performance and ability. His chances at making SWAT were good. In addition to his extraordinary performance as an officer, he had a good relationship with the father and founder of SWAT, Chief Darryl Gates. Chief Gates loved Randy. In fact, he made several visits to him while he was in the hospital recovering from the on-duty injuries he sustained while working the CRASH unit. Chief Gates saw Randy as a true cop, one who would do just about anything to take down violent street criminals.

Chief Gates not only admired Randy's courage but also his talents as a football player, so he was always present at the LAPD Centurion's football games. He knew most of the players by name, particularly those who had a major influence on a game's win.

After intensive training at SWAT School, on July 31, 1988, Randy qualified and was selected to become a member of the elite Special Weapons and Tactics team. He was ecstatic! He had accomplished a goal that he'd set for himself, and now he was a part of a highly trained specialized unit that many officers respected and admired.

To Randy, becoming a SWAT member was the most important decision of his life, even greater than his dream of becoming a professional football player, which he'd already put behind him. He welcomed the drastic change that was about to take place in his life and accepted that his social calendar, which was once set in stone, would no longer exist.

Life as Randy knew it was radically changing. There would be no such thing as a planned schedule unless he was on vacation, and even that possibility was questionable. A pager would dictate his schedule and the outcome of each day of his life.

In between intense training days, debriefs, warrants, court appearances, and unexpected call-ups such as emergency deployments to criminal activity, the unit did crime suppression in the streets of Los Angeles. Most of the seasoned SWAT officers shied away from crime suppression details, as they felt it was a duty more suitable for the younger and newer SWAT officers. They felt that they had already paid their dues beating the streets and preferred dealing with more intense criminal activity that required specialized tactics.

Randy, however, liked working crime suppression. It gave him the opportunity to put a dent in crime and to build relationships within the community. It also afforded him the opportunity to talk to young people about staying away from criminal activity, so he viewed it as a win-win prospect.

Never having any grievances about deployment assignments, Randy worked long hours and put in a lot of overtime, which wasn't optional, as overtime was usually a court subpoena, an extension of some unexpected call-up, or a deployment that Randy would be assigned. He took pride in his position as a SWAT officer, doing everything that was required of him. Thus his social life was not what it once was, as he was just too busy with work. Regardless of the change, he learned to conform and adjust to the life of a SWAT officer.

Randy with SWAT Gear on.

Randy during training at shooting range.

Only on rare occasions would Randy try to slip in a little social time with his fellow officers. Many of those were his classmates who had been promoted and moved up the ranks and were now supervisors or in highly skilled and specialized units. The only interdepartmental activity that Randy participated in outside of SWAT was the LAPD Centurion football team, and even that was getting close to ending. His age was catching up with him, and he couldn't afford a serious injury being on the SWAT Team. The hits of the younger officers seemed to be getting harder and harder as he got older and older.

## CHAPTER 8

# T.G.I. Friday's

JUST AS RANDY SETTLED INTO being a SWAT team member, his roommate and best friend, James Craig, decided to move in with his longtime girlfriend. Although the two buddies would no longer be roommates, they would remain the best of friends, still partying together whenever their schedules would permit. But after James left, it was hard for Randy to find another good roommate. He tested the waters with a few other guys, but things just didn't work out. Randy began to realize that it was time for him to step out on his own.

It wasn't long before he purchased a condominium unit in a gated community called the Cameo Woods, a complex situated at the intersection of Los Angeles and Culver City, California. Randy's condo was a cozy one-bedroom that was just big enough for him. Randy kept it immaculate. He liked nice things, and he was good at decorating and coordinating colors. Having an eye for detail, he decorated his condo with a selection of vibrant earth-toned colors. He completed the look with wall-to-wall ivory carpet and a beautiful white-and-brown tiger print rug that accented and covered a large area of the carpet. He also incorporated a cream-colored sofa and caramel-colored marble furniture.

The paintings on the walls reflected the things he loved, such as animals and jazz musicians. In addition, tall green plants stood at every corner of the condo, contrasting the earthy colors and bringing life to the white walls. Included in the mix was one photo of his little nephew he adored, David Roseberry, which sat on his television. He also had a high-tech stereo system that could blow out the entire condominium complex, which he often cranked up while playing jazz. Essentially, he was living the life of any young bachelor's dream.

However, being a thirty-three-year-old bachelor was a life that Randy was growing tired of, as being single and having flings with different women was starting to get old. He found himself living a lifestyle that was completely different from the things he was taught and how he was raised. Randy's father had contradicted the things of God, but Randy himself did not want to continue living in a way that went against his beliefs. He had a reverence for marriage and still, regardless of his father's disappointing actions, believed in the family structure.

It was during this period of contemplation about his lifestyle that Randy and I met. I was several years younger, but many say I had a confidence and a maturity that didn't reveal our age difference. Randy saw me as an attractive, intelligent, funny, and confident young woman who had "potential." I guess I must have possessed some of those qualities in order for him to take an interest in me.

As the middle daughter of Veronica and Excel Hunter, I was the most conservative of my siblings, namely Sharon, known as Cookie, and Melinda, whom we called Packa. I may have been the more reserved one, but I had my crazy, sociable side and was considered rather popular in my day. All through school, I was involved in social clubs and was a cheerleader and a member of the first black sorority, Alpha Kappa Alpha Sorority, Incorporated.

As a family, we were close-knit and enjoyed friends and social gatherings held regularly at my parents' house. Everyone loved my mom and dad, as they were easygoing and caring people. As parents, they were different, with Mom being lenient and supportive of her girls and Dad being moderately indulgent yet overprotective and strict. He would do anything to guard his daughters, and he made sure that we all respected his wisdom and his words.

After graduating from UC Santa Barbara, I wasn't sure of my next move, so I returned home to Los Angeles and got a job working at a well-known insurance company. Although I was in my twenties, I lived at home, where my dad continued to run a tight ship. Although he was mild-mannered in many ways, he demanded that as his daughter, I respect the rules of the household, which meant I had to follow a curfew. And when it came to any male friends I brought home, it was essential that they conducted themselves with courtesy and respect toward my parents and toward me. My father insisted on protecting his girls from harm, and that included keeping away any man who wasn't up to his standards.

It was right around that time that Randy and I met at T.G.I. Friday's in Marina Del Rey. The evening we were introduced started out poorly, with me being totally disinterested, but things turned around quickly and quite unexpectedly.

On the night we met, Randy and his good buddy James Craig, along with a few other LAPD officers who worked at Friday's on an off-duty detail, were playing host to some visiting Detroit police officers. James was dating my good friend Margo Willis, who was at Friday's helping James entertain his Detroit officer friends. He requested that Margo invite some of her Alpha Kappa Alpha Sorority friends to join the group, so Margo asked me to come along. She and I had been good friends since elementary school and were even college roommates and Alpha Kappa Alpha sorority sisters, so it was natural for her to ask me to join them. However, Margo's timing couldn't have been worse, as I had just broken up with an unkind boyfriend and was taking a break from relationships, men, clubs, and outings. I just wasn't up to going anywhere. Surely the last place I wanted to be was in the company of a bunch of cocky police officers.

But since Margo was the only woman in a party of all men, she felt a little uncomfortable and was in need of another female companion. She persisted in ringing my phone off the hook until I picked it up. "Hello," I responded sleepily, knowing my voice sounded somewhat disoriented and confused.

"Lisa, I'm at Fridays with a few LAPD and Detroit police officers," Margo said. "They're asking me to invite some of my friends to join us, and I need your help. I'm the only female sitting here with all these officers."

"I'm in bed, already in my pajamas and half asleep," I replied.

"This early?" Margo asked, clearly surprised. "You need to get your butt up and forget about that arrogant monster you were dating. He was boring anyway."

# T.G.I. Friday's

I chuckled. Margo was right about my ex-boyfriend being boring, but I was more upset that I had to get back out there and join the dating scene once again. Like Randy, I found the dating scene getting old.

"Come on, Lisa ... there are a few cute guys here," Margo insisted, trying to encourage me.

"I look and feel like a mess! I'm also in a funky mood, plus my eyes are swollen from crying," I responded, giving every excuse of a pathetic, heartbroken woman.

"Oh, come on, Lisa—some friend you are," she continued, pulling out her violin sermon. "When you're down and out and need your best friend to help you out ..." She spoke in a down- and-out voice. Margo was good at laying the guilt on thick.

After a lot of begging from Margo, I reluctantly crawled out of bed to get ready and prepared myself to drive to Friday's to join her. My mother was happy that I was going out, as it tore her up to see me so sad. She encouraged me to spruce myself up so that I would feel better.

During the first few weeks of my breakup despair, my sister Melinda's best friend, Denise Beaudoin, who worked with me, began to jog with me after work. The jogging helped with my stress, and it also helped me take ten pounds off quickly. As a result, I was able to fit into Melinda's clothes, so I didn't hesitate to choose her cute V-necked purple jumpsuit that I liked so much. It made my size 9 frame look every bit a size 5, and it hugged my curvaceous hips.

I then accessorized with a silver necklace, a bracelet, and earrings, which made the whole outfit stand out. I had a chic haircut, courtesy of well-known hair designer Angie Crenshaw, and my makeup was flawless. I topped everything off with my Carolina Herrera perfume, which never failed to get me endless compliments. Even though I was looking my best, I had to try desperately to fight against my blah mood. I knew I would have to make a strong effort at being sociable that night, and I wasn't really up for it.

When I arrived at T.G.I. Friday's, I walked in and greeted Margo. Not wanting to be a downer, I turned on my best and most vibrant personality, which caught the attention of a few officers. After a smile and a formal introduction to the officers by Margo, I sat down but made no eye contact. I didn't want any of the officers to think I was interested in knowing them, and I certainly didn't want to hold any lengthy conversations. I was simply there to support Margo, while her date entertained his friends. With that in mind, I focused on keeping my conversation directed strictly toward Margo.

Purely by accident, Randy was sitting next to me. Initially, I had my back to him because I was talking to Margo, but after a few minutes, I casually turned and looked straight at him, saying hello with half a smile. I didn't really focus in on him, as he had the attention of a beautiful exotic-looking islander woman who was a regular at the bar there. She had joined the table prior to my arrival and was sitting on the other side of Randy, wearing a miniskirt and a bustier, with her breasts displayed to the world. I must admit that she was gorgeous, and the officers were drooling all over her. Even so, her beauty wasn't a threat to me, as I wasn't there for anyone in particular, except for Margo. And honestly, Miss Tahiti Tango would have been tough competition.

My blah mood began to overpower my efforts at being sociable. I couldn't help but think how much I would have preferred being at home watching *Dallas*, *Knots Landing*, or *Dynasty*—or whichever TV show was playing on Friday night. Even going back to sleep seemed like a better option, at least until Randy started joking around with me. He offered to buy Margo and me a drink, and naturally, we both accepted, since money was tight back then. We didn't turn down freebies.

Randy continued joking around with me while also making me laugh. He started to flirt subtly, and to his surprise, in fun, I flirted back, mostly so that he would realize I wasn't shy. His handsome face and muscles were not intimidating to me, so in my own amusing way, I let him know that I could handle the best of them … flirty men, that is.

As the night and conversation wore on, I realized that I was with a nice group of down-to-earth officers who were easy and fun to be around. I let myself loosen up and began socializing with everyone there, including Randy and his islander lady friend, who appeared to be more interested in him than he was in her. Ironically, what I'd thought was going to be an awful night turned out to be an entertaining evening. It was just what I needed, as it helped pull me out of an awful mood.

When the night was over and everyone started to depart Friday's, Randy and the other officers said their good-byes to Margo and me. Randy's exotic islander friend, who was actually nice and funny, also said good-bye as she walked out on Randy's arm. Margo and I remained inside the restaurant, continuing to talk about Margo's newfound relationship with Sergeant James Craig, while James was outdoors saying good-bye to his Detroit officer friends.

Five minutes later, John Paul Franklin, Randy's other good friend and fellow officer, who worked security at Friday's, ran in from outside to deliver a message to me from Randy. "Listen, Lisa, my buddy Randy is interested in you. He's trying to get rid of Baby Girl so he can talk to you before you leave," he stated.

"Uh … yeah … right," I sarcastically laughed. "I'm not going down that road, and I'm not trying to compete with Miss Tahiti Fruit Punch."

"Just give him a chance to talk to you," John Paul said.

"Girl, he's handsome, with big muscles and a nice body," Margo interjected, whispering excitedly. "He's on the SWAT team with LAPD and drives a Volvo!"

"I don't care!" I exclaimed. "I don't need any more headaches. Let's go!" I said adamantly.

As Margo and I walked out of Friday's toward the parking lot, James and Randy, who were already in cahoots about extending the night of fun, greeted us. Randy talked to me for about fifteen minutes, trying to convince me that the islander woman was just a friend.

"Talking to her is like talking to a doorknob," he said. "Please come with me to James's house with Margo. I want to get to know you a little more," he continued.

I finally agreed and went over to James's place with Margo. Randy and I ended up talking for hours in between my sipping wine and he, surprisingly, sipping chamomile tea. I realized through hours of private conversation that he was a man of substance and not quite the playboy that I'd initially thought. The beautiful night and conversation led to many more dates and a very special relationship.

## CHAPTER 9

# Dating "Baby Girl"

DATING RANDY TURNED OUT TO be exciting and fun, although I was reluctant to jump into another relationship so soon. To avoid making a mistake, I told Randy that I wanted to take it slow and date casually. I still wasn't entirely convinced that Randy was serious boyfriend material and not just another playboy, especially when he would refer to me as "Baby Girl" rather than calling me by my name. I wasn't naive about the fact that many playboys used that term as a way of making sure they didn't get their different women's names mixed up. Honey or Baby Girl was a good choice to prevent this from happening, but I absolutely despised it.

In addition, Randy was so handsome that he could capture any woman's undivided attention. Not only was he handsome; he was the ultimate total package. He was single, never married, no kids, good job, homeowner, drove a nice car, and had a body to die for. He defined every young woman's dream, so I was certain he had women waiting in line. Why would I want the competition or that headache? What's more, I wasn't sure if this was going to be another relationship that ended in heartbreak.

During our first few weeks of dating, we would go out to dinner, see a movie, or sit at his house and enjoy the sounds of some good jazz. Occasionally, we would go by my house, where I still resided with my parents and younger sister, Melinda. My sister Cookie, who was married and lived across the street from my parents, would also visit my parents' house with her baby, Amia. The close-knit relationship we shared was somewhat odd for Randy, as he wasn't used to dating a young woman who still lived at home with her parents. Besides, we had no privacy, as my sisters or parents were always somewhere nearby.

In an attempt to make a good impression on my parents, Randy was always on his best behavior, making sure to be extra articulate and extremely nice. He also referred to me by my name in the presence of my parents, especially my father, who had to have a man-to-man talk with Randy about my curfew prior to our going on our first date. Having a talk with a twenty-five-year-old woman's father about curfew was unusual for a thirty-three-year-old who had been out of high school for almost fifteen years. But he really liked me, so he didn't let it bother him.

As far as I could tell, Randy was willing to humble himself and abide by my father's rules because he respected my father, who was average in stature, dark-brown complexioned, and a bit chubby in the tummy. Regardless of my dad's smaller stature, he was a cool and serious man with old-fashioned ways, and he demanded that guests respect his family and his house. He and my beautiful mother, Veronica, migrated to Los Angeles from New Orleans, Louisiana, having married within three months of meeting at eighteen years old, and they were still together after thirty-three years.

As a young couple, they struggled to raise their daughters in a proper manner, and Daddy wasn't going to allow anyone to influence their parental approach in a negative way. So he was overprotective, but he gave us all enough rope to enjoy life without being put in harm's way. He was a no-nonsense type of man, just like Randy.

Whenever we got a new boyfriend, my father seriously scrutinized the guys my sisters and I dated, and that really impressed Randy. Dad was crazy about his girls, and if men wanted to stay in our lives, they had to make a good impression. We were spoiled but not spoiled rotten. Everyone knew we were daddy's girls, and we couldn't put anything past him that he hadn't already done himself as a teenager. Randy admired my father's logic and way of thinking, especially when it came to loving and protecting his daughters.

Randy's favorite pastime was spending time with me and working out at the gym.

One evening after I attended a party, I decided to stop by Randy's house uninvited. At that point, we had only been out on a couple of informal dates, and he had no idea I was coming to his house, so he was surprised to see me standing at his door. I had only been to his house one other time, and it was for a brief visit.

On that night, Randy had worked late and had just returned home. I had had a little too much to drink at the party, and I was tired from a long day of work. My girlfriend Margo drove me to Randy's house while another sorority sister followed behind in my car. I insisted on stopping by his house in the hopes of seeing him and having a cup of his favorite hot chamomile tea.

As I entered his condo, I flopped down on his sofa and was out like a light within seconds. Randy, in an attempt to sober me up, made me some of his favorite chamomile tea, trying desperately to wake me up, but it was to no avail.

Realizing that my parents would be worried, he called my house and talked to Melinda, pleading with her to help him get me sober enough so I would wake up and drive home. My younger sister tried earnestly to get me up by screaming at me over the phone and yelling out Daddy's threats, but it just didn't work.

Randy informed Melinda that he would let me sleep it off and then gave her the wonderful assignment of telling my father about my misfortune on that night. Randy put a blanket around me and let me sleep it off until seven the next morning.

I remember that morning as if it were yesterday, waking up in a panicked state and realizing what I had done. This was so unlike my responsible, reserved behavior. I'd had one too many glasses of wine on an empty stomach and paid the price for it dearly. I knew I had gone over to Randy's house, but I didn't remember going to sleep. I sat up slowly, noticing Randy at the end of the sofa, sitting straight up with his mouth open and snoring. I looked at my watch and realized that it was early morning—and that I had slept there all night. In a panic, I yelled at Randy, waking him up. "Why didn't you wake me up? My father's going to kill me!"

"I tried to wake you up. Next time you decide to drink with the big dogs, you should know your limit!" he shouted back.

I shuffled around in a tizzy trying to locate my jacket, shoes, and purse. I then grabbed my keys and ran out of Randy's condo with my shoes barely on my feet, scampering quickly down the stairs to my car. I drove home speeding, unaware of his presence behind me. Randy was in fact following me in his take-home unmarked police car.

At one point, he pulled up next to me at a red light and asked me to roll down my window. He then warned me in a smart tone that if I didn't slow down, he was going to pull me over and issue me a ticket. I recall rolling my eyes and ignoring his foolishness, as I knew I had bigger fish to fry when I got home and had to face my dad, Excel Hunter. I knew exactly what awaited me at home. Randy followed me home.

When I arrived at my house, I begged Randy to drive away. I didn't want him to witness the wrath of my father, and being a gentleman, he did as I requested. I then sat in the car meditating and praying, trying to get up enough nerve to walk into the house. To make matters worse, I was embarrassed because some of the elders on my block were outside on that gorgeous Saturday morning, watering their grass and tending to their gardens.

In my paranoid state, I felt as if they were looking at me and talking about my wayward ways. I was certain they would know how I disrespected my parents' house by waltzing in at an inappropriate hour. Surely they could figure it out by the after-five outfit I had on, which consisted of a black miniskirt, fitted black jacket with rhinestone buttons, fishnet panty hose, and black pumps with three-inch heels, with the previous night's makeup smeared all over my face.

*Dang it!* I thought, hitting my steering wheel. *Why does Mr. Elliott have to be watering our grass this morning?*

I knew I would have to greet him before entering the house, so I braced myself for the inevitable comments and got out of my car slowly. "Good morning, Mr. Elliott," I said as I walked up the sidewalk and walkway that led to my parents' front door.

Mr. Elliott, who was about eighty years old, nodded as he sat on his stool and continued to water our grass. Mr. Elliott was kind of our next-door neighbor slash grandfather. You couldn't hide anything from him either, so I could tell by his demeanor that he wasn't pleased with my behavior, but he didn't say a word.

I turned the key, walked through the front door, and was immediately greeted by my father, who had a few choice words for me. "Do you know what time it is?" he stated emphatically.

"Yes Daddy, but I—"

"But Daddy nothin'!" he yelled. "There's only one man in this house, and that's the one with the zipper up front! There's only one king of this here castle, and that's me! This boat don't rock unless I rock it! This ship don't sail unless I'm navigating it! Don't you bring your behind up in here the next morning ever again! I didn't raise no alley cats! And I don't give a damn if he is the police!"

"Daddy, it wasn't his fault. I had a little too much to drink, and I accidentally fell asleep over at his house," I explained.

"If you can't hold your liquor, don't drink!" he replied angrily. "I'm gonna talk to him and let him know how we run things in this house."

I was nervous, as I knew Randy had a strong personality too. One bad comment or move on his part would put him at negative zero when it came to my father. Besides, Randy was already disturbed and disappointed by my rather irresponsible behavior, so I thought for sure this was going to be the end of our barely beginning relationship. However, that did not hold true.

A few hours later, Randy called my house and asked to speak to my father. He felt terrible about what happened, and he wanted to let my father know that he didn't take advantage of his daughter that night or any other night.

I nervously gave the telephone to my father, who still wasn't in the best of moods. I tried to eavesdrop on their conversation, but I could only hear bits and pieces of what was being said. When my father hung up the phone, he came directly into my room, where I was pretending to be asleep. I was afraid to hear the outcome of that conversation, but I opened my eyes to his walking around my room calmly, telling me that Randy seemed to be a nice guy and how much he appreciated him for having the decency and respect to call and explain what had happened.

My father then reprimanded me for my irresponsible behavior of drinking too much and alluded to the fact that I was not going out for a week unless I was in the company of Randy.

Randy playing football with LAPD Centurions. He received an award for Athlete of The Decade his final year playing.

Unbeknownst to me, Randy had informed my dad that he wanted to take me out and had requested his permission. Surprisingly, that very same day, Randy called back and asked me out to dinner. I agreed but under one condition: we wouldn't talk about my irresponsible behavior. I was thoroughly embarrassed and ashamed and didn't want to rehash it. Randy agreed and picked me up later that day, taking me to Stephano's Restaurant in Westwood, California, where we laughed and talked and enjoyed a great dinner.

It was our first formal date, and it went great, with the exception of Randy being a little rough around the edges when it came to table etiquette and his calling me "Baby Girl" all night. Regardless of my endless reminders that my name was Lisa, he would sarcastically apologize and then revert to calling me "Baby Girl" again. This annoyed me to no end. All I could do was roll my eyes in disgust and turn up my pointy nose.

Months passed, and after a while, I got used to Randy calling me Baby Girl. He truly seemed to like calling me that. I never did see signs of other women in his life during the entire time we were dating. He'd told me he was a one-woman man, and that appeared to be true.

I was beginning to see several different sides to Randy: happy, sad, loving, spoiled, serious, rigid, compassionate, intelligent, active, smart, tidy, knowledgeable, no-nonsense, demanding, and somewhat religious. I also noticed that he did have good table etiquette, but he only displayed it when he saw fit or in proper or formal settings. When he was with me, he treated me as if I were one of the guys, which to me meant he was relaxed and comfortable around me. I fell in love with his roughneck disposition, and the feeling was mutual. But I was still somewhat apprehensive about our relationship, as Randy was moving too fast, faster than I wanted to go, mostly because I wasn't ready. He would call me every chance he got in between call-ups, warrants, court dates, and training. On a weekly basis, he sent me beautiful roses with cards and poetry that he'd written. He purchased a beautiful long black leather coat and expensive jewelry for me. His thoughtfulness, kindness, and actions were moving at a speed that actually scared me. He was so loving and attentive toward me that it just seemed unreal. The playboy spirit that I thought Randy possessed and would eventually come out never did. My love for Randy was in overdrive, and according to my timeline, this wasn't supposed to happen so soon. I felt like I needed to put the brakes on our relationship before it crashed and I was the only one injured.

Fearing that our relationship was too good to be true, I asked Randy if we could take a break from dating because I wasn't sure if I was ready for a serious relationship. I also asked him if he would stop buying me things and sending me roses. Randy, being a macho man, was visibly hurt by my request, and he seemed more or less dumbfounded. After all, everything was going so well. We had good conversations and agreed on most things pertaining to life's issues. We enjoyed being together, and we even started working out together. Nevertheless, Randy respectfully honored my request.

When more than a week had passed and I hadn't heard from Randy, I realized that I missed talking with him, but I tried to hold out and not call him. By the second week, I couldn't resist phoning him to see how he was doing. I left several messages over the next couple of weeks, but he didn't return any of my calls. To say I was perturbed by his unresponsive behavior would be an understatement, and although I realized I'd asked him to take a break, it didn't mean we couldn't be friends. It was hard for me to believe that he wouldn't respond to my phone calls. I felt as if he had immediately forgotten about our love affair and quickly gone to the next floozy waiting in line.

I hated that I was letting my childlike behavior get the best of me, but I couldn't control my temper. So without giving it a second thought, I jumped into my car and drove over to his condo. I was going to catch him and that floozy right in the act and give him a piece of my mind!

I knocked on the door, and Randy answered it half-asleep. He had been up all night serving warrants, so he was tired and hadn't gotten much sleep. But he wasn't going to get my sympathy; I was angry with him for ignoring me, and he was going to hear it.

I tried to remain calm and not let my mother's Creole temper rear its head, but I couldn't hold back. I let him have it! "You know, I called you several times and left several messages," I said in an extremely perturbed voice.

"Is that right?" he said, lethargically walking back to his bed.

"I was very disappointed when you did not have the decency to return any of my calls," I continued, following him down the hallway to his bedroom.

I went on with my ranting. "I can't believe how quickly you just forgot about me!"

He chuckled and got back in bed, throwing the covers over his shoulders as he mocked me. "I forgot about you ... yeah, right!" he responded, turning his back as if I weren't present.

"I can't believe your immature behavior!" I yelled.

That last statement made Randy irate. "Immature behavior! You have the audacity to call me immature! Little girl, go home to your daddy!" he replied.

This condescending comment brought out of me my mother's Creole temper—as well as her mother's and all my ancestors'. This was certainly a time I wished that my father's mother's sweet, praying, calm Baptist spirit would have kicked in. But it didn't!

I was in a fit of rage, and I couldn't contain it. I picked up a pillow and threw it at Randy's big peanut head as hard as I could. I then walked out of his bedroom and down the corridor to head home. Suddenly, I felt the blow of a hit that jerked my body. Randy had taken a pillow and thrown it back at me.

I slowly turned around in a state of shock, as Randy had never displayed an ounce of violent behavior toward me. I was stunned and called him the name that is most fitting for a donkey. My feelings were hurt because even though Randy was rough around the edges, he had always been delicate with me and handled me carefully.

With tears in my eyes, I picked up that same pillow and threw it back at him. Before you knew it, a pillow fight had ensued, and Randy wasn't holding back. I was angry about his ignoring me, and he was angry about my indecisive and spoiled, demanding ways. We were both getting our frustrations out by means of a pillow fight. And to make matters worse, the angrier I got, the more Randy laughed.

I cried and yelled, "This is all a big joke to you!"

Then while laughing, he grabbed me and started kissing me in addition to expressing how much he missed me. It was a crazy love, and we made up by making love and vowing to never part ways again.

The exclusive dating scene was back in motion, and that was our last feud while dating. He was in love with me, and I was in love with him.

We spent every moment possible together, and I was always home before 1:00 a.m. Randy knew he had to bring me home at a respectable hour. He dared not violate my father's rules, and since Randy had worked so hard to get in my dad's good graces, he didn't want to spoil it. He had established a good relationship with my father, earning him a good pot of filé gumbo at every request. There was no way that Randy was going to mess up the good thing he had going with Mr. Hunter.

# CHAPTER 10

# Tying the Knot

THE NIGHTS WERE STARTING TO get cold, and Randy and I both wanted to snuggle up with each other at night rather than him having to drop me off at my house. He got tired of going home and getting in bed by himself, and I got tired of looking at Melinda's face every night, regardless of her extreme beauty. So in only four months time, on April Fools' Day, Randy did the unexpected. He took me to The Warehouse, a nice restaurant in Marina del Rey, California, for dinner. Afterward, we drove around for a while, embracing the stillness of the night. And then he parked his car near a marina that housed luxurious boats and yachts. It was a beautiful night, with a full moon reflecting off the deep blue calm water. It was so peaceful.

There was nothing unusual about this sort of activity, as Randy and I would often venture to a quiet spot to relax and talk. But then Randy suddenly started expressing his love for me. His roughneck disposition became gentle as a lamb: "Baby Girl, I really love you. You're cool. I love spending time with you. I love everything about you. You're different." And then he reached into his pocket and presented me with a little red box, simply saying, "Here."

He opened the box and proposed to me with a 2.5-carat diamond engagement ring with a gold band.

I screamed with excitement and jumped up and down in the car.

Then I grabbed his face and kissed him on the lips. I scrambled out of the car and started jumping up and down, still yelling with excitement, as the ring was so beautiful, but not as beautiful as Randy was to me on that special night. I got back in the car and hugged Randy again, who had a big smile on his face.

"I guess that means, yes, uh, Baby Girl," he said.

"Of course, silly!" I replied.

I accepted his proposal, and we drove home to share the news with my family.

When we got to the house, I ran inside, leaving Randy behind as I went in search of my parents. I found them both in bed, watching TV. Like a young girl, I jumped into the bed with them just as I had when I was ten years old. I flopped my big butt between them, wiggling my hand and showing them my ring.

It was no surprise to my mother, and she too screamed with delighted excitement. However, my father couldn't believe it. He took his glasses off and grabbed my hand, moving it close to his eyes in order to get a better look at my big diamond ring. Initially, they both thought it was an April Fools' joke since Randy and I had only been dating for four months. However, when they saw the big diamond rock on my finger, they knew it was the real deal. My family was thrilled.

It was finally happening for Randy and me. He was ecstatic about marrying me, and I was overjoyed about marrying him. We both had been in countless whirlwind relationships and believed we had finally met the person worthy of our love, someone we could settle down with and start a family.

We wanted to get married right away, but it wasn't going to be a rushed ceremony. It was going to be held in the church. We had only six months to plan the wedding, and we had to come to an agreement about our plans first, starting with the church. Randy was attending Trinity Baptist Church of Los Angeles at the time, where the devoted and loving family friend Reverend Elliott Mason was the pastor. Randy loved Reverend Mason, for he and his beautiful wife, Geraldine, had remained by his mother's side after his father left the family. They would often counsel Randy's mother with the word of God, praying with her for the healing of her broken heart.

Our Engagement Photo.

Randy appreciated their love and support, and because of them, Randy slowly began strengthening his faith under Reverend Mason's ministry. I had visited Trinity Baptist Church with Randy and his family a few times and enjoyed their services, plus I loved the Masons too. They were a beautiful family; however, I wasn't ready to convert from Catholicism. I was born and raised in the Catholic Church and was used to tradition, so we decided on a Catholic wedding with Reverend Mason participating in the wedding ceremony and extending a lovely prayer of blessings.

Nine months later, on a bright, sunny day—September 15, 1990—we were married. Randy and I exchanged vows at St. Jerome Catholic Church in Los Angeles, California. My home church, Transfiguration Catholic Church, was booked the entire month of September, and since Randy and I didn't want to wait any longer, St. Jerome agreed to marry us. It was a gorgeous round church highlighted in gold. It was centrally located in the Westchester area of Los Angeles. Father James Kavanagh provided premarital counseling, as did Reverend Mason.

Father Kavanagh was extremely nice and personable, and he delivered a wedding ceremony fit for a king and queen. In fact, Randy often referred to his wedding as "My Big Fat Creole Wedding" since many of my relatives flew in from New Orleans. Randy's family also flew in, but they came from New York. Both Randy and I knew many people, so our wedding was huge, with over four hundred guests in attendance, including family, friends, officers, football buddies, sorority sisters, and more.

On our wedding day, Randy and I were the perfectly attired couple. I wore an elegant fitted white silk lace dress with a beautiful appliqué embellished with pearl beads and glittery sequins. I would have to say that my cathedral length train ran a close second to Princess Diana's. My headpiece sat high on my head, with lots of netting, sequins, and pearls. Randy, handsome as ever, wore a black tuxedo with a white shirt, complementing his good looks.

Our wedding party was large and consisted of approximately twenty-five people. Randy's groomsmen were all police officers and one civilian worker, his soon-to-be brother-in-law, Cookie's husband of six years, Wilfred Sumlin. The groomsmen wore black tuxedos.

My bridesmaids, consisting of my sisters, my cousin, and childhood friends, wore beautiful coral-colored satin dresses. My bridesmaids walked down like beautiful gazelles, escorted by big muscular groomsmen to the sounds of the jazz single "Save Yourself for Me," by the jazz group Hiroshima.

Lastly, my cute little flower girls provided the church with the scent of fresh peach roses, while my little ring bearer, Randy's nephew, stole the show as he marched down the aisle like a miniature Randy.

My sweet, loving future mother-in-law was escorted down the aisle looking solemn and perplexed. I believe she wasn't totally convinced that I was the right one for her only son. Her lack of excitement and solemn expressions gave way to her heart and what she was feeling. After all, Randy and I had only known each other for nine months, and although Catholics are Christians, I was a different denomination than what his mother had hoped for her only son.

On the other hand, my mother was thrilled that her middle girl was jumping the broom. As a sophisticated diva, my mother was eager to walk down that aisle for her middle daughter. She was escorted looking as sexy and sassy as ever, making her presence known.

I have to admit that every person in the wedding was extremely attractive, for our wedding party represented every shade or color of the African American culture. It was a beautiful wedding.

As I prepared to walk down the aisle, I had an array of things going through my mind. I was nervous and happy about being a bride, but my heart was heavy as I held on to my handsome father escorting me down the aisle. I knew my time with my father was limited, for Daddy had just been diagnosed with stage IV prostate cancer and was terminally ill. The doctors were giving him up to five years more to live. Even with this vast array of emotions, I still gave praise to God for blessing me with a wonderful husband and for allowing my father to be alive so that he could give me away in marriage.

As I walked down the aisle, I felt all eyes on me. Randy, overwhelmed with emotion, started to cry upon seeing me. His groomsmen didn't know what to think, as many of them had played LAPD Centurion football with him and knew him as "Mud Bone" or "The Rock." He was given those nicknames for his strength and his roughneck disposition. To see him crying was strange; however, what they didn't know about were the conversations Randy had with God and the promises he had made to Him. He had promised God that he would get his life right and serve Him totally, especially since God had blessed him with a wife. His tears were tears of joy and a display of gratitude to the God that still existed and loved him regardless of the hardships he endured.

Randy and I said traditional wedding vows, and the wedding ended with laughter as Father Kavanagh said, "This is the first wedding I have ever done where just about all the groomsmen are police officers. I have never felt so safe doing a wedding in all my life!" All the guests were tickled by the priest's sense of humor. Everyone then headed over to the reception at the hotel, and we danced and celebrated throughout the night.

I had the thrill and honor of throwing my bouquet. As I turned to throw it, the entire floor was filled with women aggressively trying to catch it in hopes of someday being in my shoes as a beautiful bride. It was also their opportunity to let all the handsome single men know that they were available.

Likewise, Randy threw my garter to all the single men, but the men showed no signs of urgency in catching the garter. They were all cool, calm, and collected. I believe many of them would have liked being in Randy's shoes and finding a soul mate one day, but for the moment, their macho behavior wouldn't let them show it.

During the traditional money dance ceremony, Randy's SWAT buddies decided to go against the tradition of dancing with the bride and giving her a donation toward the honeymoon. Instead, they opted to do a group slow dance with Randy. Randy was so embarrassed and tried to run away from his SWAT brothers, but they were just as strong as he was, and they were not going to let him escape from their group hug.

Our wedding was a joyous occasion, a day that we both cherished. And afterward we realized it was time for the real work to begin: marriage and starting a family.

Our Wedding Day, September 15, 1990.

We Honeymooned in Kauai and Maui.

# CHAPTER 11

# And the Two Shall Become One

RANDY AND I PURCHASED A beautiful two-story condo in San Pedro, California. It was a block away from the city of Rancho Palos Verdes, a beautiful area we both thought was ideal for starting a family. Like any new couple, we had a period of adjustment as we struggled to find a happy medium. Randy, at thirty-four years of age, was stuck in his bachelor-like self-centered ways, especially when it came to doing things around the house. It drove me crazy. Unlike me, Randy was used to a quiet house that at most would echo the sounds of loud jazz music. He was a neat freak who demanded that everything in the house be tidy, saying that every object had its rightful place. He was also very private and only wanted to entertain people on special occasions such as birthdays or at Christmas. He took pleasure in just being around family, watching football while his mother and I cooked up a good Sunday dinner. He also liked sitting around the table discussing politics, religion, or work-related incidences. But nothing took the place of a good game of Scrabble while drinking a cup of hot Chamomile tea and eating his favorite dessert, his mother's famous pineapple upside-down cake. He embraced the simple pleasures of life, perhaps to offset his hectic work schedule.

I, on the other hand, had an upbringing that was very sociable, making my family's home one of the loudest on the block. My parents, natives of New Orleans, Louisiana, brought their Southern hospitality to California, so their culture was deeply rooted within their three daughters at an early age. During the week, there was work and school, which the family took seriously, but weekends and holidays were a different story. It wasn't unusual for family and friends to stop by the house unannounced just to socialize with my sisters, my parents, or me. We gave barbeques and parties for any and all celebrations, and there were times when an impromptu barbecue or a seafood boil party would take place for no reason at all. You can be sure that drinks other than soda and water were available, a far cry from chamomile tea: beer, wine, Crown Royal, and Jack Daniel's whiskey.

In terms of household maintenance, I wasn't as tidy as my dear husband was. While growing up, my mother, my sisters, and I made sure our house stayed presentable, with all participating in the household chores whenever needed. But no one flinched if there was a dish or two left in the sink or a bed was unmade. For me, there was no problem with my house looking lived in, but Randy was not going to accept any of my excuses for not having an immaculate house at all times.

We both eventually realized that if we wanted to stay married, we would have to learn to yield to each other. We discovered how to compromise when it came to festivities, family, privacy, household maintenance, position of the toilet paper, and how to squeeze the toothpaste. For the most part, we figured out how to deal with all the pet peeves and idiosyncrasies that most newly married couples face.

Ironically, unlike most couples, managing our finances was never a real issue for us. Randy was very conservative and wasn't a big spender. However, when he did buy something, you can be sure it was going to be of great quality. He had learned in his twenties the damaging effect of credit cards, so he made every effort to avoid irresponsible spending. In contrast, my spending sometimes would get the best of me. From time to time, I would get out of control, going on wild shopping sprees on a whim. But Randy knew how to pull the reins in on me and get me back on the priority program. I truly wanted to be more of a help than a hindrance in meeting those financial goals, so I had no problem adhering to his wishes.

Perhaps the most crucial and important matter that needed to be resolved between us was our oneness when it came to our worship. We both knew that our faith was going to be monumental in keeping our marriage alive and intact, so we needed to find a church where we could worship together. Spiritually, we were both Christians, but we were of different denominations. Randy, being raised Pentecostal, had a hard time relating to the quiet traditions of the Catholic Church, and my being raised Catholic meant that I had a difficult time adjusting to the screaming and shouting of the Pentecostal Church. We spent months visiting different churches, trying to find that special church that would help us grow closer to God and enrich our lives.

It wasn't long before I consulted with my godmother, Carol Ann Gilmore, who had left the traditional Catholic Church years ago in search of a word-based church, also referred to as nondenominational Christian church. Over the years, she introduced us to two churches where we received spiritual teachings from the Bible, along with counseling, guidance, and loving fellowship with other believers. One was Agape Christian Fellowship of Los Angeles, under the leadership of Pastor Edward Haygood; the other was Glory Christian Fellowship International, under the leadership of Pastor Alton Trimble. While fellowshipping with these churches and obtaining continued spiritual guidance from Randy's mother and Reverend Mason, we were led to rededicate our lives together in Christ. However, Randy's rededication was nothing short of a transformation in an enormous way.

In our early years of marriage, while attending Agape Christian Fellowship, Randy got extremely involved in church and started growing and developing rapidly in the things of God. He was a new man in Christ, and his life and lifestyle reflected that commitment. Trivial things like an argument over an immaculate house didn't matter to him anymore. What became more of a focal point was his relationship with God, his family and friends, community outreach, work, and football; all the other things were not as important.

I, on the other hand, was not as active as Randy was in church, as I focused more on the blessings that were bestowed on my new life. It was important to me that I find balance between church activities and managing and keeping my house in order.

Being a new wife and mother was very important to me, so I was going to cherish the blessings that God had given me. I had already experienced the misfortune of losing my firstborn to a devastating miscarriage during my second trimester, so I wasn't going to take my family or life for granted by spending too much time away from home.

Shortly after my miscarriage, I tried again to conceive another child. Fortunately, it wasn't long before I was pregnant again, and this time I took proper precautions to assure a full-term pregnancy. My doctor put me on bed rest, and I had to take a leave of absence from my job as a claims adjuster.

During this time, the Los Angeles Police Department had Randy working a lot of overtime. I missed his company a great deal and would often complain and cry of loneliness, boredom, and living so far away from family and friends. I was thirty minutes away from my sisters and parents, but it felt like hours since I could not visit them at the drop of a dime as I had in the past. I found myself filling that void with the assistance of AT&T, holding lengthy phone conversations with family and friends.

Randy's work schedule became even more demanding when an incident took place that shook the entire city of Los Angeles, including the Los Angeles Police Department, to its core. It was the 1992 Rodney King civil unrest riot. The brutal beating of Rodney King was a horrifying confrontation and served as the pivotal defining moment that would change the way the LAPD operated.

Randy had mixed emotions about everything. The excessive force that his fellow officers used to apprehend Rodney King saddened him. He was never one to play the race card, but in this particular case he felt that possibly ethnicity combined with fear played a part in the officers' actions. He was disturbed that the behavior of these officers painted a bad image of the majority of LAPD officers, an image they did not deserve. He agreed with some of the constructive criticism that was given to LAPD but was offended when the entire force was scrutinized because of this incident.

Randy knew that the greater portion of his fellow officers took their oath to protect and serve seriously, and that they worked hard every day to make the streets of Los Angeles safe. It was disheartening to hear some of the accusations and negative comments made about the police force.

Regardless, his opinion of Chief Daryl Gates never wavered or changed. In his view, Daryl Gates was one of the best chiefs he had ever worked for while being an LAPD police officer. He based this on Chief Gates's loyalty, dedication, and commitment to the LAPD and its officers as well as to the city of Los Angeles. He was a hardworking top cop, tough on crime but unfortunately slower to change on policy and procedures. Some might say he had a paramilitary style of policing; however, times were changing and the city was calling for community policing. Gates always believed in, supported and was quick to defend the actions of his officers, which perhaps later came back to obliterate his career as chief of police.

From a purely personal standpoint, Randy didn't really comment on the racist issue surrounding Daryl Gates. His thought was that if Daryl Gates was a racist, as many had claimed, that he, like the rest of the world, would someday have to answer to God for his shortcomings. He only knew Chief Gates on a professional level, and based on his knowledge of him and working under his leadership, Randy respected him as a chief. In return, Chief Gates always had admiration and respect for Randy.

For the record, Randy despised racism. He had always had a culturally diverse group of friends, and he got along with everyone. He was not oblivious to the racial attitudes that some of the officers had, but if it came out in any form when Randy was in view … God help them. Being a serious man, if or when he was offended, he was quick to let the person doing the offending get a piece of his mind. Some things he simply wouldn't tolerate, and blatant racism was one of them. He used to say something like this about racism:

"Sadly, there are some people who don't believe they are racist, but they are. They truly believe that they're doing you a favor by smiling in your face and being nice to you. But eventually something will cause that racial bigotry to raise its ugly head and reveal to you just who they truly are. Some people are better at disguising it than others, but it will eventually come out. It's just a matter of time. And they'd better be ready for the consequences."

After the Rodney King riots, Chief Gates wrote a book on his career experiences with LAPD. Randy purchased the book, as he knew Gates shared many historical events in the book, and he wanted to read what he had to say. He read it while I was in labor giving birth to our son, Matthew Excel Simmons, born on June 4, 1992.

Matthew was a nine-pound, six-ounce beautiful baby boy. Interestingly, the doctor who delivered Matthew, Dr. Maryam Bahreini of Torrance, California, was a petite, glamorous woman who stood five feet, even with three-inch heels. She was a sassy and feisty diva of a doctor who enjoyed teasing Randy about his big muscles. After delivering Matthew, she placed him in Randy's arms, still covered with blood from the afterbirth. Randy looked at Matthew and started shaking like a leaf. He was filled with an array of emotions, smiling and crying all at the same time. He was so thrilled about the birth of his son that he kept on the T-shirt that showed the bloodstains of his firstborn son. To some, that may have appeared unpleasant, but to Randy it was evidence of a miracle. He went to work to announce the news of his baby boy, bragging about his T-shirt and the evidence of his hard work and labor while delivering his new baby, Matthew. The one thing Randy forgot to share were my efforts in the birth of our son and the fact that I was foolish enough to honor his request of opting out of pain medication. Randy was a health fanatic, so he didn't want any unnecessary drugs in Matthew's system. Instead, he wanted to assure that Matthew was born a healthy baby, so although delivering such a large baby almost killed me, because of the love I had for my husband and my child, I refused the pain medication. I suffered tremendously; however, the joy of seeing my baby boy erased all memory of the pain.

Randy and I were the proudest parents in the world, as Matthew was everything to us. We both knew that our life would now be shared with this little one who demanded all our time and attention. We also knew that we had to look out for little Matthew's future, so we were committed to working hard to ensure that we could contribute to a prosperous life for our little one. Thus we got started immediately, planning for his college education.

In the interim, my joy of having my new little addition was cut short by the harsh reality of possibly losing my father, as cancer had taken its toll on my dad. I was working, being a new mother, and making visits from San Pedro to Los Angeles just to spend time with him. I also wanted my father to spend time with little Matthew. Randy would try to help whenever his schedule would permit, but time was running out for my father. The thought of Matthew never truly knowing his remarkable grandfather saddened Randy and me. My father was the only grandfather that Matthew had since Randy's father was still missing in action and did not respond to our phone calls or letters about his new grandson. We wanted to share with him that we had named Matthew after both grandfathers, giving him his first name, Matthew, after Randy's father and his middle name, Excel, after my father. However, it was obvious that Matthew Dallas Simmons did not want to be found.

During those years, Randy developed a close relationship with my father, respecting him for his wisdom and for being the patriarch of the family. He was shockingly surprised to see how quickly my father's illness took him down since no one was expecting him to die so soon. The night of his death, Randy had a warrant just outside of Las Vegas. I pleaded with him not to go, as I knew my mother, sisters, and I needed his prayers and support. However, Randy had been working on this warrant for weeks, and no one could estimate a time for my father's death. So Randy held me in his arms, and together we prayed. We knew that it was the only thing that was going to sustain my family and me, knowing my father was everything to us. He was the glue that held our family together. He was our protector, our counselor, our advisor, our mentor, and the man that we felt God put in charge to shield us under any circumstances in the earth realm. We weren't ready for him to go. We wanted him to stay with us for at least a little while longer, as he was the essence of a good father.

Randy gently kissed me, and before leaving, he said his final goodbye to my father. My dad died a few hours later, leaving us all devastated beyond words.

Following the death of my father, Randy made a commitment to me. He knew that I was brokenhearted over my loss, for my father had always taken care of my family and me and given his unconditional love selflessly. Randy also knew he would have to make it a point to spend more time with me, so he promised that he would always take care of me and love me with that same unconditional love that God requires of all of us. Knowing that his work schedule was already hectic, he decided not to work so much voluntary overtime so that he could spend more time with Matthew and me, at least long enough to get me through the grieving process.

Randy did whatever he could to cheer me up. We were constantly going to church because I was in need of spiritual healing after my father's death. During that time, Randy began to read and really study the Bible.

My father, Mr. Excel Hunter and Randy on our wedding day.

Randy, Matt and I at Agape Christian Fellowship Church.

Our son Matthew was born June 4, 1992.

While he was growing spiritually, I began growing belly-wise. After a few mornings of fighting what I thought was a bad flu bug that wouldn't go away, I was informed by my doctor that I was pregnant again. This was wonderful news, as my family and I all needed some added joy. Now the Simmons family was growing, and that meant we needed more space.

Randy and I were doing well and growing rapidly in our careers. We were both extremely disciplined people when it came to saving money, especially given Randy's goal-oriented nature. If he had an objective to achieve, he was going to be disciplined and do whatever it required to reach that goal. Consequently, we spent several months house hunting in an attempt to find a nice home before our new little addition arrived.

In November of 1993, we moved into a house just around the corner, in Rancho Palos Verdes. We went from a cozy two-bedroom condo to a lovely, spacious five-bedroom home. Randy was a realist and knew that if he wanted a comfortable lifestyle, he would have to put in some overtime, and I agreed. Our brand-new home came with a big mortgage, plus we were soon going to have a new mouth to feed, along with diapers, babysitting expenses, and the continued financial support that Randy provided his mother from time to time. Randy worked up until just a week before my due date, and then he made a decision to take off a month after I gave birth so that he could help around the house.

Randy and I always had a way of joking around with each other, just as buddies often do. One night after I laid little Matthew down to sleep, I got into bed looking forward to a New Orleans Creole brunch I was going to be attending for Mother's Day. While Randy was shaving and talking to me from our connecting bathroom, he was reprimanding me for eating too much and gaining so much weight. I had gotten so big with my second child that people were always asking me if I was having triplets. Randy would shake his head and say, "Wow, Lisa, that's deep. You'd better slow down, girl."

I would respond sarcastically, "My baby's hungry, and I'm going to feed her."

He would then reply, "You mean *him*."

Randy wanted to have another boy because, in his mind, boys were easier. As far as he was concerned, there were already too many emotional, moody, and hormonal females in our family, and since Randy had to deal with his sisters, as well as my sisters and me, the thought of having one more emotional female to care for was too much for Randy to accept. It essentially scared him. Plus he would always say jokingly, "If I ever have a daughter, I might have to hurt somebody when she starts dating," he stated.

As I continued to talk about the tasty food that was going to be served at the Mother's Day brunch the next day, a sudden pain interrupted me. I screamed and paused for a moment, getting quiet.

Randy walked out of the bathroom with shaving cream still on his face. "What's wrong?"

"I felt a pop. I think my water broke!" I said in a state of shock.

"I thought you said the baby was due on May seventeenth," he replied.

"That's an estimated due date! My water's broken!" I exclaimed, starting to feel slight labor pains and water rush down my legs.

"Then get out of the bed, Lisa, before you get the entire mattress wet!" he shouted nervously.

"I can't move," I cried. "I think she's coming!"

"You mean *he's* coming!" Randy replied, trying to help lift me out of bed.

Then I gave him one of those evil looks that many men get when they're irritating their wives who are experiencing excruciating labor pains. It was one of those looks that said to be quiet and get me to the hospital before I bite your head off.

Noticing that this was the real deal, Randy woke up little Matthew and rushed me to the hospital.

Excruciating labor pains were coming left and right. I honestly thought I was going to die, for my heart was racing out of control and I was literally out of my mind with pain. This time I asked for and got every pain reliever under the sun, and Randy dared not question me.

After a few short hours of being in labor, a bundle of joy was born to us. I recalled Randy looking confused and saying to the doctor, "Wait, I see a slit … Where's the little ding-a-ling?"

The doctor responded, "You have a little girl, Mr. Simmons."

Our daughter Gabrielle was born on May 7, 1994.

Randy replied with a big nervous smile while picking her up and holding her in his arms. He looked at this little princess, Gabrielle, and then turned around and showed Matthew his little sister, who was twenty-three months younger. Gabrielle was born on May 7, 1994. She was eight pounds and four ounces, which by the way did not substantiate my big weight gain. She looked just like her brother, Matthew, but with a browner complexion, and she was absolutely adorable. Randy didn't get another football player; instead, he got a little cheerleader who brought an additional amount of happiness into the Simmons family.

I brought Gabrielle home on Mother's Day, and I couldn't have asked for a better Mother's Day present. Randy took vacation from SWAT and hovered around the house. He found himself grocery shopping, paying bills, looking at household furniture, and working out at the gym. Before long, he became bored. It was hard for him to do so little and have a lot of free time on his hands, so he began to pick up his Bible and study some more. He knew he had to stay connected to God even more so now, as God had blessed him with a wife and two beautiful kids, so he wanted His mercy and grace to reign over his household.

Randy made a decision that as soon as baby Gabrielle and I were able to get out of the house, we would visit a new church closer to home. It was then that my godmother recommended Glory Christian Fellowship International Church.

After one month of attending to Gabrielle and taking care of me, Randy was going stir-crazy. He went ballistic when he heard the breaking news of Nicole Brown Simpson, former wife of football great O. J. Simpson, and friend Ron Goldman being found stabbed to death. The SWAT team responded and went into tactical deployment. Randy was frustrated because he wasn't there to use his negotiating skills to get O. J. to surrender. Initially, he, like most of America, couldn't imagine the all-American football star and actor, "The Juice," being guilty of such a heinous crime. What monster would commit such an evil act? Being a football admirer, Randy did not want to believe that the football legend could have anything to do with such a horrific crime; however, as the murder trial unfolded and evidence was presented, Randy's opinion of O. J. started to change.

In the end, Randy felt strongly that O. J. had killed them or had something to do with the deaths surrounding Nicole Brown Simpson and Ron Goldman. He felt bad for the Brown family, the Goldman family, and most of all, O. J. and Nicole's children. These kinds of sad events brought Randy to his knees in prayer. A senseless death of a young mother was heart wrenching to him and horrifically painful to see.

## CHAPTER 12

# Family + SWAT + Church = A Busy Lifestyle

LOOKING AT RANDY, YOU WOULDN'T think that a man with such a statuesque body and cool disposition would have such a kind and loving heart. In fact, out of all the muscles in his body, the biggest and strongest of these was his heart. He had compassion for the lost, the lonely, the sick, the poor, and the brokenhearted. While working the streets of Los Angeles, he witnessed not just crime but also the heartbreaking scene of a number of lost souls. Some parts of downtown Los Angeles were filled with homeless people, many of them in need of psychiatric help. Among them were children whose innocent lives were affected by the horrible and dreadful crimes they witnessed or experienced.

There were a number of community housing development sites that Randy patrolled, many of which were drug and gang infested. The graffiti on the walls generally marked a particular gang's territory. A drive-by shooting was typical, and the thought of an innocent bystander taking the bullet for such foolishness infuriated Randy. The panhandlers begging for money and the prostitutes walking the street and soliciting business appeared to be invisible to the young children playing in the street, as this was ordinary day-to-day community activity.

Randy felt that these areas were truly underserved and ignored. It was like a huge elephant standing in the room—while everyone looked over it, around it, and underneath it, no one wanted to deal with it. The major problems that plagued inner-city communities were something few questioned or found the answers to.

Randy believed that each new generation of innocent kids that grew up in those communities would be plagued and influenced by elements of the streets. He saw one easy fix; besides policing the streets, a solution that could change the situation would be positive role models who would reach out and show the kids a better way of life. In Randy's opinion, if there were no positive role models, the vicious cycle of criminal activity would continue.

It all became very personal for Randy. He felt a strong desire to participate in some sort of outreach, not based on some superman egocentric attitude to save the world, but through a true calling to do outreach that would influence children in a positive way. Little did he know that God would use the resources of church and SWAT to help him fulfill the purpose God had for his life.

In 1994, the Simmons family joined Glory Christian Fellowship International Church in Carson, California. The pastor, Alton Trimble, and his wife, Judith Trimble, were a few years older than Randy and I, and they were both fully knowledgeable about the Bible. Sister Trimble was a teacher, and she and Pastor Trimble had a heart for kids. They took a special interest in helping kids develop socially and academically. Pastor Trimble was an excellent teacher of the word, and Randy and I learned a great deal under his ministry. The church had an excellent worship service, with a choir that could have been nominated for several gospel Grammy Awards. Pastor Trimble himself, lead vocalist Mark English, and Shelly Pruitt were blessed with voices that made a Catholic girl like me want to shout for joy. To top it all off, the members were gracious and friendly and had a welcoming spirit. Randy and I felt comfortable there, as it had a family-like ambiance. Joining the church ultimately enriched the foundation of our faith and propelled our spiritual growth.

Over the next few years, Randy and I became busier than ever. Randy's SWAT schedule kept him on the go with call-ups, warrants, and training, while I had a hectic schedule as well. I was actively involved with motherhood, tending to baby Gabrielle and an active toddler, Matthew. Besides working at a full-time job, I was also pursuing a self-employed sales position with a renowned insurance company, which required intensive and extensive studying and training.

Randy visiting the Island of Capri in Italy. Our last big trip together.

Family photo of us at our church bible study.

Initially, Randy did not want me to pursue such a demanding sales career, especially since his occupation was already extremely challenging. He was afraid that my hectic schedule would interfere or take away from our family. As he was concerned about the kids and me, he didn't want an overwhelming career to weigh heavily on us or put extra stress on the kids and me. In addition, Randy was big on systems and structure, which we finally got on track in our household. A new career could possibly derail everything.

During our first few years of marriage, I would complain endlessly about Randy having me on such a rigid schedule. It felt as if I were in the military and he was the drill sergeant. It took years for me to conform to his style of scheduling and to understand his logic when it came to being on a timetable. Working on SWAT, Randy's schedule was always changing or being modified, depending on what was going on in the city. To prevent further chaos, he needed me to stick firmly to a plan so that personal things would get done. Randy felt that his unpredictable and complicated schedule was crazy enough. Consequently, he needed me to be the steady one, managing things at home so that the family would have some stability. Nothing meant more to Randy than the well-being of his family, and his methodical way of thinking always made things run smoothly.

I was a master at orchestrating things, especially the activities I was passionate about. I agreed with Randy in terms of stability; however, I was determined to fulfill my own dreams too. I wanted to pursue a career in sales. In support of my dreams, I took it upon myself to hire a full-time nanny to assist me during my training period. Throughout that time, I took organization to a new level. Having enrolled in an insurance agency sales program in Westlake Village, California, I made it a point to continue managing my home. I knew my husband's position on keeping the family intact, and I didn't want any conflict or confusion.

With Randy's SWAT schedule being so unpredictable, all the babysitting issues were my responsibility and affected my schedule. I committed to approximately a year of training, which meant a commute time of four hours daily, picking up Matthew from preschool, coming home to cook for the family, spending quality time with the children, studying at night, and then bedtime romance with Randy, if he wasn't called out for a warrant or an unexpected call-up. The majority of his training was during the day, while warrants were for the most part at night, and a call-up could take place at any given time. Sometimes Randy would work around the clock, alternating between an unexpected call-up and a scheduled warrant.

In the midst of our fast-paced life, we always made time to attend church, for church took priority over everything, and we only missed it if there were work-related issues. Even after work, Randy would call home to tell me that he was going to stop at church before making his way home. In a tired stupor, he would attend Bible study or prayer service. It was never a chore for him because he truly enjoyed church and wanted to learn everything he could in order to have a closer relationship with the Lord.

Once I finished sales training school, I was considered a self-employed insurance agent and had multiple responsibilities. I was able to get my own agency up and running. The kids were now in elementary school and were attending Trinity Lutheran School in Hawthorne, California, only a few blocks from my office. Everything was running smoothly, and I could now truly appreciate and understand Randy's purpose for wanting structure and systems in place.

I managed to follow the system effectively, especially where my motherly efforts were concerned, and being self-employed with flexible hours, I could come and go as I pleased. Being serious about the rearing of the kids, although his schedule was demanding, Randy made every effort to contribute to child care whenever his schedule would permit, as he was determined not to be an absentee father.

While I was building my insurance business, Randy was working on another project that was near and dear to his heart outside of SWAT. He and Pastor Trimble had been in discussion about carrying out a community outreach program. Our pastor, being familiar with the turbulent street crimes that affected youth in the community, agreed to let Randy implement a program under his leadership, a program that would minister and mentor to kids at various project sites. Randy would be the director, along with a team of site leaders from the church who would work with him to accomplish this goal. It would be called the Glory Kids Ministry, and it required a lot of love, time, and commitment.

Prior to starting the Glory Kids Ministry, Randy began conducting extensive research on how to develop and run a successful outreach program. He looked at a number of other churches that ran outreach programs, plus he went to seminars and read books. But there was something that books and seminars could not teach him: a true spirit of love, patience, compassion, and discernment. Randy knew he needed to have these essential qualities in order to be effective in a community plagued by violence.

After a year of research and driving around Los Angeles observing different project sites, Randy set his eyes on the Hacienda projects on 103rd and Compton Boulevard as the first site to test the Glory Kids program. Randy arrived in August of 1997. Hacienda was in an area of Los Angeles called Watts, which was considered one of the toughest crime areas of Los Angeles. The Hacienda projects, now called "housing development" due to the negative stigma associated with the word "projects," was relatively large. Hacienda stretched for eight square blocks, going north, south, east, and west. The streets were configured like one big square, and the homes were single-level light green dwellings, each comprised of two units, with the square holding well over one hundred residences.

Some of the dwellings lined the streets of Compton and 103$^{rd}$, while the others filled in the inner areas of the housing development. In the middle of these two-unit family dwellings was a basketball court with blacktop. Randy would use the basketball court as a stage to speak and deliver the gospel and words of encouragement to the Glory Kids and their parents.

Only someone like Randy, a strong and selfless director, would be able to lead such a demanding and benevolent ministry and mentoring program. Randy, along with the assistance of the other site leaders, went faithfully to various project sites in the inner city of Los Angeles and minister and mentor to kids. He would have his program laid out weekly so that the group would be well organized. A prayer and a scripture verse would kick off the program, accompanied by a skit that illustrated the scripture and how it applied to life today. The Glory Kids Ministry took place every weekend, and the fun would end with games, toys, candy, or ice cream treats. Randy also committed to bringing those same kids and their parents to church every Sunday.

During the first weekend program, Pastor Trimble accompanied Randy as he anxiously set up a sound system with a microphone and speakers. He was excited about starting this new outreach project, a project for which he had a deep passion. The microphone would be the major tool used to gather people over to the blacktop. However, on that first day of speaking, a problem occurred. They forgot they needed electricity in order for the sound system to work. Randy contemplated long and hard about what to do. He looked around him and focused on a dwelling that sat close to the blacktop. He walked up to the home, and Pastor Trimble remained nearby on the blacktop, watching the equipment. When he knocked on the door, a woman named Linda greeted him.

Linda, it turned out, was a recovering drug user who was in and out of rehab. She had four children, and she had just regained custody after losing her kids to the State of California. She reluctantly opened the door and was apprehensive about talking to Randy. She hadn't seen him before and wasn't sure if Randy was someone from Child Protective Services or law enforcement coming to question her about her drug use. Naturally, she wasn't very approachable and her guard was up.

Knowledgeable about the personalities of drug users, Randy was able to tune in as he recognized her fear about talking to him. He quickly alleviated her fears by talking as humbly as possible, explaining what he was trying to accomplish in the housing development. Fearing that she wouldn't participate, he didn't tell her that he was the police. When he saw that she was slightly receptive to his goals and ideas about helping the kids in the housing development, he went on to ask her if she could help him by allowing him to use her electricity and that he would compensate her in return. He then went on to ask her for help as it pertained to gathering the children who lived in the housing site. He knew that Linda could be very instrumental in helping him jump-start Glory Kids. With some hesitancy, Linda agreed and let Randy use her electricity, plus she gathered a few children and adults, and they sat and listened to Randy deliver his first outreach message.

Randy's first message was based on the love of God. He explained to the parents and children how much God loved them, and that God had a beautiful purpose and plan for their lives. He also explained that it was because of God's love that he and others would be volunteering their time at the housing development every Saturday to teach lessons from the Bible—lessons that would be used to help the kids build strong character in a positive way.

Randy with the Glory Kids.

He further explained that there would be games, prizes, and treats after every lesson, hoping it would give the kids an incentive to come and join him every Saturday for an edifying lesson and fun. He ended that first message with treats, candy, and a prayer.

When the presentation was over, Linda walked up to Randy and thanked him for caring about the Hacienda residence. She began to cry and expressed to Randy that he was like an angel sent from heaven, intervening on that particular day and rescuing her. She explained that prior to his knocking on her door, she was having thoughts of backsliding, as she was craving drugs and felt overwhelmed about being a mother. She didn't feel as if she had any purpose in life. Randy, being such a compassionate soul, gave her a warm hug, and he and Pastor Trimble prayed with Linda. From that day forward, Randy continued to encourage Linda. He kept a close eye on her, making sure she didn't go back to a life of darkness. Ultimately, Linda became a driving force in helping him gather kids every Saturday and bringing them to the Glory Kids outreach.

# CHAPTER 13

# The Balancing Act

OVER THE NEXT FEW YEARS, the Simmons family ran their lives at full speed. Randy and I juggled and sometimes struggled with balancing the multitude of responsibilities each of us had taken on. Randy was committed to SWAT and Glory Kids, which required a lot of time and dedication, while as a competitive insurance agent, I worked hard at being a top-producing agent on my insurance team. But regardless of how busy we were, we never compromised our time when it came to our children. We made sure that Matthew and Gabrielle did not miss out on anything, making sure they were involved in all sorts of activities. For Matthew, it was football, Tae Kwon Do and ice hockey; for Gabrielle, it was cheerleading, gymnastics, ice skating and modern dance. As parents, we also participated in activities right alongside our children; I taught dance at Gabrielle's school, and Randy acted as an assistant football coach for Matthew's Pop Warner football team. One might have classified us as the all-American modern-day family.

I often observed times when Randy would fight against his tiredness after extremely hectic twenty-four-hour call-ups, but it was important for him to see and have interaction with our kids every day. Sometimes he would drive up to the children's school in his unmarked police car and make unannounced visits before heading home. He would walk over to their classrooms and surprise them by looking in the classroom windows, jokingly sticking his tongue out at them. Other times he would meet them at recess or lunch, just to extend a hug and a kiss. If he had time, he would stay for recess and engage in some sports activity with Matt and his friends, shooting hoops or throwing a few football passes.

All the kids at their school knew that Matt and Gabby's father was a SWAT cop, as he wore his blue uniform proudly. The kids were impressed by his occupation and by his statuesque, brawny frame, a frame so muscular that it looked as if he might bust right out of his uniform. Parents, students, and teachers admired our family unit. I can recall the principal of the kids' school telling me that our outward display of love and affection was evidence of a close-knit family.

That same love and affection was displayed in our household as well. Whenever Randy was home for dinner, he would initiate family discussions. He would talk with Matthew and Gabrielle about making good choices in life and the consequences of one's actions. His heart and soul went into making sure that his children knew how important it was to live a good, spiritual life because he recognized that this was going to be their foundation and the key to their salvation. He made sure they knew and understood biblical teachings and how they were applicable to the things of life. It brings to mind a day when he had me type this scripture verse: *But seek ye first the kingdom of God, and His righteousness; and all these things shall be added to you* (Matthew 6:33). He then asked me to print out two copies of the verse, one for Matthew and one for Gabby. Then he took some Scotch tape and posted one of each of their bedroom walls, telling them to always remember that scripture.

I wasn't as well versed in the Bible as Randy, but I knew enough about the word of God to join in by providing our kids with some examples and expounding on specific subjects. It was important for us to instill life lessons in our children early on and give them an understanding of how the Bible would be their instruction book for dealing with life's issues.

Usually Randy would end table topics with a prayer. He loved to pray and was committed to praying daily. It was a natural practice for him throughout the day or whenever the Holy Spirit led him to pray. Whether he was praying for the family, praying for the salvation of a criminal he'd arrested, or praying for the healing of a victim who had been shot, prayer came natural to him. It wasn't a ritual where words were uttered mechanically with no heartfelt meanings associated with the prayer, as some theatrical Christians might do. When Randy prayed, whether the prayer was said softly or aloud, he prayed with passion and the assurance that God heard his prayers.

Randy was definitely the prayer warrior of the family. He wouldn't hesitate to call the kids and me in when something, being the Holy Spirit, prompted him to pray. Sometimes in the middle of the night, I would find him kneeling at the foot of Matthew's and Gabrielle's beds, praying over them while they slept. He kept pictures of them in the most bizarre places. He had pictures of them hanging on the bathroom mirror so that every morning while he was shaving or brushing his teeth, he could look at them and extend a prayer. He also kept pictures and Christian artwork the kids created at school on the inside of his closet door, so while he was getting dressed for work, he wouldn't miss an opportunity to pray for them.

And there is no doubt he prayed over me, for only soul mates could run our race, endure our active lifestyle, and remain married. I know it was his prayers and maybe mine too that gave me the strength and energy required to make it happen every day, with or without Randy being available due to his complex schedule. He loved his family, and we loved him too.

Love has many definitions and is sometimes defined in unpopular ways such as through discipline. He and I were good disciplinarians but not much for spankings. What seemed to work in our household were discussions and consequences, which were sometimes worse than a spanking. A punishment for Matthew could be a week without playing video games; for Gabrielle, it might mean missing a birthday party. These types of punishments were rare, for Matthew and Gabby exhibited good behavior for the most part, trying their best to avoid trouble, as they knew that we were not going to tolerate deviant behavior. All Randy had to do was look at them and they would straighten up their act.

As with most kids, they both knew they could easily manipulate their dear mother, as I was crazy in love with my kids, so I would do foolish things that would later come back to bite me. For example, the kids would often convince me to do things that I knew would eventually cause me trouble. Like the time when I purchased another pet for their miniature zoo that was starting to evolve at our house. Our kids had a hamster, a turtle, two bearded dragons, a dog, and a rabbit. Randy told me firmly not to purchase another pet for the kids, not even a goldfish!

But in my quest to cultivate Gabrielle's dreams of someday becoming a veterinarian, I agreed to take our friend's rabbit so that her one lonely rabbit named Penny could have a new friend, whom we named Naomi. But I learned my lesson when one morning Matthew was feeding the rabbits and accidentally let Naomi out of the cage. I had to take the kids to school, and I was running late for a breakfast I was sponsoring for a real estate board. The last thing I needed to do on that morning was chase a rabbit.

My first instinct was to wake up Randy, who was still sleeping after serving a night warrant, as I thought he would be able to capture the bunny and dry the tears of an emotional Gabrielle. Her brother had just taunted her about the neighborhood dogs eating her runaway rabbit in an attempt to continue the circle of life, which Gabby did not find amusing. But I thought long and hard about facing the wrath of Randy. I would rather risk having a neighbor call the police on me for climbing up their tree to catch a runaway rabbit; as I knew if Randy woke up and saw that we had added another rabbit to our collection it was going to be World War Three on our peaceful street. I was so mad at Matthew for letting the rabbit escape, especially since I was dressed beautifully in my new Dana Buchman suit. But what was I to do?

I took off in my new Via Spiga shoes with Matthew, the two of us running down the street with swimming pool nets to catch Gabby's rabbit. The rabbit hopped from house to house and from tree to tree, while I jumped over bushes, simultaneously scolding Matthew, who was ready to give up on saving the rabbit and let the dogs have a feast. I broke a fingernail and added several unattractive hosiery runs to my business attire.

We finally caught the rabbit and returned it to its cage. I then went on to my meeting, totally sweaty, with no curl in my hair, a broken fingernail, and runs in my pantyhose. On top of that, a few months later we had eight more rabbits, as Naomi wound up being a male rabbit. Randy hit the roof, and I got into big trouble! Nevertheless, we supported our children and knew that by keeping them interested in things they loved and involving them in various activities, it was going to keep them busy and use up any idle time.

Randy spent a lot of father and son time with Matthew. He started Matt off with fitness training early on. Even as a little boy, Randy would take Matthew to get a haircut and then sneak him into a gym so that he could watch him workout. He would beg Matt not to tell me, which actually annoyed me, as I felt the pressure of his fanatical fitness personality was being driven into Matthew from the time he was able to walk. He couldn't wait for Matt to get older and join him in his workout and football activities.

By the time Matthew was ten years old, Randy was preparing him for college football, specifically Washington State. Every year, he would take Matthew with him to his WSU football alumni reunion to encourage him about playing football. It was Randy's dream for Matt, so he started developing workout routines for him. They would lift weights and then go to the park and do pull-ups, run, jump rope, and perform football drills. I recall one night when I was up late washing clothes and Randy was up late as well, writing something. I thought it was work related because he was so intensely involved in this task. I tried to interrupt him. "Randy, do you want me to wash your training uniform?" I asked.

"Lisa, shush! I'm writing a letter to Matthew. I have to make sure my boy is right," he replied.

"You've been down here all this time writing a letter to Matthew? Are you serious? What is it about?"

"A workout assignment and some football drills," he responded.

"Is it really that serious?" I said sarcastically.

He gave me a look that said *Don't disturb me*, so I went about my business and tended to the laundry.

I later learned that Randy's letter to Mathew contained instructions about how to do his workouts, along with techniques he would need for football in case Randy wasn't available. That way, he could always refer to it through his letter. I thought it was just a few quick notes, but there would come a time when I realized that it was a heartfelt letter that Randy had carefully and lovingly written to his son.

There were times when I felt that Randy was obsessed with working out and football. Although Matthew enjoyed doing both of these activities, he wasn't as excited by them as his dad. Randy was often frustrated by Matthew's lack of enthusiasm, as Matt's first love was playing video games with his cousins. Likewise, Matthew was frustrated with Randy too, because at times Randy would interrupt a play day just for Matt to work out with him. My sisters and I used to teasingly say, "Randy needs another best friend," just so he could give Matthew a break.

For Matt, working out was just one of the many activities he enjoyed, but not the only one. Again, video games were his passion, and he especially loved the Xbox and PlayStation. This took precedence over any and every activity and became a direct competition with what Randy had envisioned. To balance out the couch potato, video kid syndrome, Randy enrolled Matthew in football.

Randy and Matthew both participated in the El Segundo Eagles Pop Warner football program, which was located in a city just north of Rancho Palos Verdes, where we lived. Randy met the coaches and liked their playing style, so he decided to enroll Matthew in their program. The location made it fast and easy to get him to practice since the city of El Segundo was less than three miles from my office and closer to the kids' school. It was also closer in proximity to Randy's job in downtown Los Angeles.

Matthew played cornerback and Randy volunteered as assistant defensive coach. This was another responsibility added to Randy's resume, but he wouldn't have traded that priceless experience for the world. He never missed a game or practice unless he was on a SWAT call-up. Randy made sure to arrange his schedule so that Glory Kids and coaching were interchangeable.

The football players loved Coach Randy, and they had the utmost respect for him. He and the coaches had a brotherly love relationship since they had big hearts like Randy. The head coach, Dean Pliaconis, was a well-known executive in the city of El Segundo. Dean's father had developed a successful family business called Plycon Transportation Group years earlier, while living in New York, and it is now a nationwide moving, packaging, and storage company. He, like Randy, made time to give back to the youth in the community. He even allowed some of the inner-city kids to live with his family in an attempt to give them a better life, far from the tough neighborhoods outside of El Segundo.

The other coach, Coach Chris Parr, was a teddy bear that roared at times and cuddled at others. He was genuinely kind and understood the importance of being a positive role model to young men. Randy loved and respected these men, primarily for their mind-sets and their outreach through the likes of football.

Randy praying with The El Segundo Eagles Football Team.

Randy Coaching Matthew.

The coaches and football players were like Randy and Matt's fraternal brothers. Randy would kid around with the players and yell out their crazy nicknames, which reflected their talents on the football field. There was Highlight, Pokey, Bow-Low, Old Man, Muffin, Skinny-B, and Chandler-Lightening Jones. Then there was the star running back, Leroy Jackson, who was constantly under Randy's eye because of his crush on Gabrielle.

Randy traveled with Matthew and his team, winning many championship games. He developed close relationships with a number of the players, especially those who didn't have fathers living in the household. He and Matt would invite them over to the house for dinner and then take them to church with the family the next morning. Randy was a unique and different kind of coach, one who extended himself to the players on and off the field, and they loved him because of it.

Matthew had played and Randy had coached for years by the time Matthew went on to play high school football. The El Segundo Eagles were true champions, and of course, Randy, like the other coaches, believed he'd contributed something to their title.

Time spent with Gabrielle was also never compromised. She was her father's princess, and Randy made time for her activities as well, for she was a cheerleader for her brother's football team. Randy found himself coaching one minute and periodically running up into the bleachers to watch Gabrielle cheer on her brother and his team. He would even drag Matthew with him to Gabby's cheerleading competitions, which were usually eight hours of loud girly screams, cheers, and dance routines. This was torture for Matthew, who simply refused to see cheerleading as a sport.

Randy and I did crazy things like creating songs to encourage our little princess. I would make up songs about Gabby and her beauty and request that everyone join in with me. Matthew couldn't stand when we sang and again felt tortured when I asked him to participate. It was so comical to hear me sing since I couldn't hold a note. And Randy the macho man would purposely sing out of tune purely to irritate me in my pursuit to develop an award-winning song.

We usually sang to Gabrielle to get her to smile while she was doing something she didn't like doing, such as getting her hair combed. The songs would go something like this:

Gabby and Daddy at Church.

"Who's the prettiest little girl in the world?"
"Gab-bri-elle," Randy would respond.
"Who's the smartest little girl in the world?" I would ask.
"Gab-bri-elle," Randy would respond again in a deep voice.
"She's smart, she's funny, and she's witty. Her name is Gabrielle—"
"And oh, she's pretty!" Randy would say, looking her in her face.

Together, Randy and I would end the song with, "Gab, Gab-bri-elle … *Yeahhhhh!*"

This became our theme song for Gabrielle. Her mischievous brother would playfully come in and change the lyrics by replacing the word pretty with ugly and run away laughing. This would prompt an immediate and unexpected wrestling match between Matthew and Randy, with Randy defending Gabrielle by catching Matthew and holding him down in a locked position so Gabrielle could tickle him for such a remark.

Randy nicknamed Gabrielle "Little Constance" because she looked so much like his mother. She had that pretty round brown face, slanted eyes, and a big smile like her grandmother. She, unlike Matthew, could get away with some of the most mischievous actions, and Randy always justified it as "girly emotional behavior" that was excusable. But I would quickly step in and correct it. It was obvious that Gabby was a daddy's girl and Matthew was a mama's boy when it came to defending their unacceptable behavior.

In between work and all the other activities, we still managed to incorporate time for our extended family members. Connie was still single after twenty years, as her healing after Dallas's departure was slow and difficult. However, she found peace and happiness in her church and the countless friends she made after Dallas's abandonment. Our family and Randy's sister Gina and her family surrounded Connie with love and attention, spending family time with her as often as possible. Randy and I would drive to Diamond Bar to attend church with Connie often, and after services, we would feast on a delicious meal that Connie would prepare for the entire family. Randy, Gina, and his mother had a rock-solid relationship that endured the test of time.

My mother, Veronica, was also still single, having lost my father when she was only fifty-two years of age, after being married to him for thirty-four years. The dynamics of my family had dramatically changed, leaving Randy in a position once again to step into a role that he wasn't ready to accept, however qualified—the new patriarch of the family.

As tragedy would have it, a family either pulls together when a storm comes or their lives are washed away. With our family, the storm only brought our two families closer together, becoming one big happy family that supported each other in all planned and unplanned events. No one was ever alone, especially the matriarchs of the family: Connie and Veronica. A new generation of grandchildren would ensure that it would continue. When Matthew or Gabrielle was involved in any activity, their grandmothers, along with Randy and I, were there to support them.

Randy, with his sister Gina, mother and Matthew.

Randy and his Mother who he adored.

Randy's 50th Birthday Party. He delivered a heartfelt birthday message of hope to his guest. He encouraged his guest to get their lives right and spend some time serving God.

# CHAPTER 14

# Committing to a Vigorous and Rigorous Life

As time went on, I became somewhat disenchanted with the busy lifestyle that extended beyond the family and our children's extensive pursuits. Randy had become inundated with Glory Kids and all their activities, plus he had added three more housing development sites to the Glory Kids program—Wilmington Arms, Avalon, and Scottsdale. He was now mentoring to over one thousand kids weekly, and he was also picking up more responsibilities with the church. Randy had a heart of gold and would often commit to helping people even if he knew it was going to interfere with a personal commitment. But I was getting tired of seeing him overextend himself. I longed for the days when our lives were simple and the only thing on our calendar was the children's' activities and a weekend spent at San Diego Zoo or Sea World.

Things had changed drastically in just a few short years, and our weekends consisted of Randy running back and forth from coaching Matt's football team to stopping over at each housing development site for outreach in between SWAT call-ups.

As the wife of a community outreach director, coach, and SWAT officer, I eventually grew into my role as his true helpmate. Together, Randy and I learned through intense dialogue and through trial and error what was going to work best for our family. Like any couple, we had our difficulties, but somehow, through the grace of God, we pushed through and made our marriage work. I would always say that my heart wasn't as compassionate as Randy's was in terms of giving myself to others. I certainly believed in helping the disadvantaged, but I didn't live and breathe it every second of the day as Randy had done. I was a young wife and mother, and there were times I just wanted to surround myself with family matters only, as I believed in balance. Perhaps it was selfish, but it's what I felt.

Randy, on the other hand, wanted everything to intertwine. He was so passionate about helping others that much of our lives were linked with the church and Glory Kids. I tried my best to fill in the gaps by supporting Randy with his ministry whenever I could, but not always willingly or with a hearty spirit. But I did what I could. Since I was self-employed, I took advantage of my flexible schedule and tried to make the impossible happen.

Randy's job did not afford him that opportunity. His pager or cell phone dictated the events of every day. So if there was anything important that Randy had to do when he had a SWAT call-up, I was there to pick up the pieces and make it happen. I had learned after years of being married to a SWAT officer that the city of Los Angeles dictated the flow of any given day. That was just the way it was.

It was at times like these that I realized how having a husband who wore many hats impacted my life as well. One day Randy called me at work and excitedly asked me if I could do him a favor. It was typical of Randy to interrupt my day asking for a favor, and I was livid, mostly because I had a million things to do that day. Being his helpmate, though, I felt compelled. He asked me to take him to an auto body shop to get an ice cream truck that he had customized and painted purple with large cartoon faces of kids displayed all over it. The auto body/paint shop was located in Burbank, which was quite a distance from where I worked and lived; however, it was worth the drive and the inconvenience because inside the truck were magical and wonderful things.

The purple cartoon-looking truck was worth more than any Rolls Royce, Bentley, or Mercedes Benz because it held the tools and resources that Randy would use to influence a new generation of inner city kids in a positive way. As a converted ice cream truck, it would deliver a message of love, hope, faith, and a life of prosperity to children and their families in the inner city of Los Angeles.

Glory Kids Truck.

Within the truck were a microphone, a stereo sound system, and a built-in stage. This cartoon truck would be the truck Randy used every Saturday to gather the kids from the different project sites to hear him speak. It was the truck in which he would deliver his messages about God's love ... and the truck that discouraged kids from a life of gangbanging and drugs. That magical truck also stored food and clothes for the homeless.

After taking Randy to pick up the truck, I drove home feeling bad for giving Randy a hard time about taking him to get the truck. But God allowed me to see that this wasn't just any truck; it was a truck that was going to be used to save souls. Seeing Randy's sincere efforts made me realize that God was using Randy to do his work, and God chose me to help him in ways that I hadn't yet understood. I began to realize that my purpose was to be an understanding and supportive wife, thus it was my responsibility to help Randy by managing our household and filling in the gaps for activities pertaining to our kids and Glory Kids whenever necessary. My help would allow Randy to reach out and help others. In essence, he needed me there whenever he could not be at one of the many things for which he was committed, and that meant I was on call too.

Randy wouldn't hesitate to call me and ask me to fill in for him on a Glory Kid assignment. Even though I was on board with the program, I would still get frustrated at one of his spur-of-the moment interruptions or a request. It appeared that Randy's days of having structure and systems in place were long gone when it came to needing my assistance. I recall a particular day when he called me and informed me that he was on a call-up. I could tell what it was by the sound of the commotion going on in the car. I could also hear his partner, James, talking on the radio to the dispatcher and the siren of the car echoing into the phone. Randy was talking loudly, trying to share with me what was going on. From what I could hear, it appeared that a suicidal man was attempting to end his life by jumping off a cliff.

Randy, speaking loudly over James's voice, asked me to go to the Hacienda housing development site to remind the kids about a big festival our church was giving. He wanted to make sure every child knew about it. I was just about to meet with a client for a big life insurance sell, but I heard the desperation in his voice.

"Baby girl, work with me. I really need your help. I need you to go over to the Hacienda projects, collect the trip slips for the festival this weekend."

With agitation, I exclaimed, "Randy, are you serious? I have to work sometimes too! I have an insurance appointment coming in an hour."

All of my reasons to get out of going over to Hacienda were unheard. In addition, guilt got the best of me. I handed over my appointment to one of my sales agents, promptly picking up my purse and heading to the Hacienda projects, where church member and good friend Ralph Mansion was scheduled to meet me.

The projects were definitely not a place for a lady to roam around by herself, especially an unfamiliar face and one in a suit and three-inch heels. Randy was big on safety, so he'd given me strict instructions to wait in my car until Ralph arrived. He told me not to park on the side street of 103rd Street but instead to park on Compton Boulevard, where there was a lot of visibility.

I arrived at Hacienda and waited for Ralph for about thirty minutes. It was dusk, and the elements in the neighborhood appeared to be attracted to the coming of night. There were gangbangers hanging out highlighting their colors and drug dealers making transactions. There was also a sad scene of a young streetwalker that put me in an instinctive motherly mood; I wanted to grab her and put some decent clothes on her to cover her petite frame. Plus several lowriders passed me slowly, their drivers bouncing their vehicles up and down, seeking to gain attention. I was starting to feel a little uncomfortable, so I decided to contact my sister Cookie to inform her of my whereabouts. I called her, but she was at work in chambers with her judge handling court cases. Then I called my younger sister, Melinda, who reprimanded me for being in the projects without Randy or the familiar faces of our church members.

"Lisa, you're over there in a Mercedes, looking to get robbed! If Ralph doesn't show up in ten minutes, you must leave," she said, clearly concerned and agitated. She continued. "Mama would have your neck if she knew you were over there by yourself. And it's getting dark too."

I asked Melinda to pick up my kids from school, as I had a feeling I was going to be late getting back to that side of town. My kids were always in the forefront of my mind, and I knew that if they were with my sister, they would be okay. I hung up with Melinda and made contact with one of the Glory Kid teenagers that I had recognized. Monica was a young mother who'd recently had a baby, who was our newest Glory Kid.

I jumped out of my car with the trip slips and a bowl of candy that I'd picked up from the store on the way to the site. I opened the trunk of my car to put on my tennis shoes and yelled and signaled for Monica to come toward me. Her face lit up with a big smile when she saw me, and she greeted me with a big hug.

Monica was familiar with all of the Glory Kids who participated in the program, so I asked her if she would help me pass out more trip slips and collect those that had been signed by the children's legal guardians. It appeared that Ralph was running late or possibly was going to be a no-show due to his work schedule. I didn't want to walk the site alone, so I felt that was the best way to handle the situation. She was more than happy to assist me, and together we walked through the complex.

I was a little nervous being that I wasn't as popular as Randy or some of the other church members; at least I thought I wasn't as popular. The kids were all around the complex, riding their bicycles, skateboarding, playing basketball, and just hanging out and talking. The minute they knew I was there, they came running toward me, screaming my name.

"Lisa ... Lisa!" they yelled. As they surrounded me excitedly, asking me about activities concerning the festival, I passed out hugs, candy, and requested trip slips. Monica and I continued to walk through the complex when we saw Marcella at a distance.

Marcella was an attractive Hispanic parent in her mid-thirties who struggled with drugs. She and her family were regulars on the bus, attending church with Randy. She was doing well, and her life was going in a positive direction, but I hadn't seen her at church lately, although her children were still on the bus, attending with other Glory Kids. Her little son, Carlos, had been shot twice during a drive-by, once in the face and the second time in the stomach. Randy was devastated. He wept and prayed to God, asking for protection not just for little Carlos but also for all the children in the area who were surrounded by violence. Little Carlos survived both shootings without any deficits. God was truly with him ... or maybe he heard Randy's and the other church members' continuous prayers.

As we approached Marcella, something seemed strange and almost demonic about her presence. Her face was pale, and her eyes were rolling back in her head. She was walking as if she were floating on a cloud. It was obvious that Marcella was backsliding into the life of drugs again, and never in my life had I seen anything like it. The kids continued riding their bikes around her, ignoring her bizarre behavior. Apparently this was nothing out of the ordinary, for none of the kids were moved by her, nor were they afraid of her scary disposition. I, however, continued to stare with my mouth wide open in disbelief. I knew Monica could tell I was shocked by what I was witnessing, but nothing shocked me quite as much as the unexpected greeting of three thugs.

While focusing on Marcella, I was caught off guard by three thugs standing nearby. One of them had just gotten out of jail for drug trafficking. They yelled something to Monica and me, and my focus left Marcella. I looked straight ahead, pretending not to hear them while Monica encouraged me to try not to look frightened, but I couldn't help myself.

As we walked closer in their direction, the thug called for Monica and me to come to him. We were right up on them, as we had no choice, so we stopped to see what they wanted. My natural reaction was to offer them some candy and ask them if their kids were going to the festival. They ignored me, looked at me in a flirty way, and chuckled.

"You Randy's wife?" one asked.

I was always proud to be Randy's wife, for that name was very common to me, especially at church. I felt as if that were my name, "Randy's wife," but this was certainly a time I could have used a pass card. Shaking, I nervously said that I was. I recognized DJ's father, who always let his son participate with the Glory Kids, but the other two men I had never seen before.

He responded, "Ah, looka here, we appreciate what the brother's tryin' to do over here, but tell him it's time for him to step back. This is our hood. We got this."

He took a puff of his joint and looked me up and down as if he were undressing me with his eyes. "Tell him we don't need him over here no mo' with all that preachin' stuff." He exhaled smoke from his mouth.

Another one of the thugs made a comment while stepping closer to me and grabbing several pieces of candy out of my bowl. "We don't mix well with the po-po. It's like oil and water. We control dis over here," he continued. "Damn! Y'all don't have any snickers in that bowl?" he said in a negative tone.

I didn't know what to do or say, and I thought about the old Chinese proverb stating that silence is golden. I knew what I wanted to say, but I didn't think it would have worked to my advantage, so Monica and I walked away. She could see that I was visibly shaken, and in her concern about me, she tried to console my inner fears. She told me that the leader of the pack was named Ace and he had just gotten out of jail. She said that he hadn't witnessed the good works Randy was doing at the site. Although he heard about Randy from people who lived in the area, he was intimidated by the fact that Randy was the police, and he wanted him to stay away.

Monica assured me that his bark was bigger than his bite, but I didn't want any part of his bark or his bite. It was my cue to leave, so I gave Monica twenty dollars for helping me, got in my car, and drove off with tears flowing from my eyes. Just the thought of someone hurting Randy sent chills all through my body. He and I were going to have a serious conversation about his swimming in shark territory every single week.

# CHAPTER 15

# Call to Duty

It would be hours before Randy got home, and I couldn't wait to tell him about my threatening experience while in the projects. But for now, Randy was at a call-up on the other side of town, in San Pedro, California, and had other matters that were far more important, so I had to wait. There in San Pedro, near the lighthouse, a lost soul had become frustrated with the issues of life and was attempting suicide. Clinging to a rock, the victim's situation was severe as he contemplated jumping into the ocean, with the waves approximately one hundred feet below, breaking against the jagged rocks of the mountain. Hanging from the cliff and threatening to leap to his death, he was sweating profusely and shaking with intense emotion. Randy, a negotiator for SWAT, leaned over the cliff above the young man and tried to talk with him via the help of a megaphone. Empathizing with this man's heartache, Randy made every attempt to convince him to surrender and not to end his life, but Randy's pleas were ignored. Not wishing to compete with the sounds of the waves, Randy asked his lieutenant if he could be lowered down in a harness.

It was an unheard of request, and Randy's lieutenant thought he was crazy. It was way too risky, plus the mountain climbers were on their way to assist the SWAT team. But Randy pleaded with his lieutenant, and he reluctantly gave in to Randy's request.

As he was lowered down in a harness, with his body slamming and knocking against the mountains by the swing of the rope and the wind, Randy showed no signs of fear, as he simply didn't care about the danger when he was doing his job.

As he approached the man, Randy gave him one last attempt at voluntarily surrendering on his own, but he refused. Randy went into action. Nicknamed "The Claw" for his ability to use his strength for grabbing and immobilizing suspects and suicide victims, he reached out and latched on to the man, wrapping his legs around the man to secure him tightly. It was as if Randy were playing a stuntman in an action movie, except in this case, it was a real-life situation and Randy needed to save his life.

The team raised Randy and the man, applauding Randy for his brave efforts, while his good friend and partner looked on in amazement. James Hart couldn't believe Randy's heroic efforts and his willingness to put himself in such a life-threatening situation. While Randy was being treated by the paramedics for abrasions, James walked over to Randy and started clapping. "Another Simmons production," he said, with admiration in his voice for his fellow friend and officer.

"Mission accomplished," Randy responded.

I admired the fraternal brotherhood found among Randy and his SWAT brothers. They were a respectable unit with a ton of expertise and, some might add, huge egos, but rightfully so. They were the best of the best! Their high-ranking expertise was only called in to handle the most serious and dangerous crimes, for SWAT individuals were known for being good at their craft and confident about their work. As a SWAT wife of seventeen years, I knew better than most about the rigorous requirements and intense qualifications that were necessary for a member to remain in SWAT.

I can recall Randy complaining about how much he dreaded going to training or having to qualify for a PFQ, better known as the physical fitness qualification test. I assumed by his reluctant behavior that it was a most challenging test, although Randy was always up for a challenge. In this instance, however, he preferred to pass, which meant it was an extremely exhausting test.

Randy relaxing after an intense workout.

Randy was fifty-one years old, but he had a body like an eighteen-year-old, and his strength surpassed that of bodybuilder Arnold Schwarzenegger back in his prime. He would share with me how the guys would kid around with each other when it came to lifting weights, but he was strong and could outlift just about any young rookie on the team. One day a handsome young officer, whom I'll call "Superman" for this particular story, bragged about how he could beat Randy in executing pull-ups. He went as far as taunting Randy by flexing and showing his big muscles and then pointing to a tattoo that reflected the image of Superman.

Taller, bigger, and not to mention younger, he put on a grandiose performance in an attempt to intimidate Randy. The guys all stood around laughing and anxiously awaiting the big showdown. But Superman was a lot of talk, and Randy was quite the opposite, not much on talking. As a man of very few words, he was more about action when it came to competing. In contrast, Superman rubbed his hands together, flexed his chest muscles, and shrugged his shoulders, jumping up on the pull-up bar and struggling to complete each set. The number of pull-ups he performed didn't give him any bragging rights, as surely Superman could do more. The old timers on SWAT who'd worked with Randy for years knew how many Randy could complete and realized he was capable of much more. They knew that Superman was up against the Hulk.

Randy, being rather modest yet confident, jumped up on the bar and did three times as many pull-ups with ease. Superman was teased terribly by the guys, and I was told that Randy didn't even work up a good sweat, yet he outperformed Superman and put him to shame. After finishing, Randy jumped down from the bar, looked at Superman, and playfully said, "Young man, age ain't nothin' but a number ... Don't forget that, son." Then he walked away with a cool swagger.

Randy represented for the veterans, whose age was masked by their fit bodies, athletic skills, talents and endurance. With the exception of a few gray hairs, you could not distinguish the seasoned SWAT officers from the younger ones. They'd pretty much perfected their skills and talents, so the younger ones were learning from the best.

There were also those tender moments when Randy would have a one-on-one with another SWAT member about life after death. In one particular incident, he shared a story with me about how one of the SWAT members was reminiscing about Louie, his dear friend and fellow SWAT officer. Louie tragically died while training on the SWAT team.

While walking on a ten-foot high catwalk during a training module, he went to sit down and misjudged the distance of the ledge as he attempted to position his hand and lean his body weight on the ledge. As a result, he lost his balance and hit his head, thus falling to his tragic demise. It was definitely what one would consider a freak accident. The team was devastated.

Randy was a master at sharing the gospel without sounding like a religious fanatic, and everyone knew he was a man of faith. He didn't have to go around saying it, as it was clearly all in how he presented himself. With his spiritual walk strong and straight, I don't think it was a coincidence that Randy could recognize the sorrow and anguish of a fellow officer. Being a devout Christian, he was able to discern things that others couldn't see. So when his fellow SWAT brother was looking for an answer about the afterlife, Randy didn't hesitate to give it to him. He assured him that Louie, if he'd been a believer, was in a better place where the streets were paved in gold. He talked to him further about being a believer and the great reward that comes with it: eternal life after death. It gave Randy's fellow officer a sense of hope and cheered him up.

I guess the people who knew him best were his partners, for over the years, there were a few that Randy loved and respected. When I first met Randy, his partner was Andy Simon. As Randy put it, Andy was a big bad-to-the-bone buff white boy, and Randy loved working with Andy.

Then there was his temporary partner, Jerry Tomic, whom Randy valued a great deal. Jerry, he would say, was like a warhorse—a diligent and hard worker. Randy admired his work ethic, but he would often joke and side with his partner's wife, Peggy, about Jerry's working too much and too long.

And there was his faithful friend and partner, James Hart. They were like the dynamic duo. Besides sharing the same faith, they also had the same compassion for people and saw eye to eye on most things. They had even intertwined their personal lives, which seemed somewhat odd since they were both very private individuals. But for some reason, they had enough trust in each other to confide about personal issues.

SWAT, known as D Platoon, David Platoon, or D Team, had

several squads in its platoon, often requiring each squad to partake in different assignments and tasks. Occasionally, they would have to work crime suppressant, which was not popular among the members that had longevity in SWAT. Many felt that they had paid their dues and that this sort of assignment was beneath their expertise. Randy, however, having a humble spirit, found none of these tests or assignments too menial or beneath him. Besides, he liked working the streets because it gave him the opportunity to mentor and minister in a subtle way to those who lived in the underserved areas, particularly the children.

As a lead officer, known as a "Plus 3," Randy was afforded the opportunity of working with several different officers. Many of the younger officers who were new to the SWAT unit were assigned crime suppressant, and Randy would eagerly go out and work the streets with them. Observant and experienced, he could foresee trouble and when some incidents needed more attendance than others.

I was told about an incident where Randy partnered with a new rookie on the SWAT team who anxiously wanted to make an arrest. He saw some gangbangers on the street corner and felt they were dealing drugs or were ready to start trouble. He didn't know Randy very well just yet, but he was sure that this old-timer was going to bust up the scene and haul those undesirable hoodlums to jail.

He and Randy got out of the car. Randy identified the gang leader and pulled him off to the side to have a one-on-one with him. Initially, the gangbanger was resistant, strongly feeling that he and his boys were being harassed because they had on their colors and were standing on the corner. He hesitated and then walked half a block down to talk to Randy. The conversation went something like this:

"Yo, homes, this is crazy. I ain't did nothin.' Just 'cause I have on red don't mean I'm bangin'," the gangbanger stated.

Randy got close up on him and said, "You're either blood or you're not. I ain't gonna deny anything that I'm proud of. Are you a blood? What's up?"

"Wearing red ain't no crime last I checked," the gangbanger responded sarcastically.

"Man, I see you and your boys over here all the time. What's your purpose in life?" Randy questioned. "Are you gonna do this forever? You gonna waste your life on the corner drinking Old Eight, saggin' and bangin', waiting on the next drive-by to take you six feet under? Or would you rather spend your life in a matchbox with Bubba?"

The gangbanger stared at Randy with a harsh look. Obviously, Randy had struck a nerve. He continued to talk with an eyebrow lifted and his finger pointed to his forehead in a thinking position. "Think, young brother ... Get a trade, work, do something productive with your life!" Randy exclaimed.

Randy could see that he had gotten the gangbanger's attention, so he got up even closer and quietly asked him, "Do you go to church? Do you know Jesus?"

The gangbanger looked at Randy as if he were crazy, but he could see that Randy was serious. He explained to Randy that he hadn't been to church since his grandmother died. He shared with Randy a bit about his life, telling Randy that he was born to a drug user and a father who was unknown and possibly a pimp. His only hope was his beloved grandmother, who kept him and his brother in the church. She was a woman of faith and raised them to trust God, but she passed away during his teen years. At her passing, he was put in the foster care system, at which time his faith diminished. Being a ward of the state was worse than being in the streets, he told Randy, as the streets were kinder to him than the family who fostered him and his brother.

Randy could see that there was still some hope for this young man, so he invited him to church. Randy told him how every Sunday he was in the neighborhood picking up people for church. He said he would pass by in the morning and take him too; he encouraged him to go. Moments later, the young rookie cop witnessed a gangbanger crying and a SWAT officer extending brotherly love. The rookie and the gangbanger's buddies were dumbfounded.

The young rookie had learned an important lesson in community outreach. He learned through that experience that everything is not always about an arrest—that a word of encouragement and empathy, if the situation calls for it, can turn things around. Randy explained to the officer that it's about helping our youth change their mind-sets.

"Sometimes you have to engage in conversation with the kids and see what's going on inside their heads," he told the young officer. "So often as officers, we want to deal with the outer man only, the criminal activity we see. But if we as officers could do more community outreach and get in the minds of these kids, we could possibly change a generation. If we can change that inner man, the spirit, the outer man will present himself in an entirely different manner." The rookie was impressed with Randy's way of thinking, as he could see that Randy had the perception of a mature and experienced officer, emphasizing that every situation was different, and that you have to deal with each situation accordingly.

Anyone who worked with Randy could tell that he was true-blue. As his partner, James Hart said so candidly when describing Randy's position as a tough cop, "Randy was no punk! He wouldn't hesitate to take down the best of them, especially when it came to innocent victims being violated directly or indirectly by street bullies and drug dealers. Randy was always ready to handle up on street business, and it wasn't going to be a pretty scene. It was showtime!"

I recall one day when Randy and James called me from USC Medical Center. Randy was to be home early on that particular day because he had to help coach Matthew's football team. The coaches were in the middle of getting the El Segundo Eagles Pop Warner football team ready for the big play-off game. Randy called home to ask me to make contact with the coaches and to let them know not to expect him because he was held up at the hospital. Naturally, when I heard the word hospital, I went into a panic mode.

"What happened? Are you okay?" I asked.

"Yeah, there was a drug transaction, and I had to chase this fool for several blocks. By the time I caught him, he had swallowed a couple of rocks."

"By rocks ... you mean drugs?" I asked, my ignorance showing.

"No, bubble gum, Lisa! I'll be home late," he said cynically.

Randy had a way about him when he was frustrated. I always knew when he was mad because his sarcastic, cynical ways would go into overdrive. During the course of our marriage, I learned to ignore it. On that day, I knew how much he wanted to step outside of his SWAT role and take on the assistant coach role for his El Segundo Pop Warner football team, so I said nothing.

Since he was on SWAT, there was always going to be interruptions. It was a way of life not only for the officers but for their families as well. And more often than not, when we did things as a family and went places, we had to go in two separate cars. If we chose to go in the same car, we had to arrange for someone in the family to bring us home in the event that Randy had an unexpected call-up. I learned to take my own car after being stranded several times because of a SWAT call-up.

When I was seven months pregnant, Randy and I were at a Lamaze class, and wouldn't you know it! His pager went off, and I was left stranded and without my coaching partner. Initially, I rebelled against this way of life, and I would argue with Randy about us not being able to drive together. I tried to explain that sometimes I liked being chauffeured by my husband; however, this concept, for the most part, was not part of our family lifestyle, at least not while he was on call, which was more often than not. I learned the hard way that it was best if I took my own car.

## CHAPTER 16

# Church, Family, and Glory Kids

In between family, SWAT, and football coaching, Randy's truest passion was the Glory Kids Ministry. Randy loved his involvement with community outreach, and he loved the kids in the various housing development sites. The feeling was mutual, as the kids and their families loved him too. As the years went by, the adult residents in the underserved areas grew to trust Randy, not as a cop patrolling their neighborhood in an attempt to see their wrongdoings, but as a cop in a uniform who truly cared about the well-being of them and their children.

Every Saturday morning, Randy and two to four other outreach staff members from church would take the little purple ice cream truck over to the site. They would circle the neighborhood and blow the horn continuously while Randy called out on a microphone: "Glory Kids! Glory Kids! Glory Kids! Come on out! Glory Kids, Glory Kids, Glory Kids are in the house!"

Kids would come running from everywhere. It was usually midmorning, so it wasn't surprising to see some kids still in their pajamas or with sleep crumbs still in their eyes. They would be so excited to see Randy and the crew that they would forget to put on clothes and wash their faces.

Everyone knew the routine, as it was an every Saturday event. They would hear Randy's horn, see the big purple truck, and run over to the basketball court. A few kids would jump on the truck with Randy, helping him yell or doing what they could to catch the attention of other kids. Others would run and knock on the doors of their friends, telling them that Randy was here. You could hear the yells of Glory Kids all over the housing development site.

Periodically, when time permitted or when I wasn't chauffeuring Matthew and Gabrielle on one of their many activities, I would go out midweek and help Randy with the Glory Kids. For a long time, many of the kids didn't know I was Randy's wife, and he wanted it that way for security reasons. I recall the times when kids would share with me their kinship with Randy, not knowing that I was his wife. Kids would say proudly, "Randy is my uncle." Another would say, "Randy's my big brother." A fatherless child would state, "Randy's my godfather."

There was such a love for Randy that everybody wanted to be somebody special to him. As far as Randy was concerned, they were all his babies. And that's how he would refer to them—his extended children. Many of the mothers and grandmothers were his family too. They appreciated that Randy and the church took such an interest in their well-being. So the adults would often help Randy gather up kids and assist him with whatever was needed if it pertained to the Glory Kids Ministry program.

Often when Randy and his team pulled up at the site, there would be the roughest gangbangers playing basketball. I have witnessed with my own eyes the gangbangers quitting their game just so Randy could do his program, or they would ask Randy if they could finish their game using half the court. Even they had an admiration for the things that Randy was trying to accomplish in the projects. I believe that many of them felt that it was too late for them to be saved from a life of crime, but they believed that there was still hope for their own kids or little sisters and brothers. Perhaps they felt that they had no goodness to give to their children, so they didn't mind Randy and his staff instilling the word of God as well as morals and values.

Randy and his site leaders prepared for the program by laying down a tarp for the kids to sit on. They would pull down a stage that was hidden away inside of the truck, also using a microphone and speakers. Puppets, toys, candy, and posters all played a part in delivering the message of the day. The respect that Randy and the other site leaders, including Ralph,

Yolanda, Emerita, Della Reese, Mildred, Lorraine, Greg, Milton, Mike Dees, Joyce, Patrick, Ronnie, and all the others received was amazing.

The kids all sat on the tarp and listened intensely to the message each Saturday. Randy kept it simple, using a message that was taken from scripture verses out of the Bible. They were typically scriptures pertaining to love, obedience, sacrifice, or edification. He would give or use simple examples, making sure the children truly understood how to live and apply these concepts to everyday situations.

Many kids came to know Jesus Christ through Randy and the Glory Kids Ministry. Unlike most adults, who were skeptical to receive anything that was good and free, the kids jumped at the opportunity to receive Jesus as their Lord and Savior.

In his examples, Randy would use people the kids could relate to, such as their parents, siblings, friends, and teachers. Then he would have a question-and-answer period, which was usually motivated by a prize or candy. And finally, he would conclude his message with a prayer of salvation. The program ended with a fun celebration of snacks, such as popsicles, chips, cookies, candy, and fruit juices, and then games such as potato sack races or water balloon races took place.

After the program was over, Randy usually made his rounds to different houses, where he would say hello to the elders. One of them was Mrs. Lois, who agreed to attend church with Randy on Sunday if Randy wouldn't condemn her for smoking her cigarettes and drinking her coffee. She recalled their conversations and shared one with me:

"Randy, I'll go to church on Sunday, but I'm not going to give up my cigarettes and coffee just yet."

"We'll take baby steps, Mrs. Lois. Let's just get you in church first," he responded, flashing that big, beautiful smile.

He would often visit the kids' parents, including Valerie, who was the mother to Jeffrey, Tasha, Keisha, and Meika; Debra, who was Maurice and Shaunice's mom; Meredith, Anthony's mom; and Beverly, who was Monica's mom and little Josie's grandma. He would even visit with Pablo's mom and dad, neither of whom spoke a word of English but used sign language through hand gestures and smiles. Then he would visit the sick, like a woman named Mimi who was battling cancer. Lastly, he would take care of serious personal business that required the Holy Ghost to be deeply rooted in him.

Randy loved the Lord, but he was human too. There were times when the Holy Ghost would leave him and the flesh would take over. At that time, he would put on his street face and go deal with a father he thought could possibly be abusive or a mother who was doing drugs around her kids.

I remember the time when he dealt with DJ and his friends. DJ was one of the roughnecks who had threatened me in the projects when I went to pass out and collect trip slips for the festival. If I had known Randy was going to go ballistic about that incident, I might not have told him about it, but he didn't tolerate foolishness, and he certainly didn't take kindly to threats, especially when made toward a family member.

Randy shared the details of the run-in he had with DJ's father and his friends. He told me he went over to DJ's house and found his father and his hoodlum friends sitting in the front room drinking. They also appeared to be high. The dialogue went something like this:

"Who threatened my wife?" Randy asked.

DJ's father, showing off, made an announcement to his friends that Randy the po-po preacher was at the door. "Ah, man," he then said, "dat was Ace. He just got out of the pen. He hadn't been hip to what's been going on over here. You cool. Apologize to the missus. No harm intended."

Ready to take DJ and all his friends down by himself, Randy got up close to DJ and gave all his friends a look that would have scared the hardest criminal. He said in all seriousness, "You tell your friend Ace that the po-po preacher said this: If he ever ... and I mean *ever* ... runs up on my wife, my site leaders, or any of these kids, he's gonna have to deal with me ... *and I mean deal with me*. You tell him that, playa."

Randy then turned and started to walk away. DJ was clearly surprised and astounded. With a beer in one hand and a cigarette in the other, DJ took another puff and challenged Randy again: "Well, that's not nice. I thought you operated from the Good Book, Po-Po Preacher," he said sarcastically, laughing with his friends.

Again, Randy wasn't one for foolishness. He turned around slowly, took off his Ray Ban sunglasses, and walked back up close to DJ. "Oh, I do ... and if I hear another threat ... you and your boys are going to be witnessing me asking for mercy and forgiveness for my actions. That's in the Good Book too." Randy shrugged his shoulders, rolled his neck around as if to crack it to relieve tension, and gave him a long, mean stare. He went on to say, "You don't want to see the other side to me. You better check your boy."

Randy walked away with a swagger, as he knew that DJ and his friends were cowards and punks. DJ just stood there looking stupid. His demeanor changed from a hard-core gangster to an awestruck wimp. He didn't dare respond this time, for he knew Randy was serious. Randy got in his Glory Kids truck and took off, blasting, playing, singing, and bobbing his head to Mary Mary's hit gospel song: "Take these shackles off my feet so I can dance. I just want to praise you. I just want to praise you."

Randy was crazy like that. He was going to make a statement, set you straight, and revert right back to the things of God. The issue between him and DJ's father had been dealt with effectively. He said what he had to say, and he was done with it. It was time to refocus on more important matters and get ready for next Saturday's event.

Although, Glory Kids was scheduled for Saturday, I assure you that Randy's good work was done on a daily basis. It seems that his heart was always on helping those who were poor in some way. I know this firsthand, as I was often reminded and reprimanded for misappropriating my funds in the wrong direction. I had to give up several new outfits, shoes, and toys that I purchased for Gabrielle and Matthew because I was accused of buying too much for our kids and not giving enough to others. It really bothered him to know that Gabrielle had a closet full of new dresses for church while some little girl over in the projects had none. Or that I would pay top dollar for Matthew to have brand-name tennis shoes when I could have bought several for little boys in the projects who had holes in their clothes and shoes. He was at times disgusted by my lack of knowledge about the poverty that existed on the other side of town.

Overwhelmed with guilt and frustrated with my own selfish behavior, I committed to cleaning out Matthew and Gabrielle's closet every six months. The rule was that if it wasn't worn within a year, they had to give it away to the Glory Kids. This happened quite often because our kids went to private school and were required to wear uniforms, which meant they didn't get a chance to wear many other things besides their school uniforms. In addition, like most kids, they had their favorite things to wear and toys to play with, and those were the items they wore and played with repeatedly. Therefore, we gave bags and bags of clothes, shoes, and toys away, some with the price tags still on. I realized that my kids weren't interested in the excessive things; it was merely my wanting them to have them. I also realized that I was spending too much money on my own kids, and that it should be shared with those who didn't have the luxury afforded to Matthew and Gabrielle.

Since our church was on a fixed budget, most of the time when Randy and I saw a family in the projects that was in need, we didn't inform our church but simply consulted with one another and purchased things ourselves. Other church members would share stories when they witnessed Randy in a store, buying things for the poor out of his own pocket. Likewise, whenever there weren't enough toys, snacks, or prizes for The Glory Kids Ministry, Randy would take care of it, even if it meant pulling it out of his own wallet.

Mr. Lewis Fisher, an usher at our church, recalled an incident when an underprivileged family was given some rotten mattresses for their children. Randy looked at the mattresses and knew that this family deserved something nicer and cleaner. He discarded the old mattresses and went out and purchased new mattresses for the entire family.

Then there was the time that Randy and I were driving in Watts, headed over to pray for Mimi, the woman challenged with cancer. In the trunk of my car was a brand-new pair of tennis shoes that I had just purchased. Unbeknownst to me, Randy had seen the tennis shoes sitting in my trunk, but more importantly, on the way to Mimi's house, he had seen a woman walking the streets with no shoes.

He asked me, "Lisa what size shoe do you wear?"

"What?" I replied, thinking that was an odd question to ask unexpectedly.

He repeated the question again. "What size shoe do you wear?"

"I wear a size eight, sometimes eight and a half. It depends on the shoe," I answered, confused by his questioning.

"Do a U-turn," and pull over by that lady pushing that shopping cart," he said abruptly.

It was a homeless bag lady pushing a basket and wearing no shoes. He got out of the car and went up to talk to her. I saw him touching her shoulder, and she seemed disoriented. Then I saw him walk back to my car, signaling for me to roll down the window. I rolled it down, and he asked me if he could have the tennis shoes in my trunk. The old Lisa would have said, "No, are you crazy! I just purchased those tennis shoes, and I paid a pretty penny for them!" But I had learned that the more Randy and I gave, the more God blessed us abundantly.

I can't tell you how many times Randy and I pulled up in front of shoe stores and other stores to buy things for the homeless. As it says in the Bible, *The poor will always be with us* ... (Matthew 26:11) and *To whom much is given much is expected* (Luke 12:48). Sometimes Randy would catch me off guard in his giving. It didn't matter when or where we were; he just handled things as the need arose.

I recall one morning when the kids and I were going to church to meet Randy. We couldn't drive together because Sunday mornings Randy would leave before us so he could get to church early enough to drive the church bus to pick up the Glory Kids and their families. When we got to the church, Randy would always be there, greeting us as we arrived.

That particular morning, he met me at the door and asked me to do him a favor. There was a Latin family that he adored because of their faithfulness and willingness to turn their lives around and do right. They were just crazy about Randy, but the wife, Vanessa, struggled with a drug addiction. She would do well for a long while but would then backslide into a life of drugs. She had just gotten out of jail and was attending church, but it was obvious that she was embarrassed by her on-again, off-again struggles.

Randy was able to see that she wasn't comfortable going into church because of her attire, so he asked me to take her across the street to a woman's clothing store and purchase something she could change into and wear to church. I could see her looking at me from afar, shame and embarrassment written all across her face. I told Randy that I would take her, and I walked over to her, giving her a hug and assuring her that she was still loved. I said to her jokingly to ease the tension, "I'm finally early to church, and you and Randy are going to ask me to go shopping ... Wow!"

We laughed, and off we went.

I bought her a few church outfits, fitting her from head to toe and accessorizing her outfits with jewelry, matching purses, and shoes. Vanessa and her husband were so grateful, and so was Randy. He knew that we were partners, and that he could count on me for anything. I may not have been the holiest wife, but I too loved the Lord and became more cognizant about giving.

I've already mentioned how Randy never hesitated to ask a favor of me. It would always start with, "Baby Girl, can you do me a favor?" I knew the minute I heard those words that my day was going to be altered. One hot Saturday, Gabrielle and I were grocery shopping, and I had planned to relax by my pool afterward. I was going to take a break from all activities to catch a little "me time." My cell phone rang while I was shopping, and it was Randy, calling from one of the sites. When I saw his name flash across my phone, I thought about not answering it, for I knew deep in my soul that I was going to have to alter my day. But I answered it anyway, knowing that he wouldn't possibly take away my long-awaited me time that day. But sure enough, he started begging me to allow about ten kids to come to our house and swim. He felt sorry for them because some of the Glory Kids had been complaining about being bored and hot. They wanted Randy to stay on their side of town and continue to have water balloon fights. So Randy came up with this grand idea of bringing them over to our house in our Toyota Sequoia truck to swim.

I hesitated for a few minutes before giving Randy the okay, but not before three to five minutes of complaining about how I never get any "me time." Randy didn't listen to my rambling. More than likely, he took the phone away from his ear so he wouldn't hear me. He was just waiting for me to say yes, which I did. He was elated! I could hear him laughing and screaming with the kids like a big kid himself, saying, "Let's go! Lisa said you guys can come over and swim!"

I hung up and was torn between putting on a happy face or a frown. But all Gabrielle and I could do was laugh and call Randy crazy. Then Gabrielle looked at me and reminded me that we would need to get food and snacks for the kids. After all, the Simmonses did not entertain without food and snacks. It worked out well since we were in the store, and we picked up burgers, hot dogs, juices, cupcakes, and cookies for about twenty-five kids, as Gabrielle reminded me again that her father was notorious for giving false head counts. He was always off by at least ten-plus kids.

When Randy arrived at the house, true to form, he had a busload of kids. He had borrowed the church bus because he couldn't fit all those kids in his truck. Some of our neighbors were outside scratching their heads and wondering what was going on, as the noise and the excitement of the Glory Kids lit up the entire neighborhood. They swam, ate, and played for hours. Our relatively small pool had shrunk to a pond by the time the kids finished swimming. They had a ball, and Randy and I had fun watching the smiles on their faces.

Soon we started getting others on board helping with the Glory Kids. Even my sisters, who attended a different church than we did, pitched in and helped. My sister Cookie offered her talent of decorating balloons at different Glory Kids events right at the sites, and my sister Melinda lent her financial support to the church for the Glory Kids by writing a check for twenty thousand dollars. Randy had us all on board, and it felt good to give. He even got members of the police department to participate. His partner, James, involved himself in plays with Randy, as James was an entertainer by nature and was always willing and excited to take part in skits and plays with Randy. He loved the Lord and loved kids too, so it was truly a labor of love.

Randy no longer asked questions about getting my support, as he knew by the countless things we had done together that it was now a given. But we still consulted with each other about financial contributions we personally made. Randy knew that the church had other auxiliaries beside Glory Kids for which they allocated money, and there were times he didn't ask the church for their support. Church members often knew nothing about our financial support to the Glory Kids, as Randy did everything from the heart.

On another occasion, Randy ran into my office excited about what he claimed to be a once-in-a-lifetime opportunity. We needed to rent a luxury bus for the Glory Kids, and it was going to cost us every bit of two thousand dollars. We were going to take a one-day trip to Anton, California, where his fellow officer friends Steve and Mary Weaver had a home ranch complete with a swimming pool and horses. The Glory Kids had never been on a big field trip, and Randy and I incurred the costs for the bus and food, while Steve and Mary extended their home and ranch to us for free. What a blessing!

As always, Randy's head count of the children was way off, so Steve and Mary were surprised when they saw so many kids. It was a long, fun day, with kids alternating between swimming and horseback riding, in addition to our barbecuing and taking pictures of the happy and exhilarating day.

Randy was so grateful to the wonderful officers who partnered with him and who were willing to extend love to the kids from underprivileged areas. He would say that he wasn't sure if they truly understood the impact their gift of love had on the children, but he knew it created memories that the kids would cherish for a lifetime.

## CHAPTER 17

# Sacrifices

OUR LIVES HAD BECOME EXTREMELY busy; however, somehow or another, we never missed taking a vacation. We traveled to places nearby, such as our families' hometowns of New Orleans and New York. We visited Hawaii several times, primarily because the kids loved it there. We extended ourselves to places in the Caribbean, including the Bahamas, Bermuda, and Curacao, and then we stretched even farther. Thanks to incentive trips I earned, we went to places like Italy, Spain, Paris, and London. We stayed in the best hotels or resorts and participated in various types of adventures, like snorkeling with big sea turtles, kayaking in the middle of the ocean, jet skiing, water surfing, and hang gliding (well, Randy did that). We never missed a beat when it came to vacations. When we traveled, we really traveled, taking it all in, but when we came home, it was back to business as usual. We were so busy that we both had to commit to scheduling dates with each other. We loved spending time together, so we had to make the time whenever we could find it.

One evening, quite by surprise, Randy came home from a SWAT call-up already dressed in civilian clothes. That didn't happen very often, although sometimes after a SWAT call-up, he would stay at the station and make sure to get in a good workout, after which he would shower and change into street clothes. On this particular night, when he returned home, he was wearing his MC Hammer pants that he and my brother-in-law, Wilfred, refused to give up. I guess I couldn't complain, because he did make an effort to improve on his attire by graduating from polyester biker shorts that fitted and outlined every contour of his lower body to the MC Hammer pants. I had thrown out the shorts, although I should have burned them because they were way too revealing and stirred up a ruckus when we went places together. I would see women, both old and young, looking at Randy and salivating.

Even more interesting about Randy's style, and what he was most famous for, were his Ray Ban sunglasses and his outdated fanny pack. His Ray Bans were one of the few things that Randy was willing to spend money on. His eyes were very sensitive to the sun, so his optometrist suggested that he always have a good pair of sunglasses handy. But nothing was more valuable to him than his treasured black leather fanny pack that he wore fastened around his waist. He used it to hold his personal belongings and his gun. I imagine he liked it because although it wasn't stylish any longer, his things were easily accessible.

Usually when Randy returned home after one of his call-ups, I would ask him about the incident. I liked hearing Randy's SWAT call-up stories, as they fascinated me, especially when I learned about the tactics the SWAT team used to capture suspects. Randy told me about several methods that SWAT would use, such as coming through rooftops, underneath floors, or busting through neighboring walls to apprehend a suspect. He would describe the devastating collapse of a building due to the destructive power of a battering ram or the use of a flashbang with its blinding illumination and explosive force, which could shake up any large building. The stories were awesome, but the missions were dangerous.

I once saw a movie where the SWAT team used a fiber-optic scope to help locate suspects that could be hiding in inconspicuous places. I envisioned Randy and the team doing these types of things, for they occasionally trained actors or took on acting roles in action, drama, and law enforcement types of films, mostly as extras. I would joke with Randy and his partner, James Hart, about the roles they would play, and I would tell them that their performance, all ten seconds of it, had earned them an Academy Award nomination.

On this night, after I heard a mouthful regarding one of his many thousands of SWAT call-up stories, Randy pulled two tickets out of his fanny pack; they were for Hiroshima, a fusion and smooth jazz band.

I was thrilled, as Hiroshima's music was played at our wedding. Randy loved jazz and could go into a meditative state when he listened to it. He just loved sitting in the dark and taking it all in. I loved jazz too, but I believe those tickets were more for him, since it helped him relax, lifting the stress and tension. Regardless, we were going to have a good time at the concert, as we both needed a break from our frenzied schedules. I'd even had the audacity to add another project to my already hectic schedule. Besides being a self-employed insurance agent, I decided to engage in a partnership with my sisters. I already had one partnership with them, called Excel Angels, which dealt with real estate investments that we owned in New Orleans. But now I was going to make myself even busier by partnering with my sisters in a restaurant venture called New Orleans Vieux Carré.

Randy wasn't too keen on the idea since I already had a full-time job as a mother, which always came first, in addition to operating an insurance sales business. I was also traveling to New Orleans to check on properties whenever time permitted. He felt that we were both already working on overload, and that the restaurant business would take away from family, ultimately sending us through the roof. Plus, Randy always said that if I had time to do anything extra, he would want me to help him expand Glory Kids. Together we could add more project sites and minister, mentor, and entertain kids throughout the week. He felt that if I really got involved with Glory Kids, we could do monumental things, especially with the connections my sisters and I had with people in the community. Honestly speaking, I didn't mind volunteering and helping out with Glory Kids on occasion, but it wasn't something I wanted to or could commit to on a daily basis. My passion was enjoying Matthew and Gabrielle and getting involved with their activities and my own business ventures. The thrill of operating a business like a restaurant was inviting and exciting.

Since both my sisters also had full-time jobs, my mother, a cousin, and my sister's husband were going to manage the restaurant, so they expected our assistance in the evenings and on weekends. Looking back, I don't really know what possessed us to think we could run a busy, hectic business like a restaurant without committing to it full time, which had been Randy's point. But as usual, we were up for a challenge, and Randy apprehensively supported us. He knew it was going to be a twenty-four-hour, seven-day-a-week operation. He also knew that it was an investment the entire family would have to participate in, and as a result, our lives would eventually be consumed with the restaurant business.

We slowed down the pace for just a moment, weaving into our schedules the Hiroshima concert that weekend. I was so excited and so was Randy. I took my time getting dressed and made myself enjoy our nice oversized Jacuzzi tub that we rarely used, mostly because it took so long to fill; a shower was usually much quicker. After bathing, I sat at my vanity feeling relaxed and stress-free. I decided to turn on the television in my bathroom so that I could listen while I applied my makeup. I took my time, meticulously putting on eye shadow and then picking up my lip pencil to outline my lips. Just as I was getting ready to apply the pencil, something caught my attention. I directed my eyes toward the television, and ironically, it wasn't what I was seeing that attracted me; it was what I heard that captivated my thoughts.

A commercial came on discussing women and calcium. I can't even tell you the brand of the medicine, vitamins, or powder they were discussing, or what they were actually advertising, but I recall the words they were saying, which caught my full attention. "Time is a silent thief" echoed loudly in my head—repeatedly. A weird vibe came over me that I could not explain. I began to feel agitated and jittery from those words, but I pulled myself together, shook it off, and continued dressing for the evening Randy and I had planned.

I decided to wear a dress that was Randy's favorite. It was all black and it showed a little cleavage in addition to hugging my now big hips. It flared out at the bottom, giving the illusion that my waist was a lot smaller. I had put on a lot of weight over the years, so I needed to accentuate my best assets and camouflage my flaws. I often told myself that I was going to lose the baby weight, but my babies were now thirteen and sixteen years old, so as Randy and I would often jokingly say, "Houston, we have a problem!" Randy, on the other hand, was as fit as a sixteen-year-old athlete. He was now fifty-one years of age but looking more like thirty-one. He was diligent when it came to working out, unlike his wife, who struggled with eating right and exercising. Over the years, it caught up with me.

Enjoying happy times at my sister's brother-in-law's wedding, Detective Maury Sumlin with Santa Monica Police Departments: sitting at table- My niece Amia Sumlin, brother-in-law Wilfred Sumlin, Randy, Me, and my sister Melinda Harleaux. Back Row: My nephew Dominic Sumlin, Sister Sharon "Cookie" Sumlin, Maury Sumlin, brother-in-law Dwayne Harleaux, my mother Veronica Hunter and her friend Harold Jackson.

In any event, I looked my best for my hubby, who adored his full-figured wife. I fixed my hair the way he liked it and put on my silver rhinestone strappy sandals that were pretty to look at but hurt like hell. It didn't matter, though, because it was what I called pretty sacrifices, and you just had to push through the pain. Randy, not being much of a dresser, wore his faded blue jeans, a silk caramel-colored long-sleeved shirt, and some cool black snakeskin boots. He looked good in just about anything he wore.

Going out on the town was weird to us, mostly because we were not used to doing things for ourselves. We were more used to giving, giving, and giving to others, often neglecting ourselves. Naturally, this was a welcome treat, as it was a special night, with no kids and no work. Randy was already getting frisky having so much freedom. He actually tried to convince me to stay home and play house, as opposed to going to the concert, but I was not going to miss seeing Hiroshima for anything, not even wifely duties. I grabbed my jacket and purse and headed for the car. As I opened the door that led to the garage, I did what Randy and I would normally do when we went somewhere together: I got in my car and was prepared to follow him. As I mentioned previously, driving in separate cars was normal for us, as a call-up could leave me stranded somewhere, calling for my parents or sisters to pick me up. Over the years, I got tired of that scenario, so I just succumbed to the fact that for the most part, I would have to drive myself.

Strangely, on this particular night, Randy wanted to risk it and suggested we ride together in the same car, as he was sure there was not going to be an unexpected call-up. I fought hard against his decision because I knew my husband wouldn't hesitate to drive to the nearest public area and drop me off if his cell or radio went off. But Randy assured me that things had been quiet lately, so he encouraged me with his words: "Come, on Baby Girl, let's drive together. Nothing's been jumpin' off. Lately the streets have been quiet," he said.

I hesitated at first but then jumped in the police car and put on my seat belt. I then asked for assurance one last time: "Are you sure, Randy? I'm not up for being stranded somewhere all dressed up with these shoes that are already killin' my feet," I stated.

All smiles at my sister Melinda's wedding on May 5, 2007 in New Orleans, La.

He put on his favorite Ray Ban sunglasses, backed out of the garage, and proceeded to drive to the concert at the Greek Theater in Los Angeles, simultaneously responding to my question: "We haven't had any call-ups lately," he said. "I doubt if we'll have one tonight."

Of course, Randy had no control over the streets of Los Angeles. It would be absurd to believe that what he was saying was the gospel truth. Nonetheless, he was going off on a hope and a prayer that his radio or cell phone didn't go off, as was I.

"You know, it seems like a lot of your call-ups have been in the Valley lately," I mentioned. "You would think that a lot of your call-ups would be in the hood ... South Central. Why is that?"

The Valley, formally known as San Fernando Valley in California, is located just northwest of Los Angeles and consists of little communities. It's also known for its blazing-hot summer weather. At one time, it was considered a quiet and prestigious area, attracting those of above-average income. However, the demographics changed drastically over the past twenty years, and the Valley's crime rate had become just as high as crimes in the inner city.

"Yep! The Valley is crazy! A lot of gang and drug activity. I can't believe how much it has changed. But it's crazy all over, Lisa. That's why we have to get out there and make an impression on these kids early on. Gang activities are spreading like wildfires," Randy said as he hit the steering wheel, speaking with passion.

We continued our drive to the concert, heading north on the 110 Harbor Freeway and talking about everything. Randy and I relaxed, feeling free and acting crazy. I started singing the Hiroshima song played at our wedding: "Save Yourself for Me." Then Randy got on the subject of football. The Super Bowl was coming up, and he was all hyped for the game. He was still riding on a high of last year's Super Bowl, when his favorite coach, Tony Dungy of the Indianapolis Colts, went to the Super Bowl and won against the Chicago Bears. Randy was ecstatic for Tony, as he admired him because he was of the Christian faith and always had the courage to display his love for God outwardly. Randy was his biggest fan. In addition, Tony made history when he became the first African American coach to win the Super Bowl title.

We were talking about things pertaining to our kids, Matt and Gabby, when suddenly the police radio came on. I could see Randy's facial expression and demeanor immediately change. He went from smiling and acting like a Disney character to a serious warrior about to go to war. As he tried to listen intensely to the radio, he told me to stop singing and be quiet. He reluctantly picked up the radio mike and responded 41 D, which was his SWAT code name. The dispatcher stated that there was a call-up. He started giving Randy the location and all pertinent details as I sat there quietly, wanting to strangle Randy and the dispatching officer. I wanted to take the radio and throw it out the window, but I remained calm and collected because I knew Randy was disappointed too. *Why add salt to the wound?* I thought.

"*Damn!*" Randy said. Whenever he swore, it was obvious that he was mad, as he'd stopped swearing rededicating his life to Christ years ago. But every now and then, a situation would force out those words of yesteryear.

"I can't believe this! We haven't had a call-up in weeks!" he exclaimed.

He continued to talk and hold my hand while alternating and flicking buttons in the police car, turning on his loud siren.

"Baby Girl, I'm so sorry. I'll drop you off at your mother's house," he said caringly, picking up speed and switching lanes abruptly, causing my body to jerk and swerve with the motion of the car.

Naturally, I understood, but I was also frustrated. I felt bad for Randy, as this was his opportunity to relax, unwind, and enjoy some good jazz. I had often been accused of throwing digs, so I tried to avoid displaying irritating behavior, but I couldn't resist. I had to say it: "I thought you said the streets were going to be quiet!" I yelled.

Randy didn't respond. He just looked straight ahead, concentrating on his fast driving maneuvers. He was driving like a maniac trying to get me to my mother's house quickly.

"Look you can still go. Call one of your sisters or your girlfriends, the *ettes*—Suzette, Paulette, Lynette, Vernette," he said jokingly, rambling off the rhyming names of some of my friends.

Randy exited the freeway, driving at lightening speed, heading west to Leimert Park and passing the sports arena and coliseum. We were at Bronson Avenue in no time flat. Randy turned the corner and flew up my mother's driveway. He gave me a big sloppy kiss on the lips and quickly began to pull out of the driveway.

Just as he started to drive off, I sprinted back to the car, yelling to him that I'd left my purse in the car. He had kicked me out so fast that I had forgotten to grab it, and I needed my purse because the tickets and the keys to our house were in it. He literally threw my purse out the window and blew me a kiss, laughing and shaking his head as if to say, *We have a crazy life.* It was a chaotic lifestyle, but it was also a good one, which we diligently tried to keep as loving and as normal as possible.

As luck would have it, Paulette, my good friend since childhood, agreed to go to the concert with me. While I waited for her to pick me up, my mother and I sat at the kitchen table and had a lengthy conversation about the soft opening of the restaurant, which we'd scheduled to have in less than two weeks. It was as good of a time as any to discuss business.

In opening the restaurant, Cookie and Melinda took on the task of purchasing the big restaurant appliances as well as getting restaurant requirements like permits and scheduling inspections as well, while my mother and I did the fun stuff like selecting colors for the booths, chairs, and carpet. All of us had been running around that entire week ordering dishes, lamps, tables, menus, and all the other million and one things that come with the decorating of a restaurant. We had fun doing it, but it was hard work. By the end of the week, I was so run down that I caught a cold. It was in its beginning stages, and it left me feeling lethargic. But, I continued to "push through it," as Randy would say, taking care of business.

I sat looking at my mother with such a profound sense of love for her as she went on about the restaurant. Without any thought or hesitation, she had always supported any and everything that my sisters and I tried to do. She showed no reluctance at jumping right in and helping us bring our dreams to fruition.

While we were speaking, quite unexpectedly, I sneezed. It interrupted her thoughts, and she looked at me and could tell I wasn't feeling well. She went on another rampage about Randy and me doing too much.

"You and Randy have got to slow down. That's why you're getting sick. You do too much," she said with a concerned look.

"I know, I know," I said. "I will slow down … after the grand opening of the restaurant. I have been so tired and worried lately."

"About what? Is it the restaurant?" my mother replied with concern.

"No, not at all. I have just been so emotional. Dr. Randy said I'm having premenopausal symptoms," I said sarcastically.

"Well, it could be. You might be experiencing it early," my mother responded.

I stood up and started walking in circles around the kitchen, as I wanted to share a few of the emotional states and feelings I was experiencing with my mother. I started to explain as my mother looked at me with concern, sipping on her bottle of water and opening a bottle for me.

"Mama, I can't explain it, but I've been feeling weird lately," I continued as I nervously rubbed my forehead. "The other day I looked at a picture with Randy and the kids. He was in his uniform, sitting in the chapel at Gabby's preschool graduation. Matt was looking up at Randy with admiration in his eyes, and Randy was looking down at him with love. Gabrielle was in the pew in front of them, looking back laughing."

"Where were you?" my mother asked.

"I guess I was taking the picture. I'm not sure, but I wasn't in the photo," I replied.

"And?" my mother said, waiting to hear the punch line.

I felt tears well up in my eyes, but I continued. "When I looked at the photo, I started shaking all over. I felt this nervous surge of energy in my body that wouldn't go away," I said, certain that perplexity was evident all over my face.

My mother responded as most mothers do when trying to alleviate their children's fears. "Oh, Lisa, you're just tired and overworked. It was a nice picture, so why are you getting yourself worked up," she said compassionately. "Try not to stress yourself out … You're tired and run-down!" she said adamantly, trying to calm me down.

I should have just ended my emotional drama right there, but I had to go on and express myself further, sharing another experience that left me feeling nervous. "Well, listen to this. I saw a commercial that came on TV. It was about women and calcium, and a phrase from the commercial keeps playing over and over in my head—'Time is a Silent Thief.' I can't seem to get those words out of my head. It's almost as if the phrase is haunting me."

My mother sat there rubbing her water bottle, taking a big gulp of the water. It was almost as if she were taking a sip of whiskey to heal her broken heart from when time snatched away my father at age fifty-four. She responded very softly, giving credence to the concern I had.

"Oh, yes, time is a silent thief. One day you girls were in diapers, and now you're catching up with me. So much has happened over the years, and I wonder where the time has gone. We have to slow down and enjoy the people and things we love," she said, looking out the window as if my comment put her in a somber mood.

She quickly snapped out of it when the doorbell rang. It was my loud, crazy friend Paulette, who was always ready to have a good time. She came waltzing in, putting smiles on my mother's and my face.

Paulette and I went to the concert and enjoyed the sounds of Hiroshima. Paulette wasn't Randy, but she was definitely one of those friends who were going to make sure we had a good time, and it was indeed a jazzy night.

# CHAPTER 18

# Time Is a Silent Thief

WE WERE A MONTH BEHIND in opening our restaurant, New Orleans Vieux Carré, having originally scheduled the opening during the first week in January of 2008. We got behind with the hiring, permits, and inspections, although it wound up working out to our advantage. We decided to have a private Super Bowl party with only family and employees so that we could test out our authentic Creole food prepared by my sister Melinda's new husband, Chef Dwayne Harleaux, a former deputy sheriff.

Randy was the first to arrive, so he sat in the best seat in the house, right in front of the television. It was Sunday, February 3, 2008, Super Bowl XLII, and he was ready to watch the New York Giants take on the New England Patriots. He wanted to see if Eli Manning was going to do for the Giants what his brother did for the Indianapolis Colts the year before, thus helping his team win a Super Bowl championship.

Randy was looking around the restaurant, absolutely amazed at what my sisters, my mother, and I had accomplished. Initially, as I already mentioned, he wasn't too keen on our opening a restaurant, but when he saw the fruits of our labors, he was impressed. He actually started to own the idea himself, giving us tips on what we needed to do in terms of decorating and making the place safer. When he gobbled down the food, he gave a thumbs-up to my brother-in-law and classified him as the best

Creole chef in the world. In all honesty, Chef Dwayne Harleaux would be tough competition for Emeril Lagasse.

In that same week, on February 5, 2008, we scheduled a soft opening for close family and friends to celebrate Mardi Gras, a festive Catholic holiday that signifies the last day of feasting before the start of Lent. It was appropriate given that my family was Catholic and our restaurant reflected the New Orleans culture. We celebrated with music, food, drinks, Mardi Gras beads, and a performance of a famous group dance that New Orleans people call "the second line." The dance was performed by a popular New Orleans club organization located in Los Angeles, called LALA. They came dressed in colorful costumes, beautiful beads, decorative hats, gorgeously decorated umbrellas and handkerchiefs, and bright smiles that brought the culture of New Orleans to life in our restaurant. They really entertained our guests, and it was a thrill to see, especially watching Randy join in by waving a handkerchief in the air, acting silly while illustrating one of the New Orleans famous dance traditions.

I'll never forget that night because Randy walked in our restaurant late due to training. He had on his tan army fatigues, big training boots, and a million-dollar smile. He walked from table to table, greeting everyone with a hug or a warm handshake. Then he walked into the back of the restaurant, where I was conducting cashier work, and said, "Well, ya'll in it knee deep now." He looked out at the packed restaurant. "I hope y'all can handle it, Baby Girl." He had a smile on his face and an obvious sense of pride, amazed by the amount of people we had at our soft opening.

"I hope so too," I said, as I was too busy and barely had time to chat with him.

The night was a success, but I was so happy when it was over, as it left my sisters and me exhausted. I was run-down, and my immune system was weak because of the last two events we'd had at the restaurant. Now it was time to get ready for the public opening of the restaurant, which was scheduled for February 8, 2008.

I decided to take February 6 off and not go into my office so I could stay home and rest. I just didn't have the energy to do anything anymore. It was as if everything in me was wiped out. So I made a few business calls from my bed and ended with a call to Cookie, who told me that

Bill Cosby was going to be at the bookstore Eso Won for a book signing. Eso Won was located just down the street from our new restaurant, and Cookie was excited that Mr. Cosby was going to be there. She wanted me to help her put together a marketing plan that would get readers to come to our restaurant after the book signing. Cookie, a social butterfly and a natural-born marketer, needed my help, but I was in no way capable of entertaining any other ideas. My body needed physical and mental rest.

I was in bed at about eight that night, which is a rarity for me. Gabrielle came into my room and announced that she too had a sore throat. Chances were she had caught my cold, so I gave her some medicine and directed her to bed; I needed her to stay well. It would be tough trying to open a restaurant while at the same time tending to a sick child.

I then went to my closet to put on my Bishop Montgomery High School Mother's Club sweatshirt that I had purchased from Matthew's school. I was freezing, feeling chills from what I believed were the early stages of the flu. I settled down in bed and called my mother-in-law, whom I hadn't talked to in weeks because I'd been so busy.

She and I had our differences in the early years, both competing for Randy's love and attention, but as years passed, we both recognized our own distinct and special place in Randy's life and in his heart—she as his mother and me as his wife. Looking at it from that standpoint, there was no competition. He loved us both dearly and gave us the autonomy to figure out our differences on our own. Randy was a no-nonsense type of guy, like my dad, so he didn't hesitate to put anyone in check. If he felt you were out of place or wrong, he did not care who you were, he was going to let you know that you were out of line or that what you did was inappropriate behavior. Likewise, he had no problem apologizing when he said or did something wrong. In this case, he wasn't going to entertain something as irrational as the two most important women in his life disagreeing. So after working out the kinks with my mother-in-law, we truly developed a beautiful relationship. We had a closeness that God intended for mothers-in-law and daughters-in-law, and we genuinely enjoyed each other's company, often taking trips, going shopping, and doing things with or without Randy present.

Family picture taken at church. Randy kept a bible in his hand or nearby.

Me and my mother-in-law established a very close bond and it grew closer after what was to come.

Conversely, I never developed a relationship with Randy's father, Mr. Dallas Simmons, although I did finally get a chance to meet him. Dallas and Randy had reunited about a year ago, when Randy went on one last hunt for him at the request of his aunt Martha, Dallas's sister. She was getting older and quite feeble, and she just wanted to hear her brother's voice. She asked Randy if he could help her locate him, and he said he would.

Initially, Randy had reservations about it, as he and I had attempted to make contact with him on several occasions, all of which ended unsuccessfully. The few times when Randy and Dallas were scheduled to meet, Dallas always came up with an excuse for not showing up. Frankly, I think Dallas just didn't want to be bothered with the remnants of a past life, but it was a constant rejection and disappointment for Randy.

I believe that the stronger Randy and his family grew in their faith, the more God gave them a peace and acceptance about Dallas's absence. They were also able to clearly see things about Dallas that they were blinded by previously. In the past, he was a strong leader and played a highly religious role that influenced all their lives, so his words were always gospel. They loved Dallas and believed in him. As the family grew in the things of God, they got wiser and were able to discern some of Dallas's peculiar ways. I could see how each of the family members progressed and came to a resolve about these issues over the years. Randy and his family had gotten to a point where they loved him still but just prayed for his salvation, putting years of sadness and hurt to rest.

It wasn't until Randy found his father this one final time for his aunt Martha's sake that Dallas agreed to meet and see the entire family. We were all very surprised; however, we weren't going to hold our collective breath, as he was notorious for backing out of meetings. But surprisingly, this time he kept his promise.

Randy picked him up for the visit and was shocked at his age progression. When he'd left the fold twenty-five years earlier, he was a middle-aged man, and now he was in his late seventies. He looked the same, much like Randy, but much older, and he had taken on the ailments and characteristics that often come with age. His thinking and movements were slower, and what used to be a loud, strong voice was now low, hoarse, and raspy. He was a complete stranger to his grandkids and to me.

Dallas met the entire family. He made his peace by apologizing to Constance and attempting to rebuild a relationship with Randy and his sisters. However, no one was pulling for Dallas any longer, as the yearning for him had died years ago. It was only a few times within that year that Randy's schedule permitted him to spend time with his father; seeing and spending time with him was no longer a priority. Nonetheless, it did bring long-awaited closure to the family.

Still on the phone talking with my mother-in-law, I blew my nose and coughed in the same breath as I gave her all the details about what was going on with the restaurant. But only five minutes into our conversation, Randy walked through our bedroom door. He could tell from what I was saying that I was talking to his mother. He walked around the room in circles, looking at the TV as CNN was discussing the close Democratic primary race between presidential candidate Hillary Clinton and presidential candidate Barack Obama.

He looked at me and whispered, "Tell my mother you'll call her back."

I did as he requested. I figured he just wanted to spend a little time with me, and he knew his mother and I could be on the phone talking for hours. I recall looking at him and thinking he looked worried, or perplexed about something. There were many serious matters going on at our church that concerned him, so I attributed his behavior that night to those issues.

Randy caught Gabrielle before she went to sleep, calling her back into our room and also asking Matthew to join us, as he wanted to say a family prayer before Gabby went to bed. Gabrielle dragged herself into the room and plopped down beside me. She clung to me because she was feeling awful and was ready for sleep. She and I probably were thinking the same thing: *Who's going to pray?* We would have preferred it if either Matthew or I said the prayer this night, as we weren't feeling well, and our prayers were usually short and sweet. We both knew that although Randy's prayers were beautiful, they were always lengthy, as Randy didn't forget anyone or anything when he prayed. On that night, Randy made it clear that he was going to lead us in prayer.

He turned off the television and told Gabby and me to remain sitting up in bed; he was aware that we weren't feeling well. He and Matthew stood around us, and we clenched each others' hands and bowed our heads in prayer. Randy prayed fervently for everyone, starting with Gabby and me, asking God to heal us from our colds. He then went on to pray for peace in our country as well as other countries. He prayed for our families, the Glory Kids, the elders, the sick, and those that were shut in. He prayed for the salvation of the sinner, the positive outcome of the presidential race, and lastly, I remember him slowly praying for God to lift the oppression and poverty in Darfur. After he prayed, he gave Gabby and me a kiss and playfully threw a punch at Matthew, grabbing him by his head and hugging him. As a caring and observant husband, he asked Matthew to fix me a hot cup of chamomile tea to soothe my scratchy throat.

It was about 9:30 p.m. when Randy went to take a long, hot shower. While he showered, I continued to lie in bed, sipping my tea and flipping channels between Anderson Cooper of CNN News and Pat Harvey of then–Channel 9 News. I recall taking a few more sips of tea before I went out like a light. I guess the Nyquil medicine I had taken kicked in; my body was yearning for some much-needed rest. I can only assume what Randy did after taking his shower. His ritual if there was no romance between us would be to sit up in bed and watch the news for a while and then turn off the television and read a couple of chapters of the Bible. Most nights, he did the same thing, either in bed or downstairs in the prayer room.

I awoke and rolled over between 12:00 a.m. and 12:30 a.m., as I had to use the bathroom due to drinking a lot of liquids for my cold. I remember turning over and reaching for Randy's hand prior to getting out of bed. We, like most couples, had our own little corny—some might say quirky—rituals. We would hold hands while sleeping; it was a habit we'd developed over our seventeen years of marriage. After reaching for his hand and not feeling it, I realized that Randy was not in bed. I assumed that he was downstairs in the prayer room, studying or reading the Bible. I dragged myself out of bed and walked to the bathroom, humming and singing a song that Joy, my pastor's daughter, sang so beautifully in church. I don't know why I was singing it. It's a nice song, but it's not one I would sing outside of church service, nor was it Sunday, when a song from church would sometimes play repeatedly in my mind. I don't know where it came from, but I can only guess that the Holy Spirit took over and allowed the lyrics to flow from my mouth. The song is called "Bow Down and Worship Him," recorded by Bishop Paul Morton. The lyrics are as follows:

*Bow down and worship Him,*
*Enter in*
*Oh, enter in.*

I continued to sing that chorus repeatedly. It seemed as if the lyrics were coming from deep down in my soul, and the song touched my heart and the lyrics exited my mouth even louder. I continued to sing: "Bow down and worship Him ..."

I washed my hands and returned to bed still singing that song. Then it turned to a whisper and a hum as I started turning off things Randy had left on in our bedroom. Interestingly enough, our television was still on. Randy normally turned it off, especially since he knew that I suffered from a mild case of insomnia and any loud commercials could wake me and have me up all night long. I thought to myself that he must have forgotten to turn it off before he went downstairs, so I picked up the remote and turned it off. I then turned off the lamp next to my bed and lay down praying I would fall back to sleep.

Minutes later, the house phone rang. I wasn't alarmed by the phone ringing in the wee hours of the night since a phone call at night was just as common in our house as a daytime call because of Randy's line of work. The SWAT call-ups happened a lot during the night, so I just assumed it was someone from the SWAT desk notifying Randy that there was a SWAT call-up.

After the second ring, I answered the phone, which was stationed on a shelf on my headboard. The voice on the other end was intense, nervous, and stern. The SWAT officer at the desk didn't ask for Randy; strangely, he asked for me. I can't recall the officer's name, so I'll call him Officer X.

"Is this Mrs. Simmons?" he asked.

"Yes," I replied, getting ready to yell for Randy. But he quickly interrupted me.

"This is Officer X from the Metropolitan Division. Your husband has been shot. We need you to get dressed quickly, as an officer will be at your house shortly to get you and bring you to Randy."

"Wait ... wait ... what?" I said, sitting up in bed and using one hand to turn the light back on. "Randy's here. He's downstairs reading!"

"Ma'am, we had a call-up to which Officer Simmons responded. There was some gunfire, and he was shot. We need you to get dressed quickly. A car should be there any minute to take you over to Northridge Hospital."

My entire body was shaking. I had a question for the officer, and I was afraid to death to hear his response, but I asked it anyway ... "Is he badly hurt ?"

"Ma'am, we don't know his condition. Please be ready to go," he said abruptly.

I turned on all the lights in my bedroom. I was scared. I couldn't even move. I then noticed Randy's Bible on his nightstand. If he were reading downstairs, it wouldn't have been there. I ran over and grabbed it, clutching it between my chest and my stomach, rocking back and forth, crying and saying, "Please, God ... Please, God ... This can't be happening." Then a thought came to me. Having insomnia, I hear everything even in my so-called deep sleep. I didn't hear the house phone ring, his cell phone going off or anything. Then I thought, *Randy would never leave the house without letting me know he had a call-up. He would never go out without letting me know he was leaving ... never!* I thought maybe it was a prank call or some bad joke.

I ran down the stairs frantically, hyperventilating, running from the prayer room to Matt's bedroom, where Matthew was sleeping soundly. I then ran around the entire house searching for Randy. I even looked in the garage. I thought maybe he was out there cleaning his guns, but there was no Randy. I ran back upstairs and peeked into Gabby's room, for I had found Randy kneeling at the end of hers or Matthew's bed many times in the past. He prayed for his children while they slept. Then I thought, *It must be true!*

Slowly, in a trance, I walked back to my room and called both of my sisters and my niece Amia, who was now a young adult. I needed Amia to come and look after Matthew and Gabrielle, who were still asleep and unaware of what happened to their father.

I called Cookie and Amia first, but my call went to their voicemail so I then called Melinda and she answered. "Melinda, call Cookie and

Amia. Randy's been shot. He's at Northridge Hospital. Ask Amia to come and get the kids, until I find out what's going on."

Melinda, in a panicky state, said, "Oh my God! Lisa, you can't drive yourself. Cookie and I will be over there to get you. Stay put."

"No. No. I don't need a ride. LAPD's coming to get me. I'll meet you guys there."

I hung up with Melinda and tried finding some clothes to wear as I called Pastor Trimble to let him know what had happened. I knew he would want to pray for Randy. I dared not call my mother-in-law or mother, as I couldn't handle their emotions right now, especially Randy's mother, who was weak from chemotherapy for her cancer (she had multiple myeloma). I thought it would be better for me to call once I saw Randy. That way, I could assure them with confidence that he was going to be all right.

I continued to scramble through my drawers, trying to find something warm, for it was a cold night and I knew I really needed to stay well for Randy's sake. I found an old burgundy velour sweat suit and threw it on with some tennis shoes.

Within seconds, Melinda called back, stating that she and Cookie were leaving the house and would meet me at the hospital. Amia was zooming down the 110 Freeway, trying to get to the house so she could be there for Matt and Gabby. Just as I hung up the phone, there was a loud knocking at my door.

*Bang! Bang! Bang!* It was the officers pounding on my door as if they were ready to do a drug bust. It scared the crap out of me, but I ran downstairs quickly, for Matthew's room was downstairs near the front door, and I didn't want him to be startled. I looked through the glass windows of my door, and standing there on the steps were two officers. There were also several police cars in the front of my house. I thought, *What the heck is going on! This is a nightmare.*

One of the officers looked familiar, and I remembered that Randy had worked with him in the past. His name was Officer Dave Perez. Dave was a handsome Latino officer I gathered to be in his late forties or early fifties. I did not recognize the other officer, and to be perfectly honest, I can't even remember what he looked like. So much of my mind was in a state of confusion; however, I do recall Dave walking into our home. He asked me gingerly if I remembered him.

"Yes, of course I remember you." Then I asked him with concern, "Dave … is Randy going to be okay?"

"We don't know, Lisa, but we have to move fast. Where's your jacket?" he said in a rushed tone.

I guess I was still in shock and in denial, walking around in circles slowly and not knowing what to do next. I needed Dave to talk to me and give me instructions as if I were two years old. I didn't have time to run back upstairs and get my coat. I opened the closet door downstairs and pulled out an old blue-and-black ski jacket. Dave helped me put it on, for I could barely move my body. I was practically moving in slow motion, but then, like any overprotective mother, I quickly snapped into reality when Dave mentioned that some officers would be staying in the house in case the kids woke up. I remember thinking what a nice gesture that was, but I immediately said no. Matthew and Gabrielle would freak out if they woke up and saw a house full of officers and no parents.

Matthew was fifteen, soon turning sixteen; he was old enough to know what was going on. I told Dave that he needed to wait so I could tell Matthew what was happening. I walked into Matthew's room and saw that he was in a deep sleep. I shook him softly and whispered in his ear, "Matthew, Matthew, wake up, honey," I said.

"What, Mom?" he responded, delirious and still half-asleep.

"There's been an accident. Daddy's been shot."

The news woke Matthew up. "What! Is he going to be okay? What happened!" He was clearly in a state of shock.

"I don't know. I'm on my way to the hospital to see what's going on. Amia is coming over to get you and Gabby. Don't wake Gabby until Amia gets here," I insisted.

"Mom, is Dad going to be okay?" Matthew asked again, wanting me to give him some assurance.

"Mommy doesn't know anything. Just start praying, Matt. I'll call and let you know what your father's injuries are as soon as I find out something." I gave Matthew a hug.

I walked to the front door with Matthew following behind me. I introduced him to the officers who were going to be staying at the house until Amia arrived, and then Matt looked out the front door at several other police cars that were going to be stationed out front. I guess for Matthew, it was all just a crazy nightmare.

Officer Dave took me by my arm and sternly said, "Lisa, we have got to go now."

I gave Matthew one more kiss, for I knew he was scared to death and wanting and needing the comfort of his mother. But I had to leave. I was glad that the officers were staying at my house until my niece arrived to get them. She was taking my kids to where my brother-in-law, Wilfred, and other family members would be around to give them support.

I rushed out the front door with Dave. I'll never forget that night. It was so cold, and I could feel the cool air hitting my feverish face. I walked with Dave to an unmarked police car parked in front of Randy's Toyota Sequoia truck and in front of my next-door neighbors' house. The officer who would be driving was already sitting in the car with the engine running. The other officer got in and sat in the front passenger seat, but not before opening the back passenger door for me. Dave joined me in the backseat behind the driver. The car was quiet, no one saying a word. It felt weird. Even the police radio seemed to be turned down low. Dave had his back turned to me as he sat staring out the window. *This is crazy*, I thought. *I need to know something.*

Thinking aggressively, I decided to reverse the roles and play police officer by going into interrogation mode. I kept thinking that somebody in that car was going to give me some answers. This quiet stuff was making me sick to my stomach, and I wanted to know about my husband's condition. I decided I would ask the questions again, in a different way.

"Dave, do you know if Randy was shot in the arm, leg, chest? Do you know if he's in surgery?" I said calmly.

Dave turned to me robotically and said, "Lisa, we don't know anything."

His response just didn't seem right. *How is it possible that you don't know anything?* I thought. I was starting to get a little perturbed with Dave, although he didn't know it. I couldn't let him see my snappy side. After all, I was Randy's wife, and I didn't want Randy to hear about his wife's rudeness later on. So I put my Dr. Phil "control your emotions" skills to work again. I was going to do some deductive reasoning that I had learned in my boring logic class at UC Santa Barbara. I knew that someday the class would be of value and be put to good use. I figured I would use my pastor as the main source to get my questions answered regarding Randy's condition. His response would tell me whether Randy was in critical condition.

"Dave?" I said calmly. "Do you think I should call our pastor and ask him to meet us at the hospital?"

Dave turned, looked directly in my eyes, and said firmly, "Yes, you need to call your pastor. Ask him to come tonight."

Those words sent chills up my body, and it wasn't due to my cold. I started crying and calling everyone, including Randy's sister Gina. She didn't answer, so I left her a voice mail. It was obvious that Randy was in critical condition, for Dave wouldn't have asked me to call my pastor in the early morning hours if he were stable. What confirmed this possible life-threatening status even more was the fact that the officers were driving me to a helipad so that I could be transported to Northridge Hospital by helicopter. It wasn't optional. We needed to get to the hospital quickly, and although I had never been in a helicopter, and hadn't ever planned to get in one, it was one of those moments when life had something in store for me that I could never have imagined.

The officers from the transportation unit put headset over my ears as they helped me up into the helicopter, which had no doors. They then buckled my seat belt tightly, and in the blink of an eye, I was up in the air, flying over the city. I was face-to-face with the dark blue sky and flying high above all the glittering lights that helped symbolize the famous city of Los Angeles. I remember thinking that as beautiful as LA looked below, this was no pleasure ride. It was cold, dark, and I was scared. I felt that Randy's condition must really be serious when a forty-five-minute drive to Northridge was substituted for a fifteen-minute helicopter ride. But I couldn't think about the flight in the helicopter ... This was my Randy, and I needed to be by his side. If he heard my voice, I'm sure it would make all the difference in the world. I wanted him to know that I was going to help him get through this horrific incident.

I remember crying and feeling my tears frozen against my face like icicles. Then, I started praying again, asking God to help Randy. After my little prayer, I found my mind going in every direction. While in flight, I went into insurance agent mode, thinking about the long-term care and the disability policies enforced for Randy. I would make contact with my office in the morning and report his injuries. Then I thought that I might even have to reconfigure our house. Worst-case scenario, Randy might be paralyzed, and he and I would need the bedroom downstairs. But I didn't want to think of that harsh possibility, for Randy was too active to be immobile. That would literally break his spirit and kill him. Looking back, the thought of death never crossed my mind, for I felt strongly that if he had passed away, surely the officers would have informed me when they arrived at my house. They wouldn't be taking me to the hospital to see him if he had died. I guess this was the one positive thought I could hold on to.

I didn't know what to think, so I just looked up at the dark sky, which almost looked like velvet. I observed the stars that sparkled so brightly and the moon that stood still, asking God to walk with me because I felt so alone and scared.

My mind was frazzled, so much so that I didn't even notice when we were landing on the rooftop of Northridge Hospital. I couldn't get out of the seat belt fast enough; I just wanted to go see my Randy. It seemed a multitude of police officers were on the rooftop, coming to greet me and escort me to Randy. I anxiously walked at a fast pace as I tried to keep up with the officers. Some were in front of me, and some were behind me, but what I remember most was Officer Dave walking close beside me, his arm entwined with mine.

# CHAPTER 19

# Welby Way

UNKNOWN TO ME AT THE time, just five miles away was the SWAT call-up on Welby Way, located in Winnetka, California. Winnetka is a district in the west-central San Fernando Valley, in the city of Los Angeles. It is positioned next to Canoga Park on the west and Woodland Hills on the south. It consists primarily of Latinos and Caucasians, with a few Asians and African Americans living there as well. This is where the infamous Edwin Rivera and his family lived.

The deranged twenty-year-old Edwin Rivera lived on Welby Way with his father, stepmother, and two older brothers. It was a turbulent household that neighbors on the block said they steered clear of because of the disorderliness of the brothers. Several resources stated that Edwin suffered from mental illness and had recently been released from a 5150 hold from a state hospital for his disturbed behavior. He also had a criminal record and was on probation, but he had no known gang affiliation.

Neighbors and other resources stated that Edwin was undeniably disturbed by the behavior and presence of his father's common-law wife. I was told they didn't have a good relationship; she would sometimes argue with Edwin and his brothers. As a result, neither Edwin nor his brothers held her in high esteem, but they had no choice or opinion about the matter, as this was their father's wife. Neighbors say that a few weeks prior to the incident, she and Edwin got into a huge argument about his mother, who had died of cancer years earlier. He was devastated over his mother's death, which appeared to have caused his mental condition to take a turn for the worse. The argument possibly sent Edwin over the edge and triggered his insane behavior.

Reports have it that the stepmother had returned home from an outing and saw her husband watching television with Edwin. A short time later, the stepmother claimed that she and her husband went to their bedroom to retire for the evening. They later heard four gunshots that appeared to have come from inside the house. Edwin's father left the bedroom to investigate the loud gunshot noise. Initially, he thought it was another drive-by shooting, which I'm told happened in the neighborhood weeks prior to this incident. But the shots sounded as though they were inside the home. The stepmother stated that shortly after the father left the room, she heard three additional gunshots. She became afraid and ran to hide in the bedroom closet, waiting for Edwin's father to return, but he never did.

In an unbalanced stupor, Edwin called 911 several times, trying to get the attention of police officers. The Communications Division stated that calls came in at approximately 8:30 p.m., with Edwin Rivera requesting that the police come and get him. The West Valley Police Division responded to the residence, unaware of what was going on at the house. The responding officers, pulled up at the home and approached the front door. As they came closer to the door, they could hear Edwin Rivera making a statement from inside the house. He said, "I have three dead in here." He continued by saying, "I've already killed three. Come inside and kill me."

Recognizing that this was a serious situation, the officers called their supervisor and an additional unit for backup. In the interim, Edwin made another 911 call, stating that he had killed three people fifteen minutes earlier. He made potentially twelve 911 calls, speaking very low and incoherently, with his speech heavily slurred. It sounded like a bunch of gibberish.

Another call came in at 10:30 p.m., when he stated, "Yeah ... tell 'em to shoot the sofa. Yes, tell them, the other guys, to exit the back door, please ... Tell the other guys to leave out the back door, please ..."

Then he called 911 again and made a comment that sounded

something like this: "This is 17277 Welby Way. Will you please just tell him to run up and shoot the window? I'm right here ... please."

Officers tried to communicate with him in both English and Spanish, but he was incoherent and continued to ramble on, using disoriented and illogical speech patterns. The West Valley officers and supervisors knew they were dealing with a maniac and recognized that a specialized unit was needed to apprehend him. More seriously, they were concerned about the possibility of victims that were bleeding out and in need of rescuing as soon as possible. One of the 911 dispatchers said she thought she heard moaning in the background. It was inaudible and hard to make out the sounds. Nonetheless, this incident required the assistance of the SWAT team.

I learned that Randy wasn't even scheduled to work that night, but he volunteered to assist, based on there being several relatively new SWAT officers responding to the call-up that night. He thought he would go in and lend his expertise.

Based on my time calculation, Randy must have left the house between 10:30 p.m. and 11:00 p.m. at the latest. Why he deviated from his normal routine of waking me up with a kiss and saying good-bye is something I will never know. I guess it could be blamed on my cold and my insomnia. Randy was always considerate, so I would imagine he didn't want to wake me up, especially since he knew I was sick and needed to rest.

I'm speculating that Randy got to Welby Way no later than 11:30 p.m. When the SWAT officers arrived at the scene, they assembled an entry team, with the element leader, John "Johnny" Verman, discussing the tactical procedures the team would be using. The lieutenant and the other supervisors agreed to the hostage rescue deployment tactics. Each was given his assignment and position. It was clearly going to be a Rapid Rescue Mission, otherwise defined as "the recovery of persons believed to be grievously injured, where immediate intervention is necessary to prevent additional injury or loss of life."

The SWAT team had developed and implemented a policy titled "An Immediate Response and Rapid Deployment Tactical Procedure," which they put into practice after the Columbine High School incident in Littleton, Colorado. Many felt that the SWAT team in Colorado took too long to respond to the injured victims in the high school, and as a result, many victims bled out and died due to the slow response. To prevent this from ever happening again, many SWAT teams across the country have since implemented this policy or similar policies that require responding expeditiously to victims in danger.

All the information regarding the shooting incident that follows is based on several officers' accounts of the incident, as well as reports I received because of my own personal investigation.

I learned that the Rivera house was completely dark and relatively small, and it appeared to have a square-shaped structure. The configuration of the interior was oddly designed and didn't coincide with the architectural blueprint. Nonetheless, it was no more unusual than other call-up scenes that Randy had been on previously. There was yellow tape everywhere, and all neighbors were asked to temporarily leave their homes. No one was allowed to come onto Welby Way or even near it, as it was considered a major crime scene.

The BearCat truck holding more tools and ammunition had not yet arrived, so moving quickly, the team used equipment and artillery that they had readily available for use when making entry into the home.

Two of the SWAT officers were responsible for the break and rake. This procedure serves several purposes, but it is primarily used as a distraction. Officer Johnny Verman was to breach the door with a shotgun, while another officer was to kick in the door. Two other officers were responsible for throwing the flashbangs, which is designed to startle and shock the suspect. Eight highly skilled officers were to follow suit in stick formation, each making entry and some tapering off to the left and some tapering off to the right with Officer Verman being number three in line and Randy being number five.

The team entered at approximately midnight, starting with the break and rake at a window in the front of the house. As soon as the break and rake took place, the suspect, Edwin Rivera, started firing back, with fragments hitting one of the officers in the face. In a motion as fast as lighting, Officer Verman breached the door, with the assigned officer kicking down the door. The flashbang was thrown but the desired effect of the device was lessen due to a pony wall at the entryway of the house, which it hit, causing the flashbang to malfunction. Quickly the entry team ran in, but not as assigned, based on findings in an investigation report. Somehow the positions were altered.

Verman, scheduled to be third in the stick, was now second; and Randy, scheduled to be fifth in the stick, was now third. Edwin Rivera was sitting and waiting for the opportune time to ambush the police and kill his next victim or victims. He was hiding in the back hallway, camouflaged under a mattress that covered his entire body. He was also armed with a 12-gauge shotgun and handgun. The minute Randy and the others entered the house, Edwin, acting out with aggressive and deadly behavior, commenced shooting. I learned that he shot Randy first and then Officer Verman—within seconds of making entry. Both Randy and Johnny Verman were shot in the face and critically injured. They went down before being able to return shots. An officer shouted, "Man down, man down! All units, officer needs help—officer down!"

The violent behavior of Edwin Rivera, and the velocity of the shootout had everyone in disarray. One officer said that everything was happening so fast that he didn't know if he had been shot. He slipped and saw blood all over his hands and uniform. He later realized that he had slipped in a pool of blood that was coming from a victim bleeding out next to him.

The suspect, Edwin Rivera, retreated to the back of the house after shooting Randy and Johnny. It was at that time that Officer Anthony Samuelson rescued Randy, and Steve Scallon made entry and rescued Johnny. Paramedics were waiting outside, ready to perform medical treatment and rush Randy and Johnny to Northridge Hospital.

## CHAPTER 20

# Press B, Please

Randy arrived at Northridge Hospital about 12:30 a.m. An emergency team was working on him in one room, while a team across the way worked on Johnny.

I entered the building about 1:15 a.m. and was instructed to head toward the elevator so I could see Randy. I was nervous but glad that I had finally arrived. I wanted to talk to the doctors to get a clear diagnosis of Randy's injuries and find out what his prognosis would be. I was looking for straight answers, not responses of "We don't know."

Dave and I entered the elevator with several other officers, and I heard someone say, "Press B, please."

I said, "Why are we going to the basement?" That seemed odd to me. The basement just seemed so drab and cold. It was a place where most hospitals stored ... I didn't want to complete that thought.

"Where's the emergency room?" I asked.

No one answered. Again, a cold chill went through my body. I specifically remember looking at one of the officers, a tall Caucasian man. He looked sad and choked up. His face and nose were red. His eyes were watery, so I knew something was terribly wrong. Based on everyone's manner, it was a strong possibility that Randy and Johnny could be in the basement fighting for their lives.

Dave and I walked off the elevator, still arm and arm, and he ever so gently led me down a long corridor. There were officers lined up against the wall, looking solemn and sad, most of them in uniform. I recall passing them one by one, trying to make eye contact, but strangely, they all held their heads down, unable to look me in the eye. And to my surprise, I saw a chaplain walking out of a room that was situated at the end of the hall. My knees started shaking, and I felt that I was going to pass out. I remember breaking loose from Dave, wanting to run back to the helicopter so that I could go home, get in my bed, and wake up from this horrible nightmare. I remember feeling almost angry and extremely scared.

I said something like, "I'm not going down there!"

Dave braced me, holding me by the arm again and asking me to walk with him into the room. I thought, *This just doesn't look good*. I felt it in my bones.

I slowly walked into a room filled with people. Some were in uniform, but the majority of the people were dressed in civilian clothes. The first of those who caught my attention were my sisters, standing on the other side of the room, farthest away from the door where I entered. I recall looking at them as if to say, *What's going on?* They were looking at me from across the room, tears rolling down their faces. Then someone touched my arm and instructed me to walk to my left, where to my surprise, I saw Randy's classmate and good friend, now an LAPD captain, James Craig standing with tears in his eyes. I immediately started crying as I waited for James to say the words, which he did almost in a whisper.

"He's gone, Lisa. We lost him."

I can still hear those chilling words that caused me to bellow out a scream that came from my innermost soul. It was as if I let out all seventeen years of our wonderful life together. My heart and my soul were aching so much, and I was desperately in need of some quick intervention or I was going to be making that journey with Randy. I have never felt a pain like that before in my entire life—a heartache that only those who have lost a close loved one knows. My sisters ran to my aid, along with other officers and officials, but none of their words could comfort me. I was in the world but out of it. I could hear everyone saying things, but I couldn't comprehend anything. Every word coming out of anyone's mouth at that time was inaudible to me, as no words could lift this pain off me. I knew I needed *Jesus*. I needed supernatural powers to intervene. I needed the Holy Ghost to help me. I needed some serious prayer, so

I asked someone to pray for me. I needed prayer in a big way, for I was hurting so much that I could barely breathe.

Someone started praying ... I can't really remember who—maybe it was the chaplain—but I knew as the minutes ticked on and as prayers went up, God was stirring things up in my spirit, which was calming me down and bringing me back to a harsh reality. As a result, I went into worship. How could I not thank God for blessing me with a wonderful husband? It may have seemed odd to some, but for Randy and me, God was real, and whether it be life or death, I was still going to thank Him and give Him glory, even in that darkest hour. I knew without a doubt that Randy would have acted on those same thoughts.

"Thank you, Jesus, for blessing me. Thank you, God, for Randy's wonderful life. I love you, God. Please don't leave me." I kept reiterating those words: "Please don't leave me, God."

I know that God loves me just as He loves Randy, but truthfully speaking, I felt that Randy had a special relationship with God. He loved God with everything he had, with all his might, and he illustrated that on a daily basis. My evidence and works couldn't compare to Randy's. Nonetheless, I knew that God had given Randy to me to be my soul mate, to cover me, to protect me, and to stand by me. As my husband, he did a great job performing the duties entrusted him by God. Now he was gone. Despair and loneliness instantly came over me. I needed God more than ever to walk me through this dark, lonely season. I wanted God to know that I needed Him.

After the dust settled, I recall sitting down and feeling extremely hot, almost as if I had broken out in a fever. James Craig had given me some water. Drinking it brought my temperature down and slowly began to cool my body, allowing my jittery soul to retreat to a somewhat normal state. I wanted so desperately to gain composure so I could be coherent enough to understand what was going on and what had happened. Keep in mind: the kids and I were just praying with Randy a few hours earlier, and now he was dead. I knew nothing about Welby Way at this time. All information I shared in the previous chapter, I learned much later. Again, I didn't know Randy had even left the house, so my curiosity about the incident was in full force.

A doctor came in to explain to me what happened to Randy. I can't remember the doctor's name, but he was a handsome middle-aged white man who pulled up a chair right in front of me and compassionately gave me the details of Randy's fatal injuries. Sitting next to the doctor was an attractive Latino man, and he was gently holding my hand as if to give me some comfort while I heard the gory details. The doctor explained that Randy was shot in the right side of his neck; the bullet exited through the back, thus severing his spine. He assured me that the paramedics and doctors did everything possible to save his life. The more he talked and explained, the more I cried. I could feel the Latino man clenching my hand tighter and tighter as the doctor continued to explain Randy's last minutes of life and how he fought to stay alive. With my face drenched in tears, I looked over at the Latino man, who had tears flowing from his eyes as well. His face looked familiar … It was Mayor Villaraigosa, only he wasn't that political figure who graced our presence on the news as he discussed issues that impacted the city of Los Angeles. Rather he was a man who was obviously affected by Randy's premature death. He wanted to extend any comfort he could to Randy's grieving widow. Recognizing who he was, I thanked him for his support with a half smile and a whisper.

Then coming through the door, eager to hear Randy's medical status, was another familiar face. It was Pastor Trimble. Naturally, he was nervous and concerned. Randy was like a younger brother to Pastor Trimble. Randy loved and supported Pastor Trimble in just about every ministry the church offered. He supported him spiritually and prayed for him on a personal level. He was grateful for his teachings and had immense gratitude for his knowledge and wisdom about the Bible. Randy learned so much under his ministry, which helped him grow in the things of God. In addition, Pastor Trimble gave him the leadership role of being over the Glory Kids Ministry and supported his vision of broadening his outreach of the ministry. Now I had the difficult task of sharing the tragic news that Randy was killed.

I knew he could see by the expression on my face that whatever words I uttered from my mouth were going to bring bad news. However, I think, like everyone else, he wasn't expecting to hear that Randy had died. The tragic news hit him hard and left him in disbelief, so much that he questioned me again, with his voice crying and trembling at the same time. "He died?" I couldn't respond and say the word yes, so he and I just hugged and cried together. Seeing my pastor's heartbroken was unusual to me. Not that my pastor wasn't compassionate, but like Randy—a big, tall, robust man—he was very confident and in control of his emotions. Seeing the pastor so upset just confirmed what I already knew in my heart: his love for Randy. My pastor offered prayer again, as he knew that it was much needed for my sake as well as for his and for everyone there who was still trying to come to grips with Randy's death.

After prayer, I just held on to and hugged everyone who came to support me. There was my good friend Paulette, whom I'd called before I got in the chopper, my brother-in-law's brother, Maury, a detective for the Santa Monica Police Department who comforted me just by his presence, and other officers that I knew. At that point, I asked no further questions about the incident, for it seemed irrelevant at the time. My only concern was Randy. I wanted to see him, regardless of his state or condition.

Captain Jeff Greer, another classmate of Randy's and now the captain of SWAT, agreed to escort me to see Randy, under the condition that I would be strong enough to handle seeing Randy no longer alive. He explained to me that Johnny Verman was in a room across the hall, still fighting for his life, so any information about Randy's death could make his outcome fatal as well. In a kind way, he was asking that I please try to keep my emotions under control for Johnny's sake. I agreed, but honestly speaking, I wasn't going to make any promises. However, I wanted Johnny to pull through, so I tried to be sensitive and remain cognizant of this fact.

Jeff, again not being just Randy's captain but his good friend, was looking out for Randy's wife. He was concerned about my state of mind and asked me again whether I was going to be okay. I told him that I would be, and with my sisters by my side, I walked in and saw my precious Randy lying on the gurney with a sheet covering his body. He lay there lifeless. His eyes were swollen and almost bulging out of his head, and there on the right side of his neck was a small hole with blood still streaming from it, onto the sheets and onto the gurney. I cried uncontrollably, rubbing his head and telling him that he didn't even tell me and the kids good-bye. I wondered aloud, saying, "Who would want to kill a man like you? If they had only known your good deeds and your spirit, they wouldn't have done this."

I just continued to ramble, talking out of my head like a psychotic person. I wanted to hold him for the last time, so I wrapped my arms around his body and laid my face against his chest. I tried to hear if there was still a heartbeat, but I heard nothing, and his chest seemed hard as a rock. I guess rigor mortis was setting in. It was evident that he wasn't in that shell or that body anymore. Randy was making his journey to heaven. He was probably knocking on the pearly gates, or perhaps he was already there, walking around on the streets paved of gold that the Bible speaks about as it describes heaven. Maybe he was fellowshipping with the Lord and all our loved ones who had gone before him. I had a quick vision in my mind of my father greeting him at the gates. Then I thought of him holding our little angel that I had lost in my first pregnancy. I took comfort in those thoughts, but unfortunately, here in my world, I was left with a broken heart and only memories of a life that once existed here on Earth.

My sisters and I stayed in the room for about thirty minutes more, and then I took one last look at Randy and walked out. I had my sisters on each side of me, holding my arms, alternating with friends and relatives who were just arriving at the hospital and learning the horrific news. I felt jittery yet lifeless walking through the corridors of the hospital as I made my way to the chapel to pray for healing. I passed my sister-in-law Gina and her son David who had just made it to the hospital. She didn't know that Randy had passed. She only knew that he had been shot; I had left her a message telling her that. She and David had rushed to the hospital only to learn of his tragic fate.

In my mind, I can still see her walking up to me and asking frantically, "Where is he? Is he okay? What happened?"

Then James Craig, again the bearer of bad news, informed her of Randy's passing. It was another disheartening scene. Sadly, I had no energy to help her with her grief, as I could barely handle my own emotions at the time. Family and friends stepped in to help Gina and the others who were distraught and needing comfort.

I made my way to the hospital chapel, where other family members were waiting. I sat down on the pew and continued to pray for guidance, asking God to give me the words, the courage, and the strength to tell my children. I started praying for their well-being because I knew the news of their father's death was going to tear them apart. Then I heard Randy's voice in my head saying, "Man up! My babies are going to need you. You know where I am ... Man up!" Anyone who knew Randy knew he had a rough edge that he demonstrated even when he was preaching. One thing he believed in was being strong and pushing through challenging times. He hated seeing me cry, as it was too painful for him to bear, so to offset the pain, he would encourage me by saying, "Come on, Lisa, you've got to man up!" This was definitely one of his favorite statements. Somehow, the psychological method of hearing him say those words always seemed to work for me. This would be a time that I would truly have to "man up" and be there for my children. I needed to get to where they were expeditiously so that I could tell them the tragic news before they heard it from someone else. However, just as I was getting up to leave, another familiar face walked into the chapel. It was my father-in-law, Dallas Simmons.

When Dallas walked into the chapel and heard about Randy's death, I recall seeing him shaking like a leaf, crying, and falling to his knees in prayer. *Really?* I thought. He seemed like the perfect candidate for me to direct my anger toward. I wanted to tell him, "You rejected and disappointed my husband for years ... and now you're standing here weeping like a baby. Where were you when he needed you most?" But of course, I didn't say it. The Holy Spirit came over me and gave me the power to restrain my mouth and have compassion. I extended my hand to touch his shoulder and then walked past him as I exited the chapel and headed home to see to my kids.

Emerging from the hospital elevator with my sisters and friends, who were walking us to the car, I met Johnny Verman's wife, Marsha Verman. She was in frantic mode. She grabbed me, introduced herself, and extended her sympathy to my family and me. I thanked her for her condolences but explained to her that I had to make it home, as I needed to get to my kids. I recall her wanting to continue talking, almost as if she didn't hear me say I needed to get home to my kids. I remember my sister Melinda taking over the conversation and stating firmly, "I'm sorry, but Lisa has to get home to her kids. She'll be in touch with you later."

I told her that I would be praying for Johnny and then hugged her good-bye. I believe Marsha was in a hysterical state, and that she was using her nervous energy through talking. I also believe we both were still in a state of confusion and shock.

When we left the hospital, it was probably around 4:00 a.m., and it was still cold and dark outside. But the darkness of the night was broken by spotlights on one side of the hospital, in the main parking lot. Little did I know that the media had camped outside to hear the outcome of Randy's and Johnny's conditions. They also wanted to get a glimpse of his now-grieving widow. Naturally, I wasn't ready or prepared to talk to anyone, so my sisters and I were instructed to go around the building to another exit. I wasn't concerned about the media, as new revelations of Randy's death were running through my mind.

I was walking with Pastor Trimble, who'd agreed to come with me to help break the news to Matthew and Gabrielle. I was grateful for his assistance, for we needed him, and I knew that Randy would want him to be by our side during this time.

As Pastor Trimble escorted my sisters and me to the car, I walked arm in arm with him and shared a thought that instantly came across my mind. I thought about that song I was singing: "Bow Down and Worship Him." *Enter in ... Oh, enter in.* I believe deep within my heart that it was precisely when Randy was transitioning from our world to the heavenly kingdom. I explained to him how I woke up at around the time Randy was shot and started singing that song for some odd reason. Now that reason didn't seem odd anymore. Randy took that bullet between 12:00 and 12:30 a.m., which was just around the same time I got out of my bed and started singing that song. The paramedics and doctors worked on him to save him, but he was already en route. He was officially pronounced dead at 12:55 a.m. Officer Anthony "Tony" Samuelson later told me that when he rescued Randy from the Rivera house, he looked at him and thought, *He's probably meeting Saint Peter at the door.*

Essentially, Tony was saying that Randy pretty much passed away at the scene. Surely Tony would know, having served time in the military. I'm sure he had a good idea as to what death looked like.

As we continued to the car, I'll never forget how my pastor so beautifully responded to me. He started singing "Bow Down and Worship Him" in his velvety smooth voice. At that moment, I looked up at the dark blue sky and saw all the white fluorescent twinkling stars that seemed to be dancing in unison as if rejoicing in the presence of a new angel entering in. Everything above just seemed so heavenly.

## CHAPTER 21

# Breaking News

My sister Cookie took off in her convertible Volvo, with me sitting up front and Melinda in the backseat. Looking out the window, my mouth flew wide open when I saw hundreds of police cars lining the streets for miles away. When I was up in the helicopter, I was oblivious to what was going on below. My sisters stated that they knew something tragic had happened when they drove up to the hospital and saw the multitude of police cars. The presence of all the police cars had them terrified. They felt terrible news could be awaiting them inside the hospital. Unfortunately, their inkling was right.

We didn't talk much, as we wanted Cookie to stay focused on her driving and get us to her house as quickly as possible. I was so afraid the kids would hear about what happened to their father before I had a chance to tell them. As Cookie drove, Melinda used her cell phone to call my niece Amia and warn her that she should keep every television set off in the house. Amia was shaken. I could tell she was curious, but she must have sensed that something was terribly wrong, so she did as she was told.

Unbeknownst to Amia, her father, my brother-in-law Wilfred, had already received the news from his wife, Cookie. Devastated, he immediately went into an emotional state of distress, for he and Randy were like brothers. Amia realized it was strange for him not to come out of his room and check on the kids, as he was a terrific uncle and a wonderful father. But instead, he was secluded in his room, and Amia could hear him sobbing when she walked passed her parents' bedroom, clearly indicating that something tragic had occurred.

It wasn't long before we reached Wilfred and Cookie's house in Leimert Park, a little district in the Los Angeles area where I grew up. Cookie and her family had lived diagonally across the street from my mother on a major thoroughfare. When we arrived, it was still early morning, and I couldn't bear to knock on my mother's door to tell her the sad news. I knew I had to stay focused, to concentrate on the hardest thing I ever had to do in my life: tell my children that their father had been tragically killed.

Once in Cookie's house, Pastor Trimble, my sisters, and I, were greeted by some officers from LAPD's Southwest Division, which responds to the Leimert Park area. Coincidently, it was also the division that Captain James Craig had overseen. Some of the officers there were Randy's friends, and I gave them each a hug and then walked back to Cookie's family room. The kids were upstairs waiting for my arrival. They walked down the steps and could clearly see that I had been crying. I looked at both of them with tears flowing freely from my eyes. Just the sight of them sent me into an agonizing state. Matthew stood there nervously, waiting for me to respond, while Gabrielle, standing behind him, could feel my grief and started shaking her head back and forth as if to say, *No! Please tell me that my dad is not dead.* I just stood there crying as she and Matthew waited for words to come from my lips. Then finally, I got up enough courage to say the words.

"Daddy didn't make it."

Matthew, shocked at what I said, repeated my words to be sure he'd heard me right. "What? He didn't make it? He's dead?" he asked shakily.

"Yes," I said, reaching out to hold him and Gabrielle.

But before I could take hold of them, Matthew took off running down the corridor in the hallway. Pastor Trimble ran after him, and I grabbed Gabrielle. Then my niece and sisters held on to Gabby as I ran to see about Matthew. He was at Cookie's front door, and luckily the door had security locks so Matthew couldn't get out. He stood there with his head against the door, crying and beating the door with his fists. I took hold of him from behind and held him with my face pressed against his back, crying with him. I could hear his heart racing, almost as if it were going to come through his back. I was tempted to call the paramedics because of the way his heart was racing. I was actually afraid he was going to have a heart attack. I stood there with Matt as Pastor Trimble gave Matthew words of encouragement, trying to soothe his broken heart and desperately attempting to get him to calm down.

When we finally got Matthew to quiet down a bit, we walked him back to the family room, where we all sat sobbing. The adults made an effort at being strong for the kids' sake, including my niece Amia, who had cried silently for hours, disguising her emotions about the turn of events. I knew at that moment, based on my kids' condition, that I had no choice but to *man up!* They needed their mother desperately, and I had to be the pillar of strength that was going to see our family through this most difficult time. I would have to remain in a state of continuous prayer, which Pastor Trimble understood.

He gathered us all together for prayer, and as always the Holy Spirit took control. Although my kids were very emotional, by the grace of God, paramedics were not needed. We were going to get through this ordeal with God's healing hands. We were going to use everything we'd learned under Pastor Trimble's leadership, reinforced through Randy's discussions, confirmed with the Bible, and sealed with the Holy Spirit and God's precious love to overcome and someday conquer our grieving emotions.

After prayer, a special friend of Randy's requested permission to express his condolences. He was waiting for me in Cookie's living room, so I went out to greet him. There he stood, tall, dark, and handsome. It was Randy's good friend and partner, James Hart, grief-stricken by the news of his dear and loyal partner. Seeing James gave me a sense of comfort but also deepened my grief, as they were a force of nature together, two men to be reckoned with, except now James stood alone in a dangerous profession that resulted in Randy's sudden death. Surely this was scary for James, as SWAT had never lost any of its members, and because it was Randy, it was hitting too close to home.

Everyone remained at Cookie's house for about another hour, just holding on to and consoling each other. I knew that we were going to be all right, for we had the support of our Heavenly Father as well as friends and family there to help us.

Later that morning, at around 7:00 a.m., I wanted to go home. I needed to feel close to Randy, so my sister Cookie and her good friend Lenora took Matthew and me home with James Hart, the others following behind us. Gabrielle stayed with Amia, who was going to join us at the house shortly.

By this time, all of America had heard the news. While we were en route to my house, my cell phone and my sisters' cell phones were ringing off the hook. I could only take one phone call at a time, and each phone call elicited an emotional breakdown from both ends of the phone line, all of which was affecting Matthew even more. I decided to turn off my cell phone and just sit quietly on the drive home, holding Matthew's hand.

As we pulled into our neighborhood, I saw police cars blocking all the streets leading to our house. The police made sure to keep the media and lookie loos at bay. When we turned onto our block, I saw neighbors looking confused by the presence of the police, plainly wondering what was going on. It was still early morning, and it was apparent that many had not yet heard the news. Randy's name had just been released to the media as the SWAT officer that was tragically killed. I remember seeing one neighbor grab his mouth in shock when a police officer told him what happened. Our neighbors were very familiar with Randy, not just as the police officer or the husband or father to the family that lived in the white house near the corner but also as the muscular, friendly guy they saw jogging throughout the neighborhood daily. Occasionally, he would stop and make conversation. Neighbors would always say what a pleasure it was to talk with him.

Our street was relatively quiet, except when our kids had their friends over. On this day, it looked like a circus, with people walking up and down the street and police cars circling the neighborhood. A few blocks over the media trucks lined the streets with their satellite antennas up. Good neighbors had set up tables in front of their houses, with coffee and doughnuts for the officers who had worked around the clock securing our home and the neighborhood. I recall looking out the car window, crying as I envisioned Randy pulling our kids in a red wagon up and down the sidewalks and jogging up the hill. I envisioned seeing his big smile at the corner street as he came to look for me at dusk when I was out walking our dog, Monique. In the blink of an eye, what once was the biggest part my life was now gone. *Time is a silent thief,* I thought. It had stolen a huge part of my life when it was least expected.

When we drove up in my driveway, a friendly face was waiting for me. It was Jimmy Fields, a middle-aged, handsome, black man of average height and weight. He was a Texas man with old-fashioned Southern ways. Jimmy was a good friend of the family's and an usher at our church. He loved Randy, and Randy loved him, supporting him with all his endeavors to become a jailer for the city of Los Angeles. Jimmy was the type that could love you in one breath but become agitated and scold you in another. Sometimes it was comical to see him getting upset, speaking fast and firmly with his strong Texas accent.

Jimmy was one of Randy's biggest fans, and he would often say that Randy was the real deal. In fact, he told me on several occasions, even prior to Randy's death, that Randy was a good man and a true example of how a man should aspire to live his life in every aspect. He would say Randy was a rarity and would even compare himself with Randy, especially when it came to having patience, as Jimmy had very little. I enjoyed hearing Jimmy talk about Randy and the Glory Kids.

Randy asked Jimmy, as he had many others, to help with the Glory Kids Ministry, but some would come up with excuses as to why they couldn't volunteer, with reasons ranging from having to work, to being in school on Saturday, or some other responsibility. But Jimmy didn't give excuses. He was always honest, firmly telling Randy in his Southern accent, "You know I ain't as holy as you are. I would have to hurt one of those bad kids the minute he got out of line."

Randy laughed and shook his head at Jimmy, saying, "You're right, brother. Stick to ushering. We all have our talents, and dealing with kids sure ain't yours."

But Jimmy supported Randy in other ways, edifying him as a man and clearly supporting his family. Being at the house at my arrival was evidence of that support. When I arrived and saw Jimmy, I broke down, crying in his arms. Everyone and everything had a special connection to Randy that was endearing, and each person who loved Randy brought forth more of my emotions.

Jimmy quickly escorted us all inside the house, instantly becoming like a bodyguard, shielding me from the press and unwanted interaction. He understood that I needed time to digest this horrific incident. I didn't realize how much I was going to need the protection of Jimmy and others, as I wasn't a celebrity or an important dignitary. I was simply Randy's wife. But little did I know that the name *Randy* held a lot of weight in itself.

The doorbell rang constantly as flowers and plants kept coming in by the dozens. And the phone continued to ring off the hook, with my sisters and friends acting as secretaries. People continued to make their way into our house, but not before being screened by the police. You either had to be family, a law enforcement officer, or a delivery person to enter the street. I later learned that some neighbors had to show proof that they lived in the neighborhood so they could return to their homes.

Reflecting back now, I can see that it was, for lack of a better term, total chaos and pandemonium. However, at that moment, I was so engulfed in sorrow that I was almost oblivious to what was going on around me. All I wanted to do was hold my children and go to sleep, just as I did when they were infants. We were physically and mentally exhausted.

Matthew's room was downstairs, and there was too much commotion for him to get any sleep, so he and I retreated to Randy's and my bedroom in the hopes of getting at least a few hours of rest. I also felt a need to be alone with Gabrielle, but she still hadn't gotten to the house. Matthew and I left everyone downstairs and went up to the bedroom, leaving my sisters, James Hart, and Jimmy Fields to handle all matters in the common area.

When we got upstairs, Matthew requested that we turn the TV on; he'd heard the commotion downstairs, with everyone running to the TV and listening to the developing news story. By now, he and I were both curious about what was going on at the call-up. The LAPD officials were going to give a news conference about the shooting. And there it was, BREAKING NEWS, with a picture of Randy's handsome face splashed across the television screen. The news anchor delivered a statement similar to this:

"Twenty-seven-year veteran Randy Simmons of the Special Weapons and Tactics team was shot and killed by deranged and possible gang suspect Edwin Rivera. His partner, Johnny Verman, twenty-five-year veteran, was critically injured but is expected to survive..."

After the statement, the actual call-up was shown live on TV, still in progress after a ten-hour standoff. The news announcer gave systematic details of the incident, bringing every viewer up to date on the latest actions made by the SWAT team and the suspect.

Between the time that Randy and Johnny had been shot and the early morning hours, the suspect had retreated toward the back of the house, reflecting minimal activity. The SWAT BearCat arrived after Randy and Johnny were shot, housing an arsenal of weapons and equipment to help assist the officers. Other SWAT officers, such as Steve Scallion, Todd Rheingold, and Keith Bacon, were called in to assist in the SWAT call-up, along with two hundred other armed officers who surrounded the home. The LAPD Air Support Division circled overhead. The sound of the helicopter propeller and tail rotor alarmed those in residences on neighboring streets.

Many of the officers did not know the fate of Randy or Johnny, although they knew it was serious. Some of them speculated based on the countenance and the emotions that were on the faces of their superiors. Still, they faithfully carried out their duties, exemplifying their motto: "Uncompromised Duty, Honor and Valor."

At about 5:30 a.m., a decision was made to deploy tear gas in an attempt to get the suspect to come out of the house and surrender. A sniper on the team noticed a woman in the rear bedroom doorway, appearing frantic as she attempted to exit the house and run to safety. It looked like someone appearing to be the suspect was keeping her from exiting, but she managed to escape with a sniper firing a round in an attempt to protect and save her. The suspect was not hit, and he remained in the house. He then went to the window and turned toward the officers, pointing a handgun toward them. Two officers fired their guns at the suspect, and he disappeared from the window. Gas and flashbangs were deployed, and smoke was everywhere, with the house appearing to be on fire. At approximately 7:30 a.m., the suspect opened the rear service porch security door and exited, giving a sniper team member the opportunity to fire one deadly and fatal round. The call-up was over.

The news conference came on, with a visibly shaken Mayor Villaraigosa, Assistant Chief Paysinger, Assistant Chief Jim McDonell, Deputy Chief Michel Moore, Councilman Dennis Zine, and others standing in a circular formation, discussing the unfolding and tragic events of the call-up.

The mayor, who only a year earlier honored Randy with the Crystal Angel Award for "outstanding community service" during the Los Angeles Police Foundation's annual True Blue Awards, was now speaking about Randy's demise. He spoke about the unfortunate incident that had happened in his city … under his leadership. His grief still mirrored that image of sadness I saw only hours earlier at the hospital. Clearly still disturbed by this horrific incident, he provided limited details about the call-up itself but gave a heartfelt statement:

"Today is a sad and tragic day in the city of Los Angeles. We lost a police officer in the line of duty—the first police officer lost in the line of duty in SWAT's history. Another officer down. All of us extend our condolences, prayers, and our heartfelt sympathy to the families and to all members of the SWAT and the Los Angeles Police Department."

He continued, with his voice cracking at times, expressing how this tragic event was personal for him, for Randy and Johnny were once assigned to his children on a detail. Randy was assigned specifically to the mayor's daughter, and Johnny to the overall detail. He also went on to explain that although many might want the details of what occurred, the case was now under investigation, and only limited information could be shared.

The news conference continued, stating that Edwin Rivera, a twenty-year-old, three-hundred-pound man of Latino ethnicity, had killed his father, fifty-four year old Gerardo Rivera; his brother Endi Rivera, twenty-five years old; and his brother Edgar Rivera, twenty-one years old. It was a quadruple homicide. Then a picture of Edwin was shown, stating that he had a history of mental illness.

I quickly walked over to the television and turned it off, as I didn't want the image of Edwin Rivera's face to stay in Matthew's head or mine before closing our eyes to take a much-needed nap. Matthew and I spoke no words about the news conference. There was nothing else to be said. It was now a matter of coming to terms with Randy's death, and I knew it was going to be a long and difficult process. But I would start by being there for my children. I held Matthew, then fifteen years old, as he lay in bed crying himself to sleep, as he had when he was an infant. I held him as tightly as I could, crying with him and wondering how I was going to help him and Gabrielle get through this unexpected and terrible time. Daddy was gone, and they desperately needed their mother's physical, mental, and emotional strength. I asked myself how I was going to help them when I am hurting too? I had no choice but to do as Randy would have expected, and that was to "man up."

# CHAPTER 22

# Planning the Funeral

I closed my eyes for about an hour, but I couldn't sleep, so I just lay in bed until I knew Matt was sound asleep. He and I were both exhausted, but I got up when I heard the doorbell. It was Gabrielle and Amia. I went downstairs to get Gabrielle, as she was in need of a nap as well. No persuasion was required, as she was tired. All three of us slept in my California king bed, with me in the middle, alternating back and forth, hugging each of them. It was a tender moment for me, especially hugging Matt. Unlike Gabby, who still liked to cuddle, Matt often pulled away from my affectionate mother hen ways, trying to resist being a mama's boy. Somehow, at that moment, the notion was nonexistent. They both needed me and didn't hesitate to embrace me back.

The three of us slept for about two to three hours but probably never entered into REM sleep. I think that for the most part, we were in the twilight zone, and it literally felt exactly like that. Restless and experiencing anxiety attacks, I got up while the kids appeared to be asleep and went downstairs to see what was going on. As more and more people arrived to pay their respects, every room in my house looked like a florist had beautifully decorated it, with plants and flowers everywhere. Oscar-winning actor Louis Gossett Jr. was the first to send a beautiful tall plant, which still sits in my foyer today. He and Randy had worked together on a committee to help inner-city kids.

As I strolled through our house greeting people, I saw a number of different faces, some known to me and some unknown. Many of the newer faces were officers that I'd never met, but I'd heard their names through conversations I had with Randy. The few officers I did know were either his partners or those officers I met while Randy played on the Centurion football team. They were all so kind to pay their respects, and I was happy for the support. With Randy having been such an extremely private man, it felt strange to have so many people in the house. He'd made every effort to keep work and home life separate. His work was tough and demanding, and his home life was his sacred haven, where everything that was precious to him dwelled. It was one of the few places where he could unwind and relax ... if only for a little while.

Later in the day, my mother came to the house. I hadn't seen or talked with her since Randy's death. Randy was like her son too, and knowing that I would have a hard time handling her reaction, I gave my sisters the difficult duty of telling her the awful news. When I saw her, she had already dealt with the initial shock and was ready to comfort me. I stood in the foyer, hugging her and crying, feeling like a little girl who needed her mother to make the pain go away. After drenching my mother's blouse with more tears than I ever knew existed, it hit me. Oh my God, I had yet to call my mother-in-law to see how she was doing. I left Gina and a few other officers with the task of telling her that her only son, the apple of her eye, the son that she bragged about continuously and admired more than words could say, was gone.

Randy's sister Gina and her son David, along with two LAPD officers, drove out to Diamond Bar, California, to see Ms. Simmons at the senior housing apartment complex where she resided. Gina was shocked and upset over her big brother's death, so she desperately needed the officer's support in telling her mother the tragic news. Surely, Ms. Simmons would have received the news by now. I cringed at the thought of what she might be going through right at that moment.

I put in a phone call to Gina, and she told me that she never heard her mother cry like that in her entire life. But she didn't use the word "cry"—she said she wailed, letting out a cry that came from so deep within her that one would classify it as the moaning of a wounded animal that had been shot by hunters.

I visualized my mother-in-law taking that hit, and the pain was too much for me to bear. I just knew I needed to see her. I wanted to see the woman who gave birth to this wonderful and courageous man, fifty-one years ago. Gina told me that they were contacting Randy's older sister Valjean and her daughters, Randy's nieces, Tanya and Tiffany, as well as family in New York and locally in California. She stated that after they made all their phone calls, they would head to our house so that my mother-in-law could be with us.

While I was on the phone talking to Gina, Melinda went upstairs to check on the kids and promptly came back downstairs looking anxious. She asked me to go up to see about Matthew, who was now awake. I could tell something had happened by the expression on her face, so I ran upstairs, leaping over steps, trying to get to him as fast as I could with my sister following me. In my bedroom, I saw Gabby still in bed asleep, but Matt was sitting at the vanity in my adjoining bathroom, reading from some papers and crying hysterically. I wanted to see what he was reading that was making him cry so uncontrollably. I tried to be gentle, but my anxiety made me act almost aggressively, as I had to see what was causing this new disturbance to my child. Matthew was shaking like a leaf as he read.

"Matt, honey, what are you reading? Let me see."

His face was soaked with tears. The emotion was too great for him to utter a response, so he just handed me a two-page letter to read. As I started going through it, I thought to myself, *Wow, there it is*. My mind flashed back to the day I was doing laundry and the letter Randy was writing to Matt, giving him instructions on working out. At the time, it seemed so bizarre to see him write a letter to his son who lived in the same house. I couldn't help but wonder why he couldn't just give him one of his football lectures as he usually did. I later realized that Randy was serious about Matt getting his workout in, so it didn't seem odd since there were times that Randy was called out to work and Matt could miss a workout. Writing a letter would enforce Randy's instructions, and Matt would have no excuses about what to do and how to do his workouts. However, I did underestimate the content of his letter. I'd thought he was simply jotting some notes for Matt, but instead, it was an endearing letter to his son. I had honestly forgotten about that night a month earlier, when I had interrupted him and asked questions about the letter. It had totally slipped my mind.

My sister was standing behind Matt and consoling him, looking at me as if to say, *What does it say?* She was curious, and I was speechless. I had already read parts of it silently and wasn't sure if I was capable of getting Randy's words out. I looked down at Matthew, who was still sitting in the vanity chair, and asked him in a soft voice if I could read it to Auntie Melinda. He nodded his head yes, and I started reading it aloud, mentioning the heading of his letter first:

*Things to do to make it to college:*
(1)   *Know that I love you no matter what happens and you can always depend on me for everything. Even if you don't get a scholarship, I have enough money from LAPD SWAT to get your education ... To God be the glory.*

I paused and looked at my sister. Matthew was holding his head down, crying and listening to me read. She and I were both shocked by his words. It was almost as if Randy were speaking from the grave.

I stopped reading the letter, as it was too much for Matt and me to handle. I needed him to digest one thing at a time. Melinda agreed and gave him a big hug, telling him that we'd read the rest of the letter at a later date. But Matthew had already read the rest of the letter, which I think broke his heart even more.

The second half of the letter was Randy giving him systematic instructions about football, the game they both loved so much, the game that united him and his father in a special way. Matthew was playing high school football, so video games were no longer his first love. They now took a backseat to football. It was going to feel weird not having his father there coaching him from the stands; now he would be coaching him from heaven above.

Randy's letter continued:

(2)   *Kickoff return:*
*You are there only because your coaches realize how good you can be even without a lot of coaching. Remember, make sure you catch the ball. Don't fumble. You are a strong boy. Do not tiptoe. Run into an opening and accelerate on your toes!*

He continued to instruct Matt to do the same thing on his punt returns, telling him, *You got more speed than you realize!*

I believe Randy's letter was a clear indication of the Holy Spirit in action. Sometimes you can do something, say something, make a move, or stray from something, and you don't know why. You might think, *Something told me to do it*. In this case, I believe that something was the Holy Spirit pressing upon Randy's heart to write his son a letter for such a day as this. I feel that Randy didn't know why he was writing that letter, but something had stirred in his spirit, and he took a pen and paper and started writing. Little did he know that death was soon to follow, and that his son needed instructions that his mother was not equipped to give. Randy admired my knowledge about many things, but he knew football was way out of my league.

By this time, Gabrielle had awakened, hearing the discussion about the letter. My niece then interrupted, telling us that Matt's and Gabby's friends from school were at the house, coming to extend their condolences. I thought that was great. They needed the comfort and joy of seeing their friends, so we put the letter away to read the rest of it at another time and we all went downstairs to join our guests.

It looked like a packed restaurant, as there was food everywhere and people had to literally squeeze their way through the house. Many of our guests were in the family room watching television, as the news was on all day, talking about the incident and flashing the faces of Randy, Johnny, Edwin Rivera, and sadly, his father and two brothers across the screen. There was now information about another one of Edwin's brothers. He wasn't at the house and was now the only surviving family member. I thought about his state of mind and knew clearly that he must be grieving too, trying to make some sense out of his brother's insane behavior and the madness that took place on Welby Way.

The media, close acquaintances, and police officers were delivering me more and more information about the incident. Everyone wanted to tell his version of what he'd heard happened. Most of the details given were secondhand and thirdhand information, and unfortunately, some of it was unclear and unfounded. The conflicting versions put me in a paranoid state, and I couldn't think or eat. I felt nauseated, and my brain was scattered; I knew I had to take in one thing at a time.

While my sisters and friends played secretary and hosts, my mother played nurse and informed me that I needed to keep my health up. She was right. I felt as if I were on Mr. Toad's Wild Ride at Disneyland, with the rough ride just getting started.

Both of my sisters had logs of messages from multiple people, including businesses and law enforcement agencies, all calling to express their condolences. They had scheduled appointments for me throughout the morning until night; there were important people that I needed to meet to discuss things pertaining to Randy's passing. I was scheduled to be super busy the following day, as I was going to be meeting with Mayor Villaraigosa, Chief Bratton, Police Commissioner John Mack, and a funeral committee. I was told that the latter would consist of officers and LAPD personnel who had formed a committee to help me plan Randy's funeral. I cringed at the word "funeral." I certainly did not anticipate having a funeral for Randy so soon. Randy was supposed to retire in three years, and we had planned to travel to different colleges to watch Matt play football, hopefully at Randy's alma mater, Washington State. We often talked about growing old together and someday being grandparents together. My future had been unexpectedly interrupted.

Thank God for family and friends, as they kept me together. My mother, sisters, and a few friends spent the night, so people were sleeping everywhere. James and Jimmy left late but assured me that they would return first thing in the morning. James encouraged me to get some rest because I was scheduled to meet Chief Bratton and Police Commissioner John Mack at about 11:00 a.m. I took James's advice, and although I'm not sure how much rest I could have possibly have gotten that first night without my spouse, I tried.

Four people were sleeping in my king-size bed: my mother, my little niece Jessica, and my sisters. Matt and Gabby were with friends and cousins in their rooms, and everyone else was sleeping in the guest bedrooms or wherever they could find a spot. I was so tired from being up almost twenty-four hours straight that I managed to fall asleep, although I slept almost sideways. Then, without warning, I was awakened by the sound of some subtle crackling noise. I thought I was hearing things, and I couldn't understand where the noise was coming from, but I sat up in my bed, trying not to wake my mom, sisters, and niece. The noise was very faint, but because I sleep so lightly, I can hear anything. When I think about how light I sleep, it still boggles my mind that I didn't hear Randy leave that night.

Still hearing this odd noise, I looked around my bedroom and focused in on the sitting area—consisting of a sofa, easy chair, coffee table, and a fireplace—across from my bed. It had all the features of a miniature den, and I couldn't believe what my eyes were seeing. My little electrical fireplace was on, and the subtle noise I heard was the log rolling around, giving off the illusion of amber lights and fire. I don't know how it came on, as it was not on when we went to bed.

I have to be honest: I was spooked at first since my fireplace works by remote control, and the remote was safely put away in a decorative container that only Randy, the kids, and I knew about. We didn't have it readily accessible because it was rare that we turned it on. In fact, I would need to tell anyone who wanted to turn on the fireplace where the remote was located in order to enjoy its cozy ambience. I thought that maybe Matt or Gabby had come in and turned it on while we were asleep. But they never had an interest in our "fake fireplace," as they called it.

Then I began to think, *Heck, somebody turned it on! It definitely wouldn't come on by itself.*

I eased out of bed and walked over to the fireplace. The amber lights lit up that section of the room, as it was still dark outside. I scrambled to look for the remote to turn it off before my mother awoke and I had to explain how it came on. I chuckled to myself when I thought about how she would react if she knew the fireplace came on by itself. Knowing my mother, she would have hightailed it out of my house as fast as possible. Normally I would too, but I wasn't afraid. I gazed into the fireplace, looking at the rolling amber logs that contrasted with the darkness in the room. It gave off a glow that was so beautiful and peaceful, causing me to embrace the stillness in the room. It was not the slightest bit scary any longer; in fact, I welcomed the thought that maybe Randy was trying to communicate with me. It was going on day two since he'd died, and I missed him like crazy.

Over breakfast the next morning, I asked Matt and Gabby if either of them had turned on my fireplace. They both looked at me and said they hadn't. Of course, they asked me why I wanted to know, but I didn't want to spook them, so I said something like, "I think we might have a short in the wiring." Being kids, it went right over their heads, but Cookie heard my question and became curious.

"Why did you ask them if they turned on the fireplace?" she asked.

I started laughing because her eyes were as big and round as if she had just seen a ghost. "Oh, the fireplace came on last night, and I was wondering if they turned it on," I responded.

"Who turned it on?" she asked with curiosity.

"I thought you did," I said jokingly.

"No, I don't even know how to turn on your fireplace. It wasn't on when we went to sleep last night," she said almost frantically.

I didn't respond. I just kept eating, and she kept staring, waiting for me to comment. I didn't want to tell her anything else, as I needed her to be on solid ground today, helping me make decisions. She couldn't be worried about whether Randy's spirit was floating around the house.

I later came to a logical conclusion that there probably was a short somewhere in the wiring of the fireplace, and I left it at that.

It was early afternoon when Chief Bratton and John W. Mack, president of the police commission, arrived. Chief Bratton gave me a hug, as did Mr. Mack, both expressing their sincere sympathy for Randy's death. I called Matthew and Gabrielle in so that they could meet the chief and the president of the commission. They were amazed at how much Matthew looked like his dad. He was definitely just as tall but a few pounds lighter. It was obvious that by the time Matt reached eighteen, he was going to be taller than and as big as, if not bigger than, Randy had been. My little Gabby was a mini-me, although Randy thought she looked just like his mom. I could definitely see a little bit of me in her. We sat and talked for a while, and our conversation with Chief Bratton and the president of the commission was pleasant, for we shared stories about Randy.

We had tons of food, and I welcomed them to it. Within an hour, the house was full again, packed with officers, family, and friends. My sweet, precious mother-in-law arrived, and once I saw her, my heart dropped. I knew how much she loved her son; Randy was everything to her. He was her only son, and although she loved her daughters just as much, for some reason, that extra something about her son made her heart leap. Maybe it was because Randy looked so much like Mr. Dallas Simmons. She would often tell me that she loved all her grandchildren, but that she was partial when it came to giving attention to the boys in the family. She was just crazy about her boys including her youngest grandson eight year old Jeremy, always getting their names confused, calling Jeremy

Matthew, Matthew Randy, Randy David, and David Matthew. The name confusion didn't matter to the boys, though, for she was their girl, and they were crazy about her too.

I embraced my mother-in-law with a kiss and a big hug, tears falling from my eyes. She wiped my tears with her hands, exhibiting so much courage and strength, and said with conviction, "Honey, you know where he is. He's with the Lord. We have to continue to trust God."

I felt a deep sense of spiritual comfort because I knew my mother-in-law had been walking with the Lord since she was a little girl. I wanted my faith to be as strong as hers, so I tried to feed off her energy and her positive attitude. I needed some spiritual encouragement because my little spirit was growing weaker the more Randy's death became a reality.

Sadly, I learned later that initially my mother-in-law had a hard time accepting reality. Gina informed me that the morning after my mother-in-law heard about Randy's death from her and the police officers, she had absolutely no recollection of being told he had died. She literally blocked it out of her mind. The next day, Gina had to tell her again about the tragic news, so it was as if she were hearing it for the first time. It was a shocker, and the reality of losing Randy was a hard pill to swallow.

People continued to come by. It seemed that everyone who came to the door had connected with Randy in a special way, and that brought me to tears again and again. My faith was strong, but my heart was shattered, especially when his newest partner, Floyd Curry, came to give me Randy's belongings. Floyd was a tall, slender, handsome young African American officer who had the utmost respect for Randy. He said that Randy was his mentor. In fact, Randy had encouraged Floyd to try out for SWAT and rooted him on all the way. He described to me that on one of the tryout days, he was growing weary during an obstacle course exercise that would qualify him to become a SWAT member. He said the exercise was very difficult, and that he found himself slowing while running … until Randy yelled at him, "Don't you dummy up on me now—finish!"

That harsh remark actually gave Floyd the fortitude and stamina to complete the task. He thought back on Randy's militant behavior and laughed with good and fond memories of his partner and mentor. But his smile quickly became a frown when he hand-delivered Randy's wallet; keys; Ray Ban sunglasses; infamous fanny pack, which safely stored his gun; and a small cross I had given him, which hung from the rearview mirror of his police car. Oh my God! Receiving those items nearly killed me. There I was accepting items that at one time had seemed so insignificant to me, yet now they held a priceless value. I tried to keep my composure, weeping a little, but inside I just wanted to let it rip. I wanted to scream, pull my hair out, or run, run, run anywhere.

Even with a house full of people, I felt so lonely. My sisters, concerned about me and checking up on me every fifteen minutes, constantly asked, "Are you all right?" They were my sisters for forty-three years, and they knew I wasn't all right. We had our own language and pretty much knew each others' real thoughts, so I knew they were really asking, *Are you about to snap?* They knew that my mind was as dizzy as a wasp being sprayed with Raid. However, I had to keep it together. I could hear Randy telling me, "Don't you dummy up on me! Man up." Those were his favorite phrases. I was always trying to listen to Randy's voice, and I could hear him say, "Man up, Baby Girl. It's time to handle business." So I did.

The funeral committee had arrived, and although I cannot remember everyone's name, there were about fifteen people sitting and standing around my ivory dining room table introducing themselves. I could see lips moving, but I was terribly nervous, and no names were registering in my head. It wasn't until later that I learned all their names as I met with each one on a one-to-one basis. I thank God my mother and sisters were by my side, with each one working in some capacity.

My cousin Gwen and Aunt Denise from New Orleans were extending their Southern hospitality by playing hostess to our guests, offering food, coffee, and tea, while Cookie sat next to me with a pen and paper, taking notes. My mother did just what I wanted her to do, which was simply to be there for me.

Other people attending the meeting included Pastor Trimble and his beautiful wife, Judith Trimble; the police chaplains, Steve Hillman and Ken Crawford; Assistant Chief Paysinger; Mary Kite, Chief Bratton's assistant; Gina Onweiler, a representative from the bereavement committee; Peter Repovich from the Los Angeles Police Protective League; Alan Atkin from the Los Angeles Police Memorial Foundation; and a few SWAT officers and other representatives I'm afraid my mind cannot recall. It looked as if we were getting ready to plan an event fit for a king.

After everyone was introduced, Chaplin Kenneth Crawford opened the meeting with a beautiful prayer. Then I sat up and put on my business face to let the department know I was ready to make funeral arrangements for my husband. I didn't want to come off as a weak, weeping widow who was incapable of making decisions, so I had to "man up" quickly. I informed them that I wanted Pastor Trimble to conduct the funeral, with Reverend Mason assisting if he was up to it. Reverend Mason was now an elderly man and had been under the weather for a while. Naturally, I wanted the Los Angeles Police Department chaplains to participate in some capacity as well. Seated at the other end of the table from me, Chaplain Steve Hillman was pretty much the lead representative for LAPD insofar as the planning of the funeral. He listened intently to all my thoughts.

I explained to those present, just in case they weren't aware, that my husband was a godly man, and that he would therefore want his funeral on holy ground, meaning a church. I knew that our church would be too small, so I informed them that we would need a church a little bigger than ours. That's when Chaplin Steve Hillman, saying something to this effect, kindly interrupted me.

"Lisa, we have already been researching churches and other venues that could possibly accommodate us for Randy's funeral. His funeral is going to be large—"

I interrupted him and said, "Yes, I know. So many people loved Randy. I have taken that into consideration, which is why I'm thinking maybe Maranatha Church or West Angeles Church of God in Christ, both located in Los Angeles. A lot of our church members were referred to these churches whenever a larger church was needed for a special event."

Chaplain Steve Hillman looked at the other LAPD representatives as if to say, *She doesn't have a clue as to how large this funeral is going to be*. He kindly interrupted me again and said something like the following: "Lisa, yes, Randy was loved by many, but not just family, friends, and officers here in Los Angeles—from all across the country and even in other countries as well. He represented a police department and a division that is highly respected and admired. More importantly, he is the first LAPD

SWAT officer to be killed in the line of duty since its inception. You're going to have people from everywhere coming to pay their respects, so we're expecting your husband's funeral to have a huge attendance."

My pastor then said, "Well, how many people are you expecting?"

Chaplin Steve, communicating through facial expressions, said in a low and serious tone, "About ten thousand."

"Ten thousand!" my sister echoed.

We all just sat there, probably thinking the same thing: *Wow! This was going to be a big funeral.* Yet I wasn't that surprised. I knew Randy had made friends all over the world from different regions of the country, from the young to the old, so I knew his funeral was going to be exceptionally large. Maybe not ten thousand people—but large nonetheless.

Chaplin Steve Hillman went on to say that the churches I had mentioned would not be able to accommodate everyone, so LAPD was looking at other alternatives, such as the Staple Center or USC's Galen Center.

I went into panic mode. I reiterated that my husband was a godly man and would want his funeral at a church. "We have to find a church that can accommodate a huge amount of people," I said.

Just as I was saying that, Fred Price's church, Crenshaw Christian Center, came into my mind, and as I thought it, Assistant Chief Paysinger said it.

"What about Crenshaw Christian Center, also known as The Faith Dome?" he asked.

"Where is it located?" someone asked.

Assistant Chief Paysinger told them that it was located right in the heart of Los Angeles, and that it would be a perfect church for Randy's funeral. Pastor Trimble and his wife agreed, and of course I did as well. The next hurdle was to find out if and when the church would be available to have such a large funeral.

Assistant Chief Paysinger stepped away from the meeting, and I watched him open his cell phone, making his way to Matthew's room with Pastor Trimble, who coincidently was his childhood friend. They were going to try to lock in a date with Crenshaw Christian Center, and I was praying that Pastor Price would accommodate us.

After a ten-minute discussion with the church's executive office, it was confirmed. Just like that, Assistant Chief Paysinger made it happen.

I was so happy and grateful that Pastor Price chose to accommodate us, and I knew Randy was saying thank you as well. I didn't want Matthew or Gabrielle ever to go to a Lakers game, a Clippers game, or a musical concert at the Staples Center and have sad memories of their dad's funeral being held there. I believe certain events need to be at certain places, and Randy's services needed to be in a church.

We went on to discuss several other things, including the program. For the most part, I was going to put the program together, along with the assistance of my family, because I wanted to show the different facets of Randy's life. His life was like a beautiful patchwork quilt, made up of many colors and fabrics. Each patch was different and represented something special about his life. Whether it was an old and faded cotton patch that represented a difficult time for him or a bright satin patch that reflected the most prosperous times in his life, they were all woven together to reflect a beautiful life.

During our conversation about the program, I also expressed that I wanted to make sure that close family would be pallbearers, including Randy's nephews—David Roseberry, Dominic Sumlin, and Christopher Meraz—and a few of his partners and close friends from church.

We went on to discuss mortuary and cemetery plans, which wasn't a hard decision. Holy Cross, located in Culver City, California, is our family cemetery. My father and other family members are located there, and our family, including the children, would decorate my father's and other relatives' grave sites every Christmas, so there was a level of comfort at Holy Cross, especially for the kids. I felt that they would want their dad near their grandfather; plus, Holy Cross is beautiful. It overlooks Los Angeles to the east and the Pacific Ocean to the west, and whenever we visited my dad, my family and I would sit there for hours, laughing and reminiscing about good memories. This cemetery gave us a sense of peace rather than anguish.

After hours of discussion, the committee adjourned. Now, it was time to get busy. A recognizable officer named Andre Dawson came over to see us. He'd accompanied the president of the police commission. I hadn't seen Andre since the Centurion days, when he and Randy played LAPD football together. He was also one of Randy's groomsmen in our wedding. Andre is so special because when Randy cried tears of joy at our wedding, Andre handed him a special handkerchief that once belonged to his grandfather. He let Randy keep it and asked him to cherish it. He felt that much love for Randy that he would give him something so personal.

Andre was there to collect Randy's clothing for the mortuary. As he asked for the clothing, a fainting spell came over me. I couldn't imagine seeing my husband lying in a casket. *No*, I thought, *not Randy*. Again, I had an emotional meltdown, but I went upstairs to get the items he requested: undergarments, uniform, badge, pins, hat, and shoes. I was able to locate everything except for his shoes and hat.

James Hart and the others were assisting me during this difficult time. I recall James looking at me with such sadness and touching my shoulder with deep compassion, asking as gingerly as possible, "Lisa, I need you to think. Where did Randy put his formal uniforms, shoes, and hats? You know, the things he would wear at formal events."

"Yes, of course. He just wore his shoes and hat recently, but I don't know what he did with them. Could they be in his locker at work?" I asked.

"No, we already cleaned out all his lockers," James said, continuing to explore Randy's closet, along with other friends, attempting to find his shoes and hat, but it was to no avail.

"I have no idea where his shoes and hat could possibly be. Can I purchase them if we're unable to find them?" I asked.

Andre and James, noticing I was getting anxious, agreed that if there were any items we could not locate, the department would purchase them. They told me not to worry.

Andre left with Mr. Mack, while Chief Bratton left prior to our conducting our meeting, so only a few officers were left at the house, along with family and friends. Just then, a breaking news segment came on TV. It was the most heartwarming yet heartbreaking scene. Just about all the news channels were showing Randy's body being driven to the mortuary with the hearse surrounded from back to front and side to side by his SWAT brothers and other Metropolitan Division officers, all escorting their fallen brother. I couldn't believe that was my Randy in a hearse. My heart still aches today when I imagine that scene. It was a loving and endearing gesture made by his LAPD brothers, but for me it was a tragic scene, knowing the man I love … my children's father … was in that hearse. *How much more can I endure?* I wondered.

Shortly after this emotional scene, I learned that I had yet another visitor, a lieutenant who needed to talk with me. He walked in with some other SWAT officers, and I realized that I had never seen him before. He was a handsome older white gentleman, of average height and perfectly fit, and he was completely bald. He had on a SWAT bomber jacket, and he looked extremely serious. There was a confident air about him, and it appeared that he was the type of man who merely by appearance alone demanded respect. I later learned that he was Lieutenant Michael Albanese, the lieutenant who supported Randy with the Glory Kids by letting him leave early or giving him time off work to do things for the children. Lieutenant Albanese had the look of a stern man but the heart of a Christian. He knew the importance of ministry, so he gave Randy favor with time off when it came to helping the Glory Kids.

When we were introduced, he expressed his condolences and went right into the matters at hand. He was there to inform me that he concurred with what Chaplin Steve Hillman had said pertaining to my young nephews being pallbearers. He wasn't sure if that was a good idea for a funeral such as this. He explained to me that the weight of the casket along with Randy's weight would be extremely heavy. He felt that because our nephews were teenage boys and because it was quite an emotional experience, they might be better off just sitting with the family. Randy would need strong men, both physically and mentally, to carry him and we didn't need any mistakes. I agreed. I think the boys were relieved too.

Lieutenant Albanese also informed me that the SWAT BearCat, which the officers initially wanted to use instead of a hearse to transport Randy's body, wouldn't represent who he was in his entirety, as Randy wasn't just SWAT; he was a Los Angeles Police Officer first and foremost. He felt that his funeral should reflect all the officers, and I agreed with his judgment. I was in total agreement with whatever made logical sense and all the things I felt my husband would want.

Lieutenant Albanese didn't stay long, and throughout his visit, he kept the same serious disposition the entire time we talked, at least until he started expressing the goodness of Randy. You could tell that he tried hard to maintain his composure, but he was really choked up as he spoke. I wanted to grab him, hold him, and tell him it was okay to let it all out, but he took hold of himself before I had a chance to say it. He went right back into his serious, militant-like disposition, saying goodbye and telling me that he would be in touch with me later. Caught up in his vibe, I adhered to his aura and stood erect. I felt as if I needed to say, "Yes, sir!" Something about the way Lieutenant Albanese carried himself made even me, a mourning widow, want to salute him.

It was a long and draining day, and I longed for my quiet life with Randy. I was exhausted and so were my children. Everyone insisted that Gabrielle and I go upstairs and get to bed early. Matt was determined to stay downstairs and sleep in his room, regardless of the loud noise that consumed our full house. My nervous energy would have allowed me to stay up longer, but I knew that Gabby was exhausted and would not lie down unless I was lying next to her. She and I retreated to my bedroom. Gabby took a shower and then fell asleep in the bed, cuddling up with her father's pillows. After I showered, I walked over to Randy's side of the bed to give Gabby a kiss and turn off the light. On a wall next to Randy's side of the bed was the main light switch, controlling all the recessed lighting in the room. I kissed Gabby and turned off the lights. When I turned around to walk back over to my side of the bed, a light illuminating from Randy's closet startled me. His closet door was cracked opened, and the light was flickering like crazy. Again, I must admit that initially I was spooked. But then I realized that it was only a lightbulb in Randy's closet. It was flickering and probably about to go out. I thought that James and the others who were searching for Randy's clothes and shoes in his closet must have forgotten to turn off the light.

I should describe Randy's closet so you can visually see my irrational behavior as I dealt with this flickering lightbulb. Randy's closet is twelve feet long, seven feet high, and two and a half feet deep. It is equivalent to the length of a bedroom wall, with four closet doors, two opening at each end of the closet. Something about my behavior was odd because my natural reaction should have been to walk over to that section of the room where the light switch was located, open his closet doors, turn off the light, and go get in my bed. However, something in my spirit told me to walk past that part of his closet where the light switch was located—to go toward the flickering light. I don't know why, nor do I understand my behavior, but something was drawing me over to the far end of his closet where the light was flickering. With my room completely dark and only the flickering light breaking through the darkness, there they were, sitting high up on a top shelf of his closet, tucked away in the corner, with the light flickering on them ... I'd found Randy's police shoes and hat that James and the others looked for and could not find. No one thought to look high up on the shelves, as it just didn't seem like a logical place to put shoes and a hat.

I stood there in a trance and cried. I was never one to believe in all that stuff about communicating with the dead because it seemed creepy to me, but this experience was beautiful. And this time for sure, I felt as if Randy *was* communicating with me. Maybe it was another coincidence, but it was the second time that some form of light and some odd experience made me feel close to Randy.

## CHAPTER 23

# The Outpouring of Love

RANDY HAD DIED EARLY THURSDAY morning, and LAPD and I had exactly one week to put this huge funeral together in the midst of emotional distress. I completely forgot about the things pertaining to our restaurant, but my sisters, realizing we needed this time for more important matters, put all of that on hold. They pushed back the opening of the restaurant for almost two weeks. My insurance business was being managed by my faithful employees who ran my office for me, as I prepared for Randy's funeral. In the interim, I had to select flowers, a grave site, coffin, speakers, singers, and pictures, plus I had to create a biography about Randy's life. I was trying to greet out-of-town guests as they came into town from New York, New Orleans, and Texas. LAPD was wonderful to the kids and me during this time, arranging to pick up and drop off our guests, taking them to and from the airport and escorting them to various locations. They went beyond the call of duty by assisting my family and me with everything we needed, and we truly appreciated their help. I can tell you with absolute confidence that LAPD has the best men and women in the city working in their department; everyone was so kind and supportive. We also had the assistance of other law enforcement agencies and organizations, schools, churches, and businesses, with the list going on and on. Everyone wanted to pay tribute to Randy in some form or fashion.

The week was going by fast. I had graphic designer Lisa Greene in a tizzy, as I was so engaged with my many guests that she couldn't get the program together. She and others literally took me up into my bedroom sitting area, locked the door, and isolated me from all the guests so I could work on the program. I recall James Hart and Jimmy getting serious with me, saying if I didn't get with Lisa Greene today, Randy would not have a program! As a result, they stood guard by my bedroom door, not letting anyone come in and not letting me go out until we finished the program.

I stepped it up and instantly got my butt in gear, as I wanted Randy to have a nice program. But it was hard for me not to show my gratitude to all the people coming by giving their love, encouragement, beautiful flowers, plants, food, or gifts. Thanking guests was a much easier task than creating an obituary. I think subconsciously, I just couldn't deal with writing Randy's obituary. It was hard for me to believe that I was writing one for him. Every time I would start writing, reading, or looking at pictures, I would just break down crying. Luckily, Randy's niece Janel and others helped me pull it all together at the midnight hour.

Randy's program was completed, and Lisa Greene did a beautiful job. However, the next three days would be the most difficult of my life, and I would need God more than ever to walk hand in hand beside my children and me.

That entire week, the tragic incident was flashed across news channels, with the media giving systematic details about funeral plans for Randy, along with an update about Johnny Verman's condition. Even in my grief, I asked if I could visit Johnny, as I wanted to see him and give him well wishes. I felt bad for him and for his family; however, LAPD advised against it, as Johnny was very fragile and heartbroken over the incident. They thought my presence might cause him to have a setback. It was totally understandable, and I was in agreement with their decision. Their priority was trying to get Johnny well enough to go home and possibly attend Randy's funeral.

The following Sunday, my family and I attended church along with many members of the LAPD, who were there for us and perhaps for themselves as well. We needed spiritual help, understanding, and healing—and we all felt a need to get closer to God. I sat up front, where Randy and I normally sat every Sunday, but this time Matthew occupied Randy's seat next to Gabrielle and me. Randy Glymph, our good friend and a member of our church, put together a beautiful video in Randy's honor, clearly illustrating his love for humanity. I think the most touching scene was a clip of him tossing a football with Matthew when he was no more than three years old. Instantly, Matt, Gabrielle, and I broke down in tears. As busy as he was, Randy always made time for the little things, like tossing a ball with Matthew, giving Gabby a piggyback ride, and meeting me for lunch. The video also showed him encouraging people to participate in his passion, which was outreach. Just hearing his voice and seeing him smile pulled at everyone's heartstrings. We were going to miss the man who completed our family structure.

The church services were good, and Pastor Trimble delivered an awesome message about the God that Randy served. Church ended in prayer and an open invitation to receive Christ. On that day, a number of people were saved, including several police officers.

Throughout the following days, the news media provided sympathetic viewers with information on several fund-raisers that were taking place across the city in honor of Randy. I cannot tell you the numbers of people who expressed their condolences through means of financial support. There was a Blue Ribbon Trust Fund set up by LAPD for our family and Johnny Verman. People we knew and did not know sent donations to show their sympathy, love, and gratitude for the ultimate sacrifice Randy had made in an effort to keep our city safe. Another fund-raiser that will always be near and dear to my heart is one the Cimmarusti brothers, Lawrence and Ralph Cimmarusti, sponsored at their Burger King in downtown Los Angeles on Cesar Chavez Avenue. On Wednesday, February 13, 2008, they announced that the proceeds from meals purchased at Burger King would be donated to Randy's family.

There were other fund-raisers across the city taking place in Randy's honor, some for our family, some for the Glory Kids, and others for children of different organizations. Randy's name instantly became a marketing tool for many businesses, with some saying Randy shopped here, Randy ate here, and Randy lifted weights here. There were vendors preparing for the day of the big funeral, selling Randy T-shirts and other memorabilia. It was, to say the least, both surprising and heartwarming.

While all the well wishes were taking place across the city, the children and I were bracing for the viewing of Randy's body and the funeral services. Randy and I were always overprotective parents, but now I was a single parent, and my mother hen ways were really kicking in. I was terribly concerned about my children, and I knew that Randy would want the kids to have the least amount of stress as possible, so I had to once again man up, directing all my attention to their needs and feelings. It was now all about the mental well-being of my children. I was prepared to set aside my own emotions and deal with them later, but for now the kids came first.

When asked if the kids and I wanted to be on the program for the funeral, I knew I wasn't capable of speaking, and I let the children make their own decisions. Gabby was like me, too upset to speak at the funeral. We both decided to express our thoughts and sentiments about Randy in the program. Being emotionally distraught, we knew exactly what we could and could not handle. Quite surprisingly Matthew, however, in spite of his emotions, decided to speak at his father's funeral. Once again, I gave my kids the space they needed to handle their father's death in the manner they chose. As I knew from my own experience with my father's death, everyone handles grief differently.

The private viewing was being held at Holy Cross Mortuary. There were probably about six Suburban trucks used by LAPD to escort my entire family to the mortuary. James Hart, who was our escort, felt compelled to take care of his partner's family, and we embraced his support, although I felt as though he and the other officers needed to be around us just as much as we needed them. Randy was our connection.

When we arrived at the mortuary, I had to get myself into the right frame of mind, so I kept hearing Randy's voice in my ear, saying, "Man up! Be strong for the kid's sake."

As kooky as it sounds, in my mind I was arguing with Randy: "You just wait until I see you in heaven; you're going to get it good for doing this to me."

I restrained from expressing my emotions and walked into the mortuary holding Matthew's and Gabrielle's hands. Representatives of Holy Cross—Chuck, Gwen, and Pastor Keith Green Sr.—met us at the door. Holy Cross definitely hired the right people for the job, for they were professional and had sweet and sensitive dispositions. Chuck gingerly asked us if we were prepared to go inside. I wanted to say, "No, how do you prepare to see the love of your life in a coffin? How do you watch your children prepare to see their big strong daddy in a coffin?"

I answered my own questions silently, thinking about the word of God. The Holy Spirit was what was going to get my kids and me through this. Just prior to entering the mortuary, I had to remind Matthew and Gabby about what our faith teaches us. I reminded them about the discussions their dad had with all of us about eternal life. My conversation with them went something like this: "Remember, guys, when we go in, we're going to see daddy's shell, but we know that he is in heaven with the Lord. Remember the scripture from 2 Corinthians 5:8: *To be absent from the body is to be present with the Lord.*"

With my nieces and nephews standing around Matthew and Gabby, all lending their support, they nodded their heads in agreement. They had heard this several times, but now it was time to put our faith to work.

As we prepared to walk in, Gabrielle stopped in her tracks. She wasn't ready to see her daddy in that state, so I didn't push her. Again, she needed to work her grief out in her own way. Matthew and I, along with other family members, walked in together. The room had soft lighting, making Randy's beautiful wooden coffin shine for miles to see. I had purchased a wooden coffin because I recalled Randy saying to me when he talked about his salvation and death that I could throw him in a wooden box and toss him anywhere because he knew where his final destination would be, referring to heaven. That was the first thing I thought about when I selected his coffin. At each end of the coffin stood two beautiful lamps, each highlighting a spread of red roses.

As we got closer and closer to the casket, we saw Randy dressed in his blues, with all his significant pins placed on his collar and chest pocket. He looked so handsome. Naturally, we all cried. It just seemed like Randy left us much too soon. Matt was a little emotional, but he felt like me, that the man in the casket didn't quite look like Randy. Gabrielle, who later gathered her courage and made her way in to join us, felt the same way. We just stared at Randy and wondered what was different about him. It wasn't drastically different—just a subtle difference. I noticed that the mortuary put too much make up on him. It was so much makeup that I asked Chuck to have someone at the mortuary remove some of it. I explained to him that my husband was a manly man, and he would have my neck if he knew I allowed people to view him that way.

Chuck sweetly responded, "But, Mrs. Simmons, under the circumstances, we had to put on a lot of makeup. We needed to cover up the bullet scar on his face."

"What bullet scar on his face?" I replied.

Chuck looked stunned when I asked him that question. His mouth hung wide open as if he didn't know what else to say. I was shocked, as this was the first I'd heard of a bullet wound to the face. You could tell he was disturbed by my reaction, so he excused himself and went to speak with SWAT Officer Steve Scallon.

Steve Scallon, James Hart, and Floyd Curry were the three SWAT officers who were considered our main escorts. Steve was a handsome middle-aged Irish man with beautiful baby blue eyes. He was as gentle as a lamb or as rough as a tiger, depending on the situation. He was a lot like Randy, a true-blue no-nonsense type of guy. He walked over to me to hear my concern.

"Steve, I'm a little concerned, as the representative is telling me that he is unable to remove the makeup because of a bullet wound Randy has in his face. Is this true?"

Steve replied, stating that the information Chuck gave me was true, that Randy had indeed had been shot in the face.

"I was told by the doctor that he was shot in the neck," I said with great concern. "Everyone around me heard the same thing. Was he shot in the neck and the face?"

"No, just the face," he replied.

I didn't want to cause a scene right there in the mortuary, so I told Steve I would deal with the miscommunication later. In the meantime, I needed them to make an effort to wipe off some of the thick makeup on Randy's face. The mortuary told me that they would make every effort to adhere to my wishes. In the meantime, my kids were looking down at their father almost in a state of shock. It was Daddy, but not a glimpse of life reflected the daddy they once knew. Their expressions and sad countenance almost killed me. I knew we had to leave soon, so I had to make a quick decision. Should I stay and allow my kids to become sick with grief and watch others cry over their father with heartache and sorrow? I clearly felt that it was almost a form of torture for them.

Besides, Randy's mom and the family from New York had arrived, and you could see how concerned the kids were for their grandmother and her reaction. Everyone was grieving for Randy, and it was unbearable.

Unexpectedly, I had an idea. I needed something to lift my kids' spirits. I heard that a lot of Matt's football friends and Gabby's cheerleading friends from El Segundo were going to be at the fund-raiser at Burger King. I initially told the kids we couldn't attend because of the private viewing. But this was the perfect solution; it would remove them from this uncomfortable situation and lift their spirits. I knew Randy would approve, as we thought a lot alike when it came to our kids. I could hear him saying, "Get my babies out of here. This is too much for them. Go lift their sprits with The El Segundo Eagles!"

I then said in an almost-cheerful voice, "Let's go to Burger King!"

Our escorts clearly didn't understand my statement, as they were just getting to know Randy's crazy wife and didn't have a clue as to my unique personality and creative way of thinking. So I said it again. "Let's go to Burger King! You know, to the fund-raiser."

I could see Matt and Gabby's faces, as they weren't comfortable seeing their father in this way. They were glad I was giving them a way out.

I recall James and the other officers pausing for a moment as they discussed the change in plans. In their SWAT mode, they quickly conferred and informed their superiors as they readjusted to the new assignment. They said, "Roger that! Let's go." We headed off to Burger King.

I could read some of the reactions of family members who had just gotten there and were getting into the somber mode of grieving. A few of them probably thought that it was not a time to eat burgers, as it was a time to grieve. I know they probably felt that my time would have best been served by standing over Randy crying until I passed out, but I felt differently. My kids and I had stayed for about an hour, and we had seen Randy, which reinforced the notion that what was lying in that casket was only his shell, for he had transitioned on to glory. I didn't want to bring further pain and agony to my kids, whose hearts were already shattered, so I made a conscious decision to leave, giving the others the option to stay if they preferred. Besides which, I knew I had another viewing to attend the next day, so the majority of family members and the officers were in agreement, while a few family members stayed behind, feeling somewhat baffled.

Immediately, we all jumped back into our assigned Suburban trucks with our assigned officers in tow and caravanned our way to Burger King. It was truly a sight to see. The SWAT officers escorted us as if we were important dignitaries, driving us all the way from Culver City to downtown Los Angeles, with traffic stopped to avoid breaking up the caravan. There were lights flashing and sirens sounding, cautioning other drivers to make way for the caravan of Suburbans. Mind you, all of this was being done while in rush hour traffic.

Looking out the window of our vehicle, we could see the reaction of drivers as they all stopped and wondered who these important officials could be. They probably thought we were the president or some highly ranked political figure. Our out-of-town family members and guests were so impressed with the kindness and support the Los Angeles Police Department bestowed on us, treating us like royalty and doing everything to show their faithfulness to their fallen brother's family.

When we arrived at Burger King, I was absolutely stunned and amazed by the crowd of people that inundated Burger King. It was an enormous turnout for the Burger King fund-raiser, with the line entering Burger King literally wrapped around the corner. I was told that it had been that way the entire day. I looked over at my kids, and they had smiles on their faces as they saw many of their friends. The El Segundo football players were sporting their football jerseys and had Coach Dean and Coach Chris by their sides. The El Segundo cheerleaders were also there, along with Coach Dani, Coach Nicole, and Coach Michelle holding up signs with words of encouragement, cheering Matthew, Gabrielle, and the Simmons family on. I cannot express how touched I was by the love and support of friends, family, the Los Angeles Police Department, the city of Los Angeles, and all of those, known and unknown, who were there for us during that time.

The media filled the parking lot with their trucks, cameras, and satellite equipment, literally taking me by surprise. While driving to Burger King, James had forewarned me that the media was going to be there, but I didn't imagine anything like this. The experience gave me a small glimpse into the lives of well-known celebrities that the cameras love. However, unlike celebrities, we were not used to all the attention.

Personally, I was scared to death. My intention was to help lift my kids' spirits and to thank the Cimmarusti brothers and the public for their support. But the crowd and the media stunned us. Nonetheless, we pushed through our state of anxiety and made our way through the crowd and into Burger King for fries and Whoppers.

SWAT escorted us into Burger King, along with Jimmy Fields, who acted as a private bodyguard for our family. We felt well protected and so loved. When we were inside, I greeted people who were in line and was surprised to see how many people wanted to shake my hand, touch me, and thank me personally for Randy's service. I remember feeling overwhelmed by this unforeseen quasi celebrity status. My cousin, Ruben, who flew in from Texas to be with the family, keyed into my nervousness, taking control of the semiaggressive Randy fans in a subtle way, diverting them away from me. He wasn't LAPD, but my once-little cousin Ruben was now tall and strong cousin Ruben, and I felt protected by him.

We sat and ate burgers, shared fries, and talked with the Cimmarusti brothers, police officers, firefighters, and others. This was the first time since Randy's death that I think the entire family smiled, laughed, and felt a little sense of reprieve. I don't know if the Cimmarusti brothers knew what attending this event did for us that day, but it truly lifted the kids' spirits and gave us all a moment of normalcy. And I mean a *moment* of normalcy because no sooner than I had that thought, James Hart interrupted me and asked me to do something that was abnormal. He asked if I would say something to the media. I gave him a look as if to say, *You've got to be kidding me!* I have never been at a loss for words, for I am quick to speak my mind, but in this case—with *lights, camera, action*—I was sure I would find myself babbling.

There were tons of people still waiting outside to get into Burger King; there were also several different news cameras and reporters, plus there were people who just wanted to see and be near the family. *How can I not say thank you to all our well-wishers?* I thought. So I slowly wrapped up my fries, due to a sudden loss of appetite, and moved into the ladies' room, where I could have my private panic attack. I then looked at myself in the mirror and saw a woman who was in need of a hair stylist and a makeup artist. I looked terrible having cried earlier at the viewing. I could hear my crazy husband saying, "Where's your hair stylist, Robin Wilson over at Trinity Beauty Salon? Call her to fix your hair!" Then I broke down and began to pray. I realized that this whole thing was not about my hair, my clothes, or even me; it was about the generosity and hearts of people who stood in line for hours to honor Randy's life of service and support his family. I asked God to give me the words that would express my heart and my gratitude. I then walked out of the bathroom, gathering my kids, mother, mother-in-law, sisters, and the rest of the family so we could be escorted out by LAPD. This was going to be the first of many news appearances that I would make.

I walked out into the darkness of night with bright lights shining in my face and cameras and microphones positioned where I would be speaking. I saw familiar and unfamiliar faces, and suddenly calmness came over me. My emotions of gratitude were riding high, and although I can't remember all that I said, I spoke from my heart. I know I thanked everyone for coming to the fund-raiser, with special thanks to the Cimmarusti brothers for putting together a wonderful event. But I also wanted to thank the public, whose acts of kindness were greatly appreciated. I was adamant about letting the public know that whatever they gave to my children and me in honor of Randy, whether it was a nickel, a prayer, or a thought, it was invaluable, and I was grateful for their support. I then stepped aside and let my mother-in-law have a few words. She expressed her gratitude as well. The night ended with our making it through another difficult day. Now it was time to prepare for day two, the public viewing.

The public viewing was held at our church, Glory Christian Fellowship International in Carson, California. Having it there was significant and symbolic, as Randy had loved his church, having spent years participating, serving, and worshipping there. Our church members were like his extended family members, and he loved them just as they loved Brother Randy. Without a second thought, we knew his viewing wouldn't be anywhere else but at that church, especially since Randy's funeral service was being held at another church for accommodation purposes. Pastor Trimble agreed with me and opened his church from midmorning to late evening to assure that all who wanted to, whether they knew Randy or not, could pay their respects and say their final good-byes.

Earlier that day, I attended to other business matters involving the funeral and chose to attend the viewing in the late afternoon. I knew it was going to be an all-day viewing, so the timing situation worked out perfectly for me. As usual, the entire family attended together. My mother, sisters, and other relatives who were staying in Los Angeles met us at the church. Randy's family opted not to attend since the next day was the funeral and my mother-in-law needed to preserve her strength for the long day ahead. And sadly, Matthew decided not to go. I could tell his father's absence was kicking in, and it was clear that he wanted to grieve alone, so I didn't press the issue, although it was difficult to leave him home alone in that state.

Driving Randy's truck, Jimmy Fields escorted us to the viewing. It seemed strange for another man to be driving his truck, but Jimmy was definitely a good alternate. Ironically, when we got into the car to drive to the viewing, one of Randy's favorite songs—"Gravity," by John Mayer—was playing in his CD player. Our entire family loved that song. I began to reflect back on the last time Randy played it, just weeks earlier, when the kids and I were in his truck coming back from having dinner at our favorite family restaurant, Coco's, which was just around the corner from our house. After leaving the restaurant, which we visited often, we would drive around the neighborhood just singing and listening to music. I was going to miss the little things like that.

It wasn't long before we got to our church, which was less than fifteen minutes away. We pulled up in the parking lot, where we were greeted by dozens of police officers, their standardized navy blue uniforms contrasting with the most beautiful sight you would ever want to see. Outlining the perimeter of the church building were hundreds of bright, colorful flower arrangements. There were so many flowers that the church could not accommodate them all, so instead they lined many of the standing arrangements outside the church. It was an incredible sight to see. I walked around the entire church before going in, looking at the arrangements and reading some of the cards. The flowers were from police departments and other law enforcement agencies, fire departments, businesses, and personal acquaintances. The ribbons around the flowers colorfully displayed a name or a city, with flowers from as far away as Hawaii's police department and Canada, France, and London. The flowers were delivered from people around the world, which was truly amazing.

I walked into our church and found it packed with people. Some were standing in line waiting to view Randy's body, and some were sitting in church socializing. Randy's body was in front of the church, with two police honor guards standing at attention at each end. There was a red rope separating his coffin from the viewers, a much-needed precaution because without a doubt, there would have been people who loved Randy so much that they would have attempted to touch him, kiss him, and do what grieving people do. Pastor Trimble knew that the viewing was going to last all day, and the church needed Randy to remain presentable.

Only Gabby and I were allowed beyond the rope, and we took advantage of our status and left some personal belongings with Randy. I placed a red rose in his coffin and wished him a Happy Valentine's Day. It didn't seem fair that I should have to spend Valentine's Day viewing my sweetheart in a casket, but as Randy would say, "It is what it is." I was glad I wasn't a big fan of Valentine's Day, as it always seemed so commercial, superficial, and hypocritical to me to express love only on one day of the year. Our love was unconditional and expressed 365 days a year ... and now for eternity. More important than the Valentine rose was the family photograph I placed in Randy's chest pocket, close to his heart, along with his wedding ring, as I wanted to make sure he had those things with him. I also put Matt's football next to him. Matt wanted me to leave him with a football that he and his dad had thrown. Gabrielle had a musical stuffed animal that played the song "Wind Beneath My Wings," which she placed next to her daddy. These acts may have appeared to be peculiar, but it just seemed right to leave him with things that reflected a piece of each of us.

Emphasizing his beautiful wooden casket were dozens of standing flower arrangements that took up the entire church stage and pulpit. And there right in the middle were my flowers. I had purchased a white heart-shaped arrangement with red roses protruding from the center of the heart, signifying a bleeding heart. The flower arrangement was lovely, and I think I purchased it based more on the name of the arrangement, which was Bleeding Heart. It was so symbolic of what I was feeling, for I felt that my heart was bleeding—and there wasn't anything that could or would ever stop it.

Flowers were constantly pouring in, and I recall a church member making a comment about how Randy would have much preferred that people send money for the Glory Kids in lieu of flowers. I had to agree and disagree. I believe Randy would have preferred that too, because he was always thinking of others. But as his wife, I felt that Randy deserved something just for him this one time. This man had given so much of his life in helping and doing for others, so in his death, I thought that people should be allowed to do whatever they wanted for him. I felt like he deserved the honor of having every flower, every petal, and every stem that God ever created to honor his service.

The viewing ended at about 8:00 p.m., and everyone left the church sanctuary except for the SWAT team. They were going to end the viewing with a private and special ceremony for their fallen comrade, but not before Gabby and I said our final good-byes. This would be the last time any of us would be able to see Randy in his earthly state of being. I gave Randy one final kiss on his forehead as Gabrielle looked on. I then went back to sit in a seat placed in front of Randy's casket, while Gabrielle and I had the honors of remaining for the ceremony. The entire SWAT team was in uniform, with the exception of his dear partner, James Hart, who was assisting the family all day and had worn civilian clothes. Without giving too many details, they all gathered around the casket and said their farewell to their fallen brother in a special way. It was the most heart-wrenching salute that one could ever witness. They then performed some other acts of love and gently closed the casket as Gabby and I sobbed and mourned for the man we loved and cherished.

After the viewing, I rushed to get home to Matthew. We had been gone for hours, and I didn't know what state of mind he was in. I felt guilty for leaving him alone so long, although people said they were going to stop by and check on him. When I got home, I saw some videos of Randy on the family room table. I never asked Matthew about the videos, as any conversation about Randy was just too painful. In my mind, I knew that if we discussed anything, it was going to be very emotional. I can only assume that Matt spent his time alone mourning his father in his own way, by watching videos, for he appeared somber and quiet.

James and Jimmy had escorted us home, and they encouraged everyone to retire to bed early. They were good at knowing when to discipline me like a child, as they had noticed my hardheaded ways early on. They knew exactly when to hold me by my arms and look me straight in the eyes, particularly when they wanted to get an important point across to me. In turn, I knew when they meant business, so I didn't hesitate to be obedient; I knew they were looking out for my well-being. Before the night ended, I did one final clothing check for the kids and me, took a shower, and went to bed, with my guests following suit.

## CHAPTER 24

# 41D–End of Watch

It was Friday, February 15, 2008. I awakened early and lay in bed for about an hour. I had a conversation with the Lord, asking Him to be with my children and me today. I asked Him to make our burden light so that we could get through this very sad and long day. I then had a conversation with Randy. Initially, I didn't want to get out of bed, as I was depressed and just wanted to sleep. Of course, I cried for about thirty minutes straight trying to get up to attend my husband's funeral, as the realization of being a widow hit me hard that morning. Just that word, "widow," sounded so depressing; it was a category I hadn't signed up for. Unfortunately, it was now my title.

My mind went everywhere while I lay in bed. I thought about the poor Glory Kids and what they might be thinking. I knew they all probably had questions for God. Some may have even questioned or blamed God for allowing this to happen to Randy. I was hoping and praying that they remembered everything that Randy taught them, especially about eternal life. I took peace in knowing that the Glory Christian Fellowship site leaders, Yolanda, Roxanne, Lorraine, Joyce, and Ralph, as well as other members of the church, would be out there consoling them and reemphasizing the things that Randy and the other leaders taught them.

I finally got up to shower, and that's when I began to think about my sweet, precious daddy ... and how I wished he were here for me.

I started reminiscing about a conversation I once had with him. We were talking about tragic experiences. I remember saying to him how I couldn't imagine anything tragic ever happening to me. My life was so easy and ... almost stress-free. I recall my dad responding to that statement by saying, "You just keep on living. Life will bring you the good, bad, and the ugly."

He was right. I wasn't prepared, though, as I surely didn't think life would leave me fatherless at twenty-eight years old or sadly make me miscarry my first child, and I definitely didn't think it would bring me such a tragedy wherein I would be widowed at age forty-three. *What a shocker*, I thought.

I gradually got dressed and went downstairs to grab a bite to eat. My good friend Margo was already up, fixing everyone a little breakfast. Our friend Denise Beaudoin had been up all night, working diligently on car and funeral coordination. She was an LAPD family contact person for our family, and she was in charge of coordinating limousine arrangements. Denise, a tall, attractive, well-organized attorney, prided herself on taking on the most difficult tasks, so coordinating transportation and seating arrangements was right up her alley. I can't remember how many limousines we had, but I believe it was eight. I recall LAPD representatives having a disagreement with the number of limos, believing that eight was too many. However, Denise and I had to explain to them that our family was huge and did everything in a big way. We also explained that many of our family members were coming from out of town, so I did not want to worry about them getting lost in an unfamiliar city. I agreed to pay for all limousines, as LAPD was kind enough to foot the bill for Randy's funeral expenses. However, money was not the problem when it came to the limousines. Unbeknownst to me, Randy's funeral would mark one of the longest processions in Los Angeles history, and city transportation was trying to reduce family cars. However, Denise worked out a fair compromise wherein the family would have eight limousines and other family members and close acquaintances would be transported in minibuses. I thank God for all family and friends who assisted during this time, for I truly needed their help.

Police escorts came to pick up the kids, our guests, and me at our house in Palos Verdes. I was dressed in my black suit, with a cream-colored silk lace blouse underneath my jacket. Randy loved pretty and dainty things on me, so I also draped myself in pearls. Knowing Randy was particular about the things Gabby wore, I was also careful to make sure she looked like his little girl, so Gabrielle had on a black dress with a white sweater. I also remember that the curls in her hair were a little tight, but she looked exactly how Randy would have wanted her to look, like his little girl ... except now she was a teenager.

As far as Matthew, his handsome face left me speechless. It looked as if he went from a little boy to a young man overnight. He walked into my room looking just like his dad, wearing Randy's black suit, complete with one of his white shirts. He also wore his father's black shoes, and then he asked me to tie one of his father's neckties around his neck. I smiled hard, fighting back tears, and I wanted to scream as loud as I could, "How in the heck do you tie a stupid tie! I need my husband!" I literally wanted to drop to my knees and scream for Randy, as I knew my children were hurting. I didn't scream. Instead, I kept my fake yet strong composure and simply told my son he looked so nice in his father's suit. I told Matthew and Gabrielle that their father would be so proud of the way they were handling his death. And like most teenagers, Matt responded with sorrow etched across his face.

"What happened to Dad sucks, Mom."

"I know, Matt, but don't use that word," I replied. But then again, I had to agree with Matt. It did suck. "You know what, Matt? I have to agree. This does suck, but we're going to be all right. I promise you."

I hugged him and Gabrielle and put his tie in my purse. I thought to myself that I was going to have to learn new things, like how to tie a tie. Coming from a family of all girls, I knew nothing about that particular act, so for now this was a job for Uncle Wilfred or Uncle Dwayne to handle.

We had agreed that the limousines would meet in Los Angeles at my sister Melinda's house in View Park, which was centrally located. It was where the family repast was going to be held, which seemed logical. This also made it easy on my in-laws who were coming from Diamond Bar, about forty-five minutes away. I wanted to make things as easy as possible for my mother-in-law, who had finished chemo treatment just prior to Randy's death. She said she was feeling fine, but it was obvious the cancer had taken a toll on her, and at times it made her feel tired. But she was always a trooper, never complaining and instead just enduring and pushing through tragedy.

While driving to Melinda's house, I noted signs on the streets and electrical posts about certain streets being blocked off at particular times because of a huge funeral. I also observed air transportation flying around Los Angeles, preparing for the big day. I was stunned to see these things because Melinda's house was several miles away from the Faith Dome. Jimmy and the other officers had emphasized that this was going to be a big funeral.

The families met at Melinda's house, where her entire street was lined with limousines, shuttle buses, police cars, and motorcades. Denise and childhood friend Dayna Dorris gave instructions to our guests who crowded the sidewalks, listening for their assigned vehicles. They also passed out VIP badges that would permit the family and close friends to be seated in a certain section of the Faith Dome. Once in our assigned vehicles, we drove to Randy's funeral with air traffic control hovering over us the entire way.

The funeral was supposed to start at 11:00 a.m., but the family had to be at the Faith Dome at 9:00 a.m. We arrived early and were placed in a holding room, where the church was kind enough to have prepared a continental breakfast for us. As we sat waiting, other VIPs entered, with one very public figure arriving early. It was Governor Arnold Schwarzenegger. Matt and Gabby's eyes lit up, not so much because he was the governor but because he was "The Terminator" and he was at their dad's funeral. He was truly a nice man, walking up and handing over his favorite DVD collection to Matthew, along with a teddy bear for Gabrielle. His beautiful wife, Maria Shriver, was unable to attend the funeral, but she sent her condolences in the form of a lovely letter and a book she'd written, called *What's Heaven?* The book offered explanations to young kids about death and events surrounding it. I really appreciated both of their expressions of sympathy.

Standing alongside Governor Schwarzenegger was Chief William Bratton and Mayor Antonio Villaraigosa. There were other dignitaries and a few celebrities as well; however, the most special guest that I longed to see was Johnny Verman.

It was heartwarming to see the SWAT team huddle around Johnny and protect him as the Secret Service protects the president.

To some degree, I felt as though they were even protecting him from me. Naturally, I would ask him no questions at a time when he was still healing and my husband was being laid to rest. I was introduced to Johnny Verman a few minutes before the start of the funeral as a few officers, his wife, Marsha, and my family stood around witnessing our first encounter together. Johnny appeared to be under the weather as well as heartbroken. Naturally, he was sad and emotional. I gave him a hug and tried to encourage him, but he couldn't really talk, as he had just had extensive surgery on his jaw. It looked as though his mouth was partially wired or just closed tight. He seemed to be in excruciating pain, and it was likely that he was on some sort of pain medication. We said our hellos and our good-byes as we prepared to walk in and honor Randy.

Randy's funeral was a big production, unlike any funeral I'd ever attended in my life. There were several official coordinators from LAPD and coordinators from our church and Crenshaw Christian Center. Our church ushers helped assist Crenshaw Christian Center's ushers, as Randy's funeral required a lot of manpower based on the multitude of people in attendance. I was told that the Faith Dome seated over ten thousand people ... and every seat was occupied. People were even standing in hallways and outside. Unfortunately, because the church had reached its seating capacity, many people had to be turned away. Randy was being honored in an enormous way.

As Jimmy Fields ushered me in, I requested to hold my kids' hands. I wanted them close to me and on each side of me, symbolizing that we were still a family. Slowly we walked into this huge, magnificent church, and Matthew, Gabrielle, and I took our seats. My mother was sitting on the other side of Gabrielle, with my mother-in-law nearby, under the watchful eye of her daughters and family. My father-in-law was also present with his wife and new family. The whole issue surrounding Dallas was awkward and uncomfortable for my mother-in-law, so LAPD made sure they sat in another section. I appreciated their accommodating us regarding this issue, as I wanted assurance that my mother-in-law was comfortable at her son's funeral—the funeral for her son who called her "Mommy," like a little boy, up until the time of his death. But there was no need to worry about confusion, for God was present and His Glory showed through all the people who came to honor this heroic man.

I believe that because of Randy's faithfulness to God, he truly had a funeral fit for a king. The funeral hadn't even started, and it was already beautiful as the love of God shone through on Randy's home going day. One might question how there could possibly be anything beautiful about a sad event like a funeral. My response would be that it's the celebration of a beautiful life one lived, the contributions he made, and the legacy he left behind.

Randy's life was displayed throughout the church, for each section of the church represented a segment of his life. There was a section for his immediate family and close friends, a section for his church family, and a section for dignitaries and high officials such as Governor Arnold Schwarzenegger; Attorney General of California Jerry Brown; Mayor Antonio Villaraigosa; Chief William Bratton; former chief and founding father of SWAT, Chief Darryl Gates; John W. Mack, president of the Police Commission; Los Angeles County Sheriff Leroy Baca; and others. Also present were his fellow police officers, comrades, and law enforcement agencies from all across the country and different parts of the world. The Glory Kids that he'd mentored occupied another section, with T-shirts of Randy bearing the words OUR HERO, THE WIND BENEATH OUR WINGS. The El Segundo Eagles football team that he coached wore their jerseys in honor of Coach Randy, with Gabrielle's cheerleading squad sitting next to the El Segundo football team. Matthew's high school football team, Bishop Montgomery, was also there, wearing their football jerseys in honor of the dad who'd coached and yelled from the stands. The Washington State University Cougar alumni, including the football team, was represented, and people known and perhaps even unknown to Randy filled the Faith Dome. I also saw Johnny Verman sitting up front to my left with his wife, Marsha Verman.

Again, highlighted for all eyes to see, was Randy's gorgeous wooden casket with the American flag draped across it, accented with red roses spread all across the top. On a white pillar sat his police hat and his white gloves. There was a picture of Randy in uniform on an easel, with Randy literally in the spotlight as lights from the church picked up every colorful item on the stage.

The funeral started with his SWAT brothers carrying his casket with such pride and honor, giving him a salute. The salute was led by active lead pallbearer Sergeant Steve Gomez, who gave commands to active pallbearers Ozzy Crenshaw, Floyd Curry, Guy Dobine, James

Hart, Tim McCarthy, Dave Perez, and Steve Scallon. As they saluted, their grief was both disguised in their stoic faces and clearly visible at the same time. Johnny Verman, extremely emotional and fragile, struck a strong and bold hand salute along with other officers and public servants. The pallbearers placed Randy's casket down on the round stage that served as a pulpit for the church. They then marched away to their respective seats.

Opening the ceremony and welcoming our guests was Pastor Alton Trimble. Following Pastor Trimble was Shelly Pruitt, our beautiful church member and songstress. Shelly had a golden voice that was beyond amazing. I requested that she sing a favorite song of Randy's from one of his much-loved artists, Randy Crawford, called "Knocking on Heaven's Door." It just seemed fitting for his funeral. After Shelly sang that heartwarming song, there was a special presentation from Mayor Villaraigosa, Chief Bratton, and Dr. Basil Kimbrew. Mayor Villaraigosa spoke of Randy's heroism. Chief Bratton spoke of Randy's character as an officer as well as his community outreach as a servant in the community. He caught the attention of everyone when he defined Randy's good deeds through a quote from our sixteenth United States president, Abraham Lincoln: "No man stands so tall as when he stoops to help a child." The quote was simple, but it was profound and appeared to be a revelation for many to start giving back and helping in the community. I believe God was using Randy's funeral as a means to send several messages to thousands.

After Chief Bratton spoke, Dr. Basil Kimbrew, a fellow classmate and football teammate, called up all Washington State alumni classmates and teammates. I was shocked to see so many of them there, as it had been years since Randy was out of college, but there they were, representing Washington State and paying homage to their fellow Cougar. And then a wonderful video montage of Randy's family life was shown, with Celine Dion's ballad "Because You Loved Me," my dedicated song, playing in the background. Following our family video was a SWAT video with the theme song from the old television series *S.W.A.T.* playing in the background as his work in SWAT was displayed. The videos made everyone laugh and cry.

Next to take the stage was James Hart, Randy's friend and SWAT partner. James spoke about Randy as a friend and as a partner. James was known for his telling good stories, and he shared stories that had the guests swaying back and forth between sorrowful tears and emotional laughter. He talked about how Randy was so proud to be on the SWAT team, and how he, James, would get a kick out of his bragging about being on "D Team." He said Randy expressed the enthusiasm of being in a special division and, perhaps even in his own mind, having favor for holding such an elite position. "D Team, baby ... D Team!" James said he found Randy's egotism funny, but he too felt the same pride. Randy just had an awesome way of verbalizing it.

Many others reflected on Randy's life, including Randy's sister Gina; my sister Sharon, "Cookie," and her husband, Wilfred; my other sister Melinda; and soon-to-be new director of Glory Kids, Patrick Davis, all who were close to Randy and devastated by his death. However, I think the most heartbreaking speech came from our son, his boy ... Matthew. His little princess Gabrielle and I were too emotional to speak, but Matthew insisted on doing so.

He gathered his courage and bravely stepped on center stage. Initially, he couldn't get the words out, breaking down and crying, but after a strong hug from Pastor Trimble, he began. He spoke about his father's character as a great father and leader in our family. He also spoke about his father's unconditional love and his strong Christian faith. Then he left the guests with a wonderful testimony that he revealed about his father. Matthew said, "Christianity wasn't a religion but a way of life for my father, and that's how it should be for all of us."

After Matthew's heartfelt speech, Randy's cousin Gregory Mays from New York read his obituary. Then there were a few more song selections from Joy Trimble, including "I Surrender All," and from Danisha Gutierrez, "Great Is Thy Faithfulness." Pastor Trimble then delivered the eulogy as he spoke about Randy and how he had the blessed assurance of eternal life. Between Matthew's speech and Pastor Trimble's eulogy, many people, including dignitaries and highly respected public figures, stood up and accepted Jesus as their Lord and Savior.

Spiritually speaking, several scriptures came to mind that I thought would be fitting. I thought of the scripture *Well done, my good and faithful servant* (Matthew 25:23) as it pertained to Randy's mission, for he'd witnessed diligently in his effort to bring people to the saving knowledge of Christ. I thought, *His work is done.* He earnestly tried to do everything as a Christian that we all were instructed to do, based on the word of God. Randy's heart's desire was to get as many souls saved as possible. That was his mission and purpose in life.

I also thought of this scripture: *And the Lord said to the servants, Go out into the highways and hedges and compel them to come in, so that my house may be filled* (Luke 14:23). Randy obeyed this scripture and performed his Christian duties of witnessing. However, through his death, millions of people could now hear the gospel of Christ as it was televised throughout the world. Everyone had an opportunity to obtain salvation. I don't believe Randy would have been able to reach that many people in his lifetime had he lived out a full life. As Randy would say, "To God be the glory!"

Ending the funeral were Grammy Award–winning gospel singers and sisters from Mary Mary, Tina Atkins-Campbell and Erica Atkins-Campbell, singing their hit song "Can't Give Up Now." The crowd was fascinated by their entertainment, their lyrics leaving us all with an encouraging message that simply said, "We can't give up now. We have to keep living because God didn't bring us this far to leave us."

Following Mary Mary, Chaplin Kenneth Crawford prayed and gave us final instructions. Mrs. Foresten Dupree sang the last song, "Soon and Very Soon," at the request of Randy's mom. It played during the recessional. The pallbearers came up again and gave a farewell salute to Randy before lifting him up and carrying his casket to a beautiful white hearse.

We all stood there outside the Faith Dome making sure Randy was carefully placed in the hearse. The media were everywhere. There were news reporters, photographers, and camera crews scrambling about trying to get pictures and information about the funeral. However, we had no time to discuss anything, as we were on a time schedule, and the service had lasted longer than anticipated. We were now preparing to partake in the second half of Randy's home going, and it was quite obvious that the second part was going to be just as long, based on the number of vehicles.

Firefighters extended their ladders in his honor.

LAPD Motorcade helped control traffic while paying homage to Randy.

We were all escorted to our limousines, which followed behind Randy's. The fire department graciously honored Randy by extending two ladders in a sky-high forty-five-degree angle, touching in a peak triangle-like formation, with the American flag draped down the center of the ladders at each exit. This was the outward displaying of their support, given in an honorable, patriotic way. It was amazing to see. Every car drove underneath the ladder formation as we all made our exit and fell in line for the procession. There were police motorcades and cars everywhere, from all different cities in California and outside of California, all lining the streets. I saw officers from London and Canada paying their respects to Randy. There was even a news station from France that wanted to interview me. Obviously, the news of Randy's death had gone abroad.

After the service, Randy's body was ready to be taken to his final resting place, Holy Cross Cemetery. Randy's white hearse, followed by the SWAT BearCat, led the procession. Eight limousines, hundreds of civilian vehicles, police cars, and motorcades followed behind the hearse. An unforeseen parade of civilians suddenly took place while en route to the cemetery. People were waving at the family, holding up signs, wearing T-shirts with Randy's face on them, and screaming, "Thank you, Officer Simmons." One resident was showing his talent by standing on the corner and airbrushing a fabulous picture of Randy on a T-shirt that hung from an easel, while a homeless man released a cageful of pigeons as his own unique way of paying homage to Randy.

I remember looking at Matthew and Gabrielle to see their mouths wide open; they couldn't believe all the attention their dad was getting. To them, he was just Dad, but to the public, he was a hero—a hero who gave back to society. I remember feeling so proud. I murmured softly, saying to Randy, "This is unbelievable. Do you see this, Randy? Do you see all the people who love you and appreciate your dedicated service?"

I told Matt and Gabby, "People love your father because he was an ordinary man who did extraordinary things. He helped people, so God saw to it that he would be honored for it."

My mother-in-law added with a big smile, "It's hard for me to be sad right now. I'm so proud of my son. His father and I raised him to be a good boy."

LAPD'S SWAT team carried their fallen
brother to his final resting place.

Randy had the largest funeral in LAPD history,
perhaps even in the city of Los Angeles.

The kids laughed and smiled when their grandma made that statement. They knew their dad was a mama's boy, so they would often tease their dad about still calling his mother "Mommy." It was so comical to the kids, but Grandma Simmons ate it up.

As we continued on our route, I saw employees from State Farm who had stopped working for a minute to display signs to me, reading, LISA, WE LOVE YOU. I was shocked to see it, and tears rolled down my face. Many of them had known Randy since the day we were married. And while en route to the cemetery, I recall seeing a preschool with all the toddlers lined up at the gate with pictures they had drawn of Officer Simmons. Displaying their artwork, they yelled, "Thank you for sharing him with us." I remained in a state of gratitude.

When we arrived at the cemetery, the limos were totally backed up. The major thoroughfare, Slauson Boulevard, was used as a parking lot with police cars parked as far as you could see. There were so many cars that the cemetery and the streets surrounding it became gridlocked. I learned that the nearby freeways were gridlocked as well. In fact, it was so crowded that public transportation and buses were required to escort people to the cemetery. The cemetery was unable to accommodate the large number of vehicles, and all streets were blocked off in every direction. Once the cemetery could no longer let in any cars, the guests had to park across the way at the neighboring Westfield Mall and take a bus to the cemetery. Buses were coming into the cemetery from all directions, dropping people off. It was so busy that it was hours before the actual burial ceremony took place, but people didn't mind waiting because it was something to see.

Later my family and I were escorted out of the limos to take our proper seats and prepare for the burial. We all made one gigantic circle around Randy's casket. I say gigantic because besides all the civilians surrounding the area, there were also thousands of police and public service officers present. There was a wave of law enforcement officers representing each department, division, city, county, state, and country. They all gathered around in their uniforms and paid homage to their fallen brother.

Within minutes, the bagpipers began playing "Taps" and then "Amazing Grace." The Air Traffic Support Unit demonstrated the missing man formation, with jet planes in the sky all in formation and then one slowly drifting away, signifying Randy's departure. This demonstration was so sad it made my heart palpitate. Later the riderless horse entered, guided by an officer. There was no one on the horse, but there were boots in the stirrups, turned backward, symbolizing the death of a fallen hero.

Police Chaplin Kenneth Crawford explained the stripes of the American flag as it was folded up tightly and handed to Matthew. Chief Bratton delivered the cross to me, along with the key from Randy's coffin, a bronze flower to Gabrielle, and the Blessed Mother Mary in bronze to Randy's mom. Pastor Trimble gave Randy his last rites, and then the most beautiful scene ever occurred: Gabrielle walked toward a birdcage and released a dove from her hands as if to say, *Have a peaceful journey to heaven, Dad.* A twenty-one gun salute followed, and a police car radio signed Randy off with a voice saying, "41 D, end of watch." The ceremony was over, and we left Randy there, where he would take his eternal rest.

After the funeral, my family and I were exhausted, as were many of our guests. It was a long day, but guests were now able to join us at any of the three repasts that were going on across the city. LAPD had a repast, the family had a repast, and our church was holding a repast. I attempted to make every one, but I just couldn't do it time-wise or physically. I went to LAPD's repast first, where I greeted people and had something to eat. I was able to extend a thank-you greeting to the Canadian police officers, who informed me that they had their flags flown at half-mast for Randy. Other officers also informed me that the FBI in Baghdad held their flags at half- mast. The Canadian police and the FBI both felt it was an honor well granted, based on the things Randy had done for them. I could not help but think what an awesome gesture was being displayed in other parts of the world. Often Randy and other members of the SWAT team were asked to train or teach other law enforcement agencies in other cities and countries. Randy never hesitated when it came to sharing knowledge and participating in training activities. He would also come back talking about what he'd learned from a different agency. It was obvious there was a great respect for each others' professions. Randy would say things like, "That's how we all stay ahead of the game, by working together for the good. Everybody lends their expertise to each other in order to bring down the bad guys and ultimately make this world a safer place to live."

A picture speaks a thousand words, grief stricken is merely one.

Gabrielle releasing a white dove. A moment we'll never forget.

By the time we finished with LAPD, I knew we weren't going to be able to make the repast at the church, for it was already late and we hadn't even gotten to our own repast. When we arrived at my sister's house, many of our guests had already left, but many were still there, so I had to go through the greeting process again. In a way, I was thankful that so many people were already gone because I was so exhausted. It's hard to keep a smiling face on all day, especially when your heart is broken, but I managed to pull it off.

I then sat down and joined our guests as they were discussing how Deputy Chief Kenny Green had been feeling weak at Randy's funeral. The emotional stress, I'm assuming, really got to him, and I learned that he also passed out at the cemetery. I remembered seeing the ambulance as he was attended to during the funeral and at the cemetery ceremony, so I was glad to hear that he was feeling better. Randy's death had shocked everyone, so it was no surprise to me that the news had affected a good friend's health.

At one point, I recall a few of our guests jumping around in conversation, talking about different subjects and asking me if I found out what happened. Initially, I thought they were still speaking about Kenny's condition, so I said, "No ... I don't really know."

"Aren't you going to try to find out?" one of the guests asked.

I could tell by the way she looked and the expression on her face that we were on two different subjects, and by then I was too tired to figure out what she meant. I changed the subject and started talking about how lovely Randy's funeral was and how the LAPD did an outstanding job in honoring him. I said to our guests, "LAPD has been so wonderful to me and my kids. I know Randy would be so proud of the way they helped us. I can't thank them enough."

Almost immediately, one of the guests said, "But, Lisa, what do you think really happened that night? It wasn't like this call-up was something unusual for Randy and them ... right?"

"I don't know," I responded, concern and perplexity in my voice.

I excused myself and walked away, pondering the thought and wondering myself what did happen that night. I knew I would need to talk to Floyd first since he was there and actually witnessed Randy being shot. But then again, Floyd was sensitive to the subject and was having a hard time with Randy's death. I thought maybe I could get James or

Steve to help me, but James wasn't there that night. Surely he could put me in contact with the investigation team. Then I thought, *Steve Scallion was there, having entered the Rivera house late.* However, I said nothing because although I was sure he had some information about what took place prior to his arrival, I still felt I needed to talk to someone who was part of the entry team. I knew the person who would put my curiosity to rest would be Johnny Verman, and I really wanted to talk to him. I needed answers as well as understanding about what actually happened that night on Welby Way.

## CHAPTER 25

# The Aftermath

AFTER WE LAID RANDY TO rest, I made every attempt to settle into my new role as a single mother and a widow. My family and Randy's family clung to one another like glue, needing to hold on to each other. I tried to resume the normal household activities as soon as possible because I wanted things to get back to normal. But I was only fooling myself. Randy's death made it difficult, if not impossible, for anything ever to be normal again.

After February 7, 2008, our family took on a new form. The reality was that if I continued to think in terms of Randy, things would always feel abnormal. The best advice anyone gave me during that time was from Officer Gina Onweiler. There is no other way to say it: Gina was heaven sent. She worked on the bereavement team with LAPD and it was clear that they selected the right person for the job. Gina was compassionate, understanding, and *truthful*. She didn't tell me things she thought I wanted to hear; she told me what I needed to hear and know. She had the gift of knowing when it was the right time to say certain things. I recall crying to her and telling her that I just wanted things to be normal again. She responded with a simple sentence that hit me like a ton of bricks. Very delicately, she said, "Lisa, if you want things to be normal again, you and the kids are going to have to find your *new normal*.

What she essentially was saying was that our family structure had changed, and that I couldn't expect my present to resemble my past. It simply wouldn't work. The reality and the truth was that Randy was gone, and now it was time to adjust my thinking and deal with the here and now, which meant a new present ... with the possibilities of a great new future. The sooner I accepted that fact, the easier the transition into my new life was going to be. So I tried desperately to meditate on the concept of finding my new normal, but little did I realize that Randy's popularity was going to slow the process down quite a bit.

Soon after the funeral, James Hart called me on the phone and asked if he could meet with me. He had a calendar of events that he needed to share, as I was going to be a big part of these events. There were several memorials, organizations, law enforcement agencies, clubs, schools, civic organizations, as well as nonprofit organizations and media interviews all requesting that the kids and I participate. Each of these organizations was honoring Randy for his heroism as an officer and for his humanitarian efforts as a man of service. Of course, I agreed to meet with James; I wanted to do anything that would honor Randy's memory and perhaps help leave a legacy for generations to come.

While I was on the phone with James, I asked him if he would do me a favor. As always, James was extremely kind, saying that he was willing to do anything to help the family and me. I asked him if he could schedule a meeting with the investigation board so that I could gain insight into the details of what happened that night on Welby Way. James was a little baffled at first because he assumed I was talking about Edwin Rivera shooting Randy and Johnny Verman. But there was nothing to discuss, for that part was straightforward: Edwin killed Randy. He later realized what I was really talking about. I wanted details about what took place that night. In essence, I wanted to know everything about the tactics that were used on Welby Way. He agreed, saying that he would talk to the captain and lieutenant and get back to me. Before James and I hung up, we scheduled a date and a time to meet to go over the plans for the scheduled events.

Later that night, I talked with Floyd Curry, the young relatively new SWAT officer who also worked with Randy as his newest partner. Floyd had stayed in close contact with the family after Randy died. Since he and Randy were new partners, they'd spent a lot of time together beating the streets, taking down bad people, and discussing the Bible. I remember one Sunday at church when Randy came in late, looking worried. He told me he was outside the church looking for a friend named Floyd who worked with him. He had invited Floyd to church, and Randy was excited that he was coming. But when Floyd hadn't arrived, Randy was concerned, thinking that perhaps he was lost and unable to locate our church. He kept getting up throughout the service, walking outside to see if he could find him. Halfway through the service, Randy realized that Floyd was a no-show, and he looked very disappointed.

As fate would have it, after Randy's death, Floyd became a brother-like friend, attending church with the kids and me almost every Sunday. After church, we had the best discussions about the sermon. Somehow, our conversations would always be directed back to fun stories about Randy. I believe it was spiritual therapy for Floyd and me, as we were both still looking for God to heal us in mind, body, and spirit. I was missing my husband, and he was missing his fallen partner. Ironically, besides Floyd's rededication to his Christian faith, Randy's death led many people toward a more intimate relationship with God, including me.

Floyd and I became extremely close, bonding as brother and sister in Christ and close friends. However, I still tiptoed around the idea of asking him to provide me with details of that dreadful night. He openly provided me with basic information, but there were still a lot of missing pieces and many unanswered questions. But I wasn't going to press the issue. I would just wait, hoping that someone of authority would provide me with the information I needed.

One week after Randy's funeral, I told my family that it was time to open our restaurant. Originally, our opening day was scheduled for February 8, 2012, the day after Randy was killed, so our employees were now two weeks behind in their employment and compensation. My mother and sisters were waiting for me to give them the signal, and I told them that I believed Randy would want us to open our dream restaurant and get busy. I knew my family felt somewhat guilty, just as I did, for continuing on, but looking back, it was the best thing that could have happened to us. In addition, I went back to my office putting on my agent hat, attempting to carry out insurance sales duties and supervisory responsibilities. Still deeply in the process of grieving, I felt like Lisa in Wonderland, busy, busy, busy, and for the first time in my life, I truly wanted to be busy. It kept my mind occupied, for I thought a little less about my current state of being.

It was on a Saturday morning that my family and I were excited about opening the restaurant. Local radio announcers mentioned the opening of our restaurant, with the news media making their way to New Orleans Vieux Carré, publicizing the restaurant by announcing that slain officer Randy Simmons's family restaurant, located in Leimert Park, was opening. Needless to say, business was good. It was a lovely, cozy restaurant with mustard-colored walls, French provincial lamps, and beautiful paintings by artist Michalopoulos of New Orleans, Louisiana. All paintings by Michalopoulos reflected different French colonial homes and places in the French Quarter. The bright and vibrant colors gave a New Orleans feel to our relatively big restaurant. In addition, there was a large chandelier in the middle of the restaurant and a wall draped in Mardi colors—purple, green, and gold—with a gigantic mask topping off the restaurant and bringing the French style and character to New Orleans Vieux Carré. We added a handsome portrait of Randy on the wall in the front of the restaurant, which was quickly noticed as one walked through the front door. We wanted something to be a constant reminder of Randy, and we wanted people to know that he was and always would be a part of our family.

Life was busy. I was working at my insurance agency Monday through Friday, helping at the restaurant occasionally at night and every weekend, and now I was planning to meet James Hart and add more activity to my already busy schedule.

On the day I was scheduled to meet James Hart at our restaurant, while waiting for him to arrive, Randy's good friend Captain James Craig and his officers from Southwest Division came in to dine. It was great seeing James Craig, as he was one of Randy's dearest friends and Matthew's godfather. He was still clearly shaken by Randy's death. He then showed me a big framed picture that his staff at Southwest Division had given him as a present. It was a picture of Randy and James at our wedding. James was Randy's best man, and in the picture, they were shaking hands like brothers. His staff knew how devastated he was about Randy's death and they wanted to give him something to help cheer him up. It was good seeing James, but I had to say good-bye, as I was meeting with the other James—James Hart—Randy's partner.

James Hart walked into the restaurant dressed casually in civilian clothes, complete with a T-shirt and basketball shorts. We were going to have lunch and go over the schedule of events, but little did he know that my motivation for meeting him was more because I was hoping he would give me some information on the investigation. I saw from a distance that James Hart nodded at James Craig, and then he sat down at a booth and waited for me to join him. I thought that their lack of interaction was odd. I had expected the two to greet each other with more brotherly love, but they kept their distance, respecting each other's space. I had forgotten that James Craig was a part of Randy's younger years, his classmate and partner when he worked CRASH as well as his partying buddy and roommate. James Hart was part of his LAPD Centurion football and SWAT years. Thus the two knew each other primarily because of Randy.

I was happy to see James Hart, as I hadn't seen him since the funeral. We gave each other a big bear hug and went right into discussing business. James was excited regarding the details he was about to give me, and he spoke quickly, practically stuttering with excitement.

"Lisa, you and the family are going to be busy up until May of next year ... and probably thereafter."

"Busy doing what?" I replied.

"Oh my God, Lisa! Randy's huge! People and organizations from all over want to honor him," he said.

He opened a black eight-by-ten calendar book with dates, events, and times scribbled in it. He slid it over to me so I could see what was in it, continuing to talk. "They would like for the entire family to be there, plus there will be representation from SWAT as well. Floyd, Guy, Steve, and me will be your primary escorts. The other guys will help out too."

My mouth was wide open. I didn't know what to say. James had presented me with a rigorous schedule that showed us attending countless events such as memorials, banquets, dinner parties, meetings, conventions, organizational meetings, ceremonies, club activities, sorority and fraternity events, sporting events, school events, law enforcement agencies, and other recognitions. The list went on and on. I glanced up at James and saw him watching me with a look of amazement.

"Can you believe it, Lisa? People loved Randy!"

"Yes, they did, James, and the family and I will be at every last event. We are all extremely honored."

James went on to say that for each event, he was going to need a head count in order to let Captain Greer of SWAT know how many Suburban trucks and officers would be needed to escort the family, starting that week.

I was very proud of the fact that so many people wanted to pay tribute to Randy, although I realized I had just added another job to my already busy schedule. However, this job was near and dear to my heart, and I could not compare it to anything of monetary value. Honoring Randy was priceless. I was proud to be his wife and proud to attend.

After we talked about this matter, I asked James about my inquiry into the investigation on Welby Way. James had already looked into it; he was good at handling business and making inquiries for me. That was going to be his next table topic. He informed me that he had talked to "the powers that be," and they were sending over detectives to meet with me midweek. I felt satisfied knowing that they were coming to talk with me. Some may have thought I should have been satisfied with the obvious—Edwin Rivera shot Randy—but I have never been one to accept surface-type information. So surely I wasn't going to accept something on the surface when it came to the death of my husband. I wanted details. I wanted minute-by-minute details of what happened or didn't happen that night. I genuinely did not think that as a widow, I was asking too much. James agreed and told me to have the family over when they came, so all the information could be conveyed and all questions could be answered at the same time. I was looking forward to this meeting, assuming it would bring closure and I could move on and truly begin to find my "new normal."

James gobbled down one of our famous shrimp and catfish po'boy sandwiches and left. My sisters and I remained in the restaurant, greeting guests and helping the new servers get acclimated to their workflow. It was tiring but fun. We stayed extremely busy that week, with friends, officers, and other unknown people patronizing our restaurant. During this time, I was easily recognized and on display, for Randy was now an icon, a public figure that everyone admired and remembered as that wonderful officer who was killed, the one who had the big, beautiful funeral that made the city of Los Angeles weep. People were coming into the restaurant weeks later, wanting to meet me and pay their condolences. It was overwhelming, but I sincerely appreciated the heartwarming concern for the family and me.

One Saturday night while I was working at the restaurant, three huge men walked in and asked to see me. I was nearby, helping one of our employees, when I heard them ask for me. Feeling nervous about their presence, I ran to the back of the restaurant, for I had recently learned about an incident that occurred just prior to Randy's funeral. Some SWAT officers had flown to Boston to capture a man who was calling the police station and threatening the kids and me. From what I gathered, he heard about Randy's death, which prompted his irrational behavior. Members of SWAT flew to Boston and apprehended him, and although I never found out the details, I just knew it was handled. But as a result, I found myself feeling leery of people I didn't know, and since I didn't recognize these men and they did not say with whom they were affiliated, I felt nervous. They said they wanted to see Randy Simmons's widow. While I was hiding in the back of the restaurant, blocked by an eight-foot wall, a server pointed me out to the guys and called, "Oh, here she is!" I wanted to strangle her, but I put on my fake smile and walked out to see how I could help them. Maybe they just wanted a booth, so I greeted them with that intention.

"Hello, welcome to New Orleans Vieux Carré," I said.

"Yes, we were walking past your restaurant and saw your husband's picture in the window. We just wanted to express our condolences," one of the big guys said. He extended his hand and I noticed a big ring on his finger. It looked like some sort of sports ring.

"Thank you. I appreciate your condolences. By the way, do you play sports?" I asked, attempting to change the subject and make general conversation.

"Yes … well, I used to play for the New York Giants. I heard your husband played college ball," he said, smiling.

"Yes, he did," I replied, my guard slowly came down.

One of his friends, who spoke with an African accent, interjected. "I just want to say that your husband had a beautiful funeral. My mother called me from the Congo and told me she was watching it … and how she was touched by his life." He extended his hand to hold mine. He then compassionately added, "My friends and I were just discussing your husband the other day. We were saying how his life made us all want to be better men."

Concurring, the third man commented, "Yes, we just wanted you to know that so many people are praying for you and your kids."

"Thank you ... Thank you," I said, my eyes welling up with tears as I watched the three wise men walk out of our restaurant.

I felt silly for running to the back. These men were so sincere about Randy leaving a positive impression on their lives. They were a few among many who stated that Randy made them want to become better. I thought what an impact he left on the lives of others, and it's still being conveyed and delivered through his death. The imprint of his life reminds me of that old spiritual song: "May the works I've done speak for me. May the life I live speak for me." Randy's life spoke for him, and it touched the lives of many.

Randy's name carried a lot of weight, so much so that I was hearing that different organizations were using his name, some for good and some for their own personal profit and gain. There were signs in front of businesses reading OFFICER SIMMONS SHOPPED HERE. I was told that some makeshift vendors were selling T-shirts of Randy in uniform, T-shirts with Matthew holding the American flag, and T-shirts with Gabrielle releasing a white dove, depicting pictures taken at the funeral. There was jewelry being made with Randy's initials and Internet requests for personal donations from people alleging to be family members. It was crazy, and a part of me was becoming paranoid and distressed over the Randy mania. I gave a lot of thought to how I could control or protect my husband's face or name. Unfortunately, my attorney informed me that Randy's death and popularity had made him an extremely public figure, and that controlling the actions of others would be difficult at best.

As the weeks passed, my house began to look more and more like a storage facility. I had rearranged the house to make room for many gifts and mementos that had come in from people all over the world. I received things locally, such as book reports on Randy and thank-you posters from young elementary school kids, and I even received holy oil from someone's grandmother as far away as Jerusalem. I received countless letters, cards, pictures, blankets, paintings, plaques, awards, crystals, and SWAT memorabilia. The majority of the gifts were lovely, and I incorporated the items into my home, with many other great gifts

I had received. Unfortunately, some sent morbid letters and other things, confirming the fact that there are some mentally ill people among us. I prayed, continuously asking God to protect my kids and me, as many complete strangers knew exactly where we lived. Based on that nutty person who threatened my kids and me from as far away as Boston, not everyone had our best interests at heart, and I was feeling a little mistrustful.

To alleviate my fears, I called my good friend Lazaro Merino, a man who was introduced to our family a long time ago by Andy Simon, Randy's partner at the time. Lazaro started off as our painter, and in later years, he became family, someone we called on for a multitude of things. We had known Lazaro for sixteen years, and he was as good as gold. In fact, he would do anything for our entire family, and I considered him my El Salvadorian brother.

Lazaro was devastated by Randy's death and promised to be around for my mom, my sisters, and me whenever we needed him. He felt a personal burden and a terrible hurt because Edwin Rivera's family was from his country. In an odd way, he felt ashamed. I wanted him to remove that absurd notion from his head, but he still made it his mission to look after us. And I took him up on his offer, especially now that I was in a paranoid state. I asked him to secure my house by putting up equipment that might also serve as a diversion. I guess Lazaro could detect that my personality was changing. As a once trusting and worry-free woman, I was now freaking out over the smallest things.

I remember him looking at me while he was putting up the cameras, and he had a very sad face. I could tell by his demeanor that he felt sorry for me and could see that Randy's death was taking a toll on me mentally. He said with his strong El Salvadorian accent, "Lisa ... no one's going to hurt you. God and Mr. Randy are looking over you and the kids."

It was obvious by the look on his face that my feelings of paranoia were getting out of control. It was an eye opener, as it made it obvious that I needed to find a way to relax and trust God. Lazaro wasn't the only one who was able to see that Randy's death was taking its toll. Unbeknownst to me, the stages of grieving were in progress, and others noticed that I was going on a heavily active rampage, attempting to occupy every second of my day so that my mind wasn't idle. I was embarking on an unwanted season in my life, and I couldn't get myself in gear for the changes that came from being alone.

Even though I stayed busy at my office, the restaurant, and with all the event ceremonies, I hadn't realized that the seasons were changing, even where it concerned my children. I was starting to feel the teenage life syndrome. In one sense, my kids needed me desperately, but in another sense, they weren't as involved with me as they had been when they were younger. It seemed like yesterday when Randy and I had to schedule private time away from the kids, for they loved being under our feet constantly. But now they were doing what teenagers do, driving and hanging out with their friends, going to the mall and the movies. They definitely didn't want their mommy following them around, and I had to respect their space, as I clearly remembered my own teenage years. Every once in a while they would lie in bed and watch a movie with me, as they knew I was missing their dad, but they would soon resort back to other matters that seemed so much more interesting to them, like Facebook and texting.

I found myself doing things like looking on the other side of my bed and envisioning Randy lying there eating his doughy sugar cookies while we watched and talked about the news. I know it sounds crazy, but you do crazy things when you miss someone you love.

One night while taking a shower, I started giving myself the pity party of the century, and the only person invited was myself. There was a spot in my shower where I could sit, so I seated myself and began crying my eyes out for a good thirty minutes. There I sat, sobbing and talking to God and Randy, asking for forgiveness for all the times I requested "me time" away from Randy and the kids. I knew I had been a good wife to Randy, but I just felt like torturing myself. I was angry with myself, and I was wishing I had done more with Randy, helped him more with the Glory Kids, been a better wife, adhered to his complaints about cooking with less salt, and everything else I could think of that made me feel even sorrier for myself.

When I finally got myself together, I stepped out of the shower and looked at myself in the mirror. The ugly sight of my swollen eyes and my big red nose made me cry even more. I put on my favorite cotton pajamas and decided to keep my pity party going for a while longer. What did I have to lose? The kids were spending the night out, and I was home alone: the sad, pathetic widow.

    I hadn't changed anything since Randy's death. His toothbrush and cologne were still in the same place on his side of the bathroom. His closet still held all of his clothes lined up perfectly, unlike my disorganized closet. I looked at his clothes, taking each item and moving it back on the rod where it hung. I then grabbed them all together and hugged them, trying to smell his scent, and then I started crying again. I cried and I cried and I cried … until I realized that I was on the floor smashing some Italian-made shoes that Randy had purchased when we were in Italy. By that time, I was exhausted from crying, so I got up and decided I'd had enough. It was time to finish off this party by falling asleep.

    As I was getting up from his closet, I looked at the notes he had scribbled and tacked on the inside of his closet door. There was a picture that Gabby drew in class, a letter that Matthew wrote about God, and close-up pictures of the family and one of me. I thought, *My husband loved his family so much that he even had us inside his closet.* I stared at that picture of me posing with a big smile, thinking back to when it was taken at my company's party. I started reminiscing about how happy we were and how much fun we had that night. And then for some odd reason, my hand pulled out the tack that attached the picture firmly to the door. I noticed there was a little card, smaller than my picture, stuck behind it. I almost didn't notice the card because it was so small. I slowly opened it, and as God as my witness, it read, "We both deserve each other's love," and it was signed, "From Randy." He kept that small card he had given me with flowers on our anniversary years ago. I remember it as if it were yesterday because that card reflected the title of the song we danced to on our wedding day. It was called "We Both Deserve Each Other's Love," by R & B group L.T.D., with Jeffrey Osborne as the lead vocalist. Oh how I loved that song … and the love it represented between Randy and me. In that moment, the joy that sprang up in me as I read the card was astonishing. My tears of pain became tears of joy. I thought, *Is this just another coincidence? Did I just happen to stumble on this hidden card?* I don't know the answer, but I do know that we loved each other dearly and were truly soul mates.

The photo and card that was on the inside of his closet door.

The week after my meltdown, I made it a point to get Randy's medical records. I was curious to see if the time he died actually coincided with the time I woke up singing that song about entering into God's presence. I was also eager to clear up the mix-up about the location of Randy's gunshot wound. By myself, I drove out to Northridge Hospital in Randy's Toyota Sequoia truck. I entered the hospital trembling with fear, trying to make my way to the medical department. Part of me was anxious to get them, and the other part of me felt scared; however, the part that was anxious superseded my fears. I couldn't get back up in the truck fast enough so I could read the medical notes.

I sat in the parking lot and pulled the records out of the envelope. I was instantly ticked off. Initially, I thought the record clerk had given me the wrong records, as the name of the patient on the envelope was a woman named Stephanie Pears. Ironically and strangely, Stephanie was brought in on the same night as Randy, with a gunshot wound. Enticed, I continued reading. Gradually, Stephanie became John Doe, and then John Doe became Randy. The medical notes were bizarre. Everything in them, including the blood results, were based on this fictitious woman named Stephanie Pears, including age and gender. They were then converted to Randy's age and gender. Then I noticed that there were donors listed, waiting for Randy's organs. By this time, I was totally baffled by all the things that were mentioned.

After reading the notes, once again I called my old faithful James Hart to see if someone could tell me what was going on. The only response I got was that to protect Randy's identity and for security reasons, they had to change his name and identity. That was it! The truth of the matter is that it may have been all there was to this identity thing, but it would have been much better if I had received a formal explanation ahead of time instead of hearing it from an endearing third party such as James Hart.

I felt bad for James because while he tried to help me with several requests, his responses would sometimes generate an earful of complaints from me. James was stuck between a rock and a hard place, for there were just some things he had no control over.

I called the doctors to make sure the records were accurate and to get some clarity on the gunshot wound, but much to my surprise, I received no return call. I also called the donor organization, known as One Legacy. I was trying to figure out if Randy's organs had been donated to the names that were listed. After careful research, the organization informed me that they were unable to receive Randy's organs. The one thing that was confirmed was his time of death. It was just as I thought. Officially, Randy was pronounced dead at 12:55 a.m., but all evidence pointed to the fact that he was transitioning the moment he was shot.

# CHAPTER 26

# The Unsubstantiated Investigation

MIDWEEK ARRIVED QUICKLY, AND THE homicide detectives were scheduled to be at my house at about 2:00 p.m. The family had arrived early, anxious to hear what happened that night on Welby Way. My brother-in-law's brother, Detective Maury Sumlin, with the Santa Monica Police Department, and James Hart were present to further assist, as were my sisters and Randy's younger sister Gina. His older sister Valjean had returned to her home in Winona, Minnesota shortly after the funeral. The elders of the family elected not to come, as they couldn't handle hearing all the details. But I wanted all the facts.

The detectives arrived and sat down at my dining room table, which seemed to be the regular meeting place. I had shuffled around boxes and boxes of things sent in honor of Randy just to make sure there was a place to walk. Both of the detectives were probably in their midforties. They were both dressed in suits and appeared to be uneasy, but they were disguising their discomfort with serious dispositions. It was awkward at first because I knew that no one felt comfortable for some reason. I guess it was because of the sensitivity of the subject matter.

My sister Melinda offered the gentlemen a cup of coffee or tea, and they both politely declined. You could tell they just wanted to handle the current business, and no one was more anxious to get started than I was. For this purpose, I will refer to the lead detective on the case as Detective #1. He began by saying that he and the other detective, whom we will call Detective #2, were sorry for our loss. He went on to say that neither one of them knew Randy, but they had heard only great things about him. Detective #2 acknowledged that they were aware we had a lot of questions, and he stated that they were here to answer our questions and also give us all pertinent information. They continued by saying they hoped they would be able to bring some closure to this tragic event. Then, after a matter of a few seconds, Detective #1 made a statement that immediately rubbed us all the wrong way.

He firmly said, "I want to assure you that nothing on our part was done wrong."

I became instantly agitated because this meeting was not intended to be accusatory but for the family to obtain information. I gathered from his comment that it was in the forefront of his mind before he entered the house. But I wanted to set the record straight right from the start. Part of Randy's no-nonsense personality had rubbed off on me, and today was not the day for foolish accusations. I wanted to make myself clear on why we were having this meeting, so I began to interrupt him before he went any further, but my sister-in-law beat me to it. She became upset and said something like the following:

"Wait ... wait ... wait ...! My brother was killed doing something he has done hundreds of times, and you're telling us nothing went wrong?"

Detective #1 apologized for starting the conversation incorrectly, and he attempted to be as sensitive to our feelings as possible, while also remaining straightforward. I suggested to everyone that we listen to what the detectives had to say first, without interrupting, and then we could ask questions. That allowed Detective #1 to take back control of some of the conversation and explain what happened and why the SWAT team reacted to the incident the way they had.

He discussed Edwin Rivera's behavior and the 911 calls. He further discussed the urgency for the SWAT team to act expeditiously. He explained that the Hostage Rescue Immediate Response Policy states that if LAPD feels there are victims being held hostage and they are in immediate danger, SWAT has to quickly go in and rescue them. He then firmly said the words that pierced my heart.

"Even if it means giving up your own life. This is what your husband got paid to do."

You know that old saying "It's not what you say but how you say it"? Well, Detective #1 could have used a little more tact and possibly showed a little more sensitivity. But because he didn't, I snapped! I remember saying to him, "This isn't about compensation, Detective; this is about preserving human life. I am well aware that my husband got paid 'to serve and protect,' and with that in mind, Detective, I just want to know if all necessary tactical equipment and resources were made available to the SWAT team so that they could effectively do their jobs while saving lives and attempting to preserve their own as well."

Detective #1 knew he'd hit a nerve. I saw James Hart holding his head down and Melinda's and Gina's rising. I knew James was thinking, *Oh boy, he's in for it now.*

"I heard the SWAT truck wasn't there. Is that true?" Melinda asked.

"The SWAT truck wasn't there initially, but it arrived later," Detective #2 responded.

"So you're saying the SWAT truck was not there ... but did the officers have all the equipment necessary to do their job effectively and safely?" I asked.

The detectives looked as though they were at a loss for words, so James Hart spoke up, giving them some reprieve from the questioning. James explained that SWAT members always have in their possession some equipment they can use when needed. In this case, the SWAT truck hadn't arrived and they needed to act expeditiously, so they had to rely on the equipment they had on hand.

Again, Melinda spoke up, saying what everyone else was probably thinking. "Is it safe to say that there is a possibility that maybe some other tactic may have been considered had the SWAT truck been there? Do you think there was a rush to judgment in going in?"

James, listening intently and clearly wanting to deliver the best answer, admitted that it was possible that if the SWAT truck had been there, maybe some other tactic(s) could have been considered and possibly used, but all things were based on the hostage rescue policy, so they had no choice but to go in and attempt to rescue victims.

I needed more understanding, so I continued with my questioning, trying to be as sensitive to them as possible without coming across as accusatory. I was just trying to make sense of things, so I said compassionately and slowly, "Detectives, please help me understand ... Randy has told me several stories about different tactics the SWAT team uses when trying to apprehend a suspect. I've heard stories about SWAT going through every crevice of a house or a building to gain access. I understand you all use diversions and all sorts of things to help you locate the suspect prior to entering. Shouldn't you have some knowledge of where the suspect is located so you won't be an open target? Were any of these factors considered?"

Detective #1 attempted to give me an explanation. He said that the house was completely dark, and there was no activity inside. The suspect would not communicate with them, and they had no choice but to go in. He further explained something that I already knew, which is that SWAT trains hard for hostage situations like this. However, based on some of the things I was currently hearing, I wasn't convinced that enough had been considered before making entry.

"I'm sure they could have used some tactic to help them get a general idea of the suspect's location before entering," I stated. "That could have taken possibly a matter of seconds." I then added, "I'm still trying to find out why the SWAT truck wasn't there."

Again helping the detectives answer questions they were unprepared for, James explained that there are only two guys licensed to drive the SWAT truck. They both lived near the call-up in San Fernando Valley and both had to leave their homes in the Valley and drive downtown, get the SWAT truck, and bring it back to the Valley, which is why it took a long time for it to arrive.

Everyone was quiet and just looked at each other. Then my sister Melinda said, "I heard the flashbang didn't go off like SWAT anticipated. Did it malfunction?"

James again tried to offer an explanation to her question. He explained that the house was poorly designed and didn't match the blueprint SWAT was given. So the flashbang hit an unforeseen wall, thus not performing to its full potential.

"On TV, it looked like the house caught on fire. Is it still standing?" I asked.

Detective #1 stated, "No, it burned completely down. There's only a fence surrounding an empty lot."

I could tell the questioning was starting to get to James. His eyes were red, as if he was getting emotional, so I gently put my hands on his arm, letting him know how sorry we all were ... and to forgive us if our questioning was out of line.

James emotionally said something like this: "Lisa, we're the ones who are sorry [referring to himself and the SWAT team]. We feel as if we failed Randy and you ... the family. We're all taking this very hard; some of us are even in therapy trying to get ourselves together. And Johnny Verman is really having a hard time with it, which is why he can't talk to you."

We all surrounded James and gave him a hug, as the last thing we wanted was to place guilt on any of the SWAT officers about what happened. By no stretch of the imagination were we trying to minimize their talents and skills as SWAT officers. I had and still have the utmost respect and admiration for their profession. I know firsthand how hard they work and how much they train to be the best; however, I did have questions and concerns regarding their tactics as it pertained to the hostage rescue policy and their safety. Also, a delay in receiving additional resources and equipment to help them do their jobs effectively needed to be addressed. I thought of other questions that warranted logical explanations that might or might not have given me a sense of satisfaction, and which I felt would bring closure to my curiosity, but our meeting was over.

I thanked the detectives for coming, as I felt enough had been said. I definitely wasn't comfortable with their answers, for they simply didn't know enough. If James weren't there helping them answer questions, I probably would have disregarded the meeting in its entirety. For that reason, I had a serious conversation with James about my dissatisfaction regarding the deficient information given to me. I couldn't solely blame the detectives, for they were instructed by someone to meet with me and provide me with basic information, possibly thinking it was sufficient to put my mind to rest. I explained to James that I appreciated him and the other officers, but I had a deep yearning to know the details of what really happened. James, without a doubt, understood how I felt. He knew how much I loved Randy ... and that I deserved to know step-by-step details of what actually happened. LAPD was a part of Randy's life, but he was my life.

In the meantime, while James inquired about my meeting with a formal investigative or debriefing committee, I was still in search of someone who could give me answers about Randy's medical reports. I left several messages with a few doctors who provided Randy with medical attention. Unfortunately, I received no return call. I wanted to clear up some ambiguous things in the medical report, yet no one was available or cared enough to take the time to go over the records with me. I wanted to have an understanding or a logical explanation about the possibly incorrect information given to me at the very beginning.

Because I got no response, I decided to go another route. I gathered my courage and decided to order his autopsy report, thinking that nothing was more detailed and defined as that would be. When I called the county of Los Angeles and asked to obtain a report about my husband, to my dismay, the staff and lead supervisor informed me that I would be unable to obtain the report until the homicide investigation was completed. It was legally placed on hold. I didn't want to interfere with the investigation process, so I chose not to challenge their response or try to pull rank as his wife. Not that it would have mattered, for the answer still would have been the same. I had to wait until LAPD lifted the hold.

Months passed, and I constantly checked to see if the autopsy report was available, but it was still on hold. I waited to hear something about the final investigation debriefing, but that too was still in progress. The more I thought about how long it was taking the investigation to be completed, the more puzzled I became about LAPD sending over the detectives at a stage when the investigation was just getting started. Why would they give someone factual information when an investigation hadn't been done? I would have rather someone said that the information they were giving me was only preliminary, for it was going to take several months, and once the investigation was completed, they would have someone contact me. I felt that would have been the proper thing to have said and done.

Nevertheless, I tried to be patient and maintain positive thoughts. After all, every organization operates differently. I truly believed that once the investigation was completed, I would have my closure. So my family and I stayed focused and continued to attend events in Randy's honor while the investigation was still in progress. As a family, we were running here and there, jumping in and out of cars, sometimes going to back-to-back events. Occasionally, my childhood friends and relatives would lend their support and attend these events as well. There was no doubt in my mind that they loved Randy, but I was also aware that some of my friends liked the fact that many of Randy's officer friends were single and handsome. I applaud the fact that the officers all remained professional and demonstrated self-restraint. Whenever complimented, they would just smile and continue focusing on their duties.

Unlike Randy, who leaned more toward the conservative side, I was more ... well, let's just say I was a little more moderate. Some might even say my family and my friends were more on the crazy side. We were loud and loved to have fun. Randy used to scratch his head and wonder about us when he would hear us cackling about something. He would then retreat to a secluded place in the house, somewhere far from our craziness. Then he would come over and interrupt our conversation by saying something sarcastic like, "When was the last time y'all been to church?" I would say something to top his sarcasm, like, "Okay, Moses, you gonna lead the way?"

I surprised him and invited my sisters and some of my good friends to join his Bible study class based on Pastor Rick Warren's Book *The Purpose Driven Life*. Initially, he was supposed to be a facilitator for an all-male group, but as the Bible says, *"My thoughts are not your thoughts, and my ways are not your ways,"* declared the Lord (Isaiah 55:8–9). God was taking Randy out of his comfort zone. He was now going to head a Bible study along with me and all the other cackling women who needed Jesus! It was so funny to see him facilitate because he was used to working with and being around men. To see him out of his element and interacting in a woman's group probably was more challenging than any SWAT training he had ever done. Eventually, he got used to our ways and enjoyed leading our group, but he didn't stick around after the meetings. As soon as they were over, Randy would vanish, knowing the cackling was going to start back up again.

Those were fun times we shared with Randy, and now we were giving his SWAT brothers a taste of what Randy had endured for years with all the women in his life. James Hart used to say jokingly, "Poor Randy ... I know Randy had headaches being around all you women," and we would all laugh in response. Truthfully, my wild high-maintenance personality is what kept our marriage fun and interesting.

My family and I enjoyed the SWAT team, and I think they enjoyed us as well. After Randy's death, we developed many enduring relationships with those who stood by our side during our darkest hour. Many of them who joined us on this difficult journey attended personal events, including Matthew's and Gabrielle's graduations, Matthew's football games, and Gabrielle's sixteenth birthday party. I am eternally grateful to them all, for all of them were truly there for us.

We spent so much time with them that we got to know some of them very well. My family and I even gave some of them nicknames: We nicknamed Jaime Rubalcava Al Pacino because with his handsomeness and cool disposition, he resembled him. There was Sergeant Chuck Batutti, whom Randy nicknamed Bambi because he was a fast runner and leaped when he ran, just like the deer Bambi. Lou Reyes and Bill Cassy were nice and humble men whose warm smiles always lifted our spirits. Then there was Bobby Gajos Jr., who was sweet as pie. I found him on my doorsteps one day, delivering birthday flowers to me from the team. Bobby was second-generation SWAT. Randy worked with him and his father, Bobby Gajos Senior. Funny man Ozzie, a natural-born comedian, helped raised funds for Randy's foundation through a 5K run. Ozzie, his beautiful wife, Marcy, and his handsome sons would all participate in the event. And there was the ever-so-fine Guy Dobine, who was always challenging Randy about something, whether it was working out or analyzing the Bible. Soon after Randy's death, Guy started attending church with his mother. I know Randy is smiling down on him. There was also Keith Bacon, who shared fond memories with me about when he and his brother, Kevin, spent summers hunting in Texas with their grandfather. Keith was as down-to-earth as they come. Sergeant Gomez warmed my heart when he and other SWAT members ran a race called Baker to Vegas. It's a grueling race that usually lasts twenty-four hours, with each runner running a few miles, or legs. Sergeant Gomez and his team brought the torch home to the finish line running with full SWAT gear, a heavy vest, and boots. I could see the anguish on his face as he struggled, but he made it to the finish line in record-breaking time. Sergeant Gomez, like Randy, was one of the seasoned guys on SWAT, and he was in good shape.

Captain Jeff Greer, Randy's classmate, worked so hard. He never broke away from his work ethic unless he was talking about his children

... or his love for watches. I remember him telling me that he liked watches because of how they functioned. The mechanics of watches fascinated him. I thought about buying him a Mickey Mouse watch and leaving him a note reminding him about valuing what the watch symbolizes, which is having fun times.

And then there is Lieutenant Michael Albanese, a classic example of not judging a book by its cover. If I didn't know him, I probably would have wrongfully prejudged him. His militant appearance contradicts his sweet spirit. He's a good and humble man whom I have the utmost respect for because of how he lives his life. He truly is one of few on the workforce who understood that Randy had a special calling in his life, so while Randy was on duty, he aided him in fulfilling it by allowing him some flexibility.

Todd Rheingold, an awesome man ... someone who has many of Randy's qualities. He has a passion for interacting with kids while on duty. Todd would often share his childhood experience of growing up in the rough parts of LA. Street bullies often challenged him and his brother. Seeing Todd now, those guys would run clear across the country, praying that Todd and his brother didn't seek revenge, for Todd is six five and strong. However, it's lucky for the street bullies that Todd has a modest nature and a compassionate heart. He's a gentle giant and, I promise you, one of the nicest guys you could ever want to meet.

Then there's my Irish lucky charm, Steve Scallon. Steve is amazing. From what I know, he's an example of a dedicated and loyal police officer and is always doing something with LAPD or assisting some other civil service organization like the FBI or the Navy SEALS. It appears that he really loves his job, but he would do away with those things he feels can get in the way of real police work. As I stated earlier, Steve is as gentle as a lamb but can be as fearless as a tiger if you rub him the wrong way. I witnessed his mode of operation firsthand when he escorted me to an invitation lunch I received from Palermo Ristorante Italiano Restaurant in Los Feliz.

This comical scene happened shortly after Randy's death, at a time when I didn't know Steve as I know him today. As Steve and I were entering the restaurant's parking lot, the valet stopped us. Steve rolled down his window and said to the young attendant, who took his job very seriously, "I'm with LAPD, and this is a police Suburban. I have to park it myself."

The young attendant just dismissed what Steve had to say and asked Steve for his keys again. Steve took off his sunglasses and looked the guy in the face. He tried explaining it again, speaking in his low, strong Irish accent, flashing his identification and providing him proof of being LAPD. "I'm sorry, but I can't let you park the car. I'm with LAPD, and we have to park our own cars for security reasons."

I couldn't believe this guy's dim-witted behavior, for he replied by again adamantly requiring Steve's keys. This time, Steve didn't reply. The next thing I knew, I felt as if I were on a roller coaster at Six Flags. Steve put the pedal to the metal and took off, sounding off at the attendant with words that he definitely deserved. When Steve pulled into a parking spot, my head was still stuck to the headrest. He apologized for taking me on the wild ride, but there was no need. I think Steve was more than patient with the young attendant, who, by the way, ran after us, still trying to get Steve's keys. He was truly a nut case, and he's lucky that Steve didn't crack his shell. It makes me laugh whenever I think of that incident. It was so funny.

From that day forward, I knew Steve and I were going to be the best of friends. Steve and I have remained in contact throughout the years, and he has made it a point to be at my front door every Christmas, delivering gifts from his family and the SWAT Team.

I wish I could personally name every SWAT member in this book, as they were all so kind, with each one of them participating in the countless events honoring Randy. There were lifelong memorable events like the Los Angeles Marathon, which was dedicated and run in his honor, with Matthew running along with them, carrying the torch, while Gabby and I stood at the finish line and cheered them on. As a souvenir, I was given the actual torch. How awesome is that?

There was also the Eagle and Badge ceremony, sponsored by the Los Angeles Police Protective League; the Chinese Association ceremony; the Los Angeles Rotary Club scholarship ceremony; the Smokey Robinson Foundation ceremony; the West Valley Legal Association; and recognition presentations with the Federal Bureau of Investigation and the Drug Enforcement Administration.

The Los Angeles Marathon plaque in honor of Randy.

Me, Matthew and Gabrielle honoring Randy's memory at The Eagle and Badge Foundation Gala at the Hyatt Regency Century Plaza Hotel.

Gabby honoring her father at a Dodger game.

There were private meetings with Governor Pete Wilson and members of the Navy SEALS; sports presentations with the Los Angeles Lakers, allowing Matt and Gabby on the court to toss the ball and take pictures with Kobe Bryant and Derek Fisher; the Los Angeles Dodgers, with Matt and Gabby throwing the first pitch; the Anaheim Ducks, honoring Randy with a standing ovation; elementary, high school, and college presentations; sorority and fraternity breakfasts and dinners with memorial after memorial after memorial. Regrettably, I cannot mention every organization or event that took place, but I will tell you that there were occasions when I attended three in a day, with the majority of requests coming through LAPD and some by personal request. Having a flexible work schedule made it possible for me to attend them all, but I could not have done it without the LAPD and the support of my office staff.

## CHAPTER 27

# Mixed Emotions

I KNEW THAT MANY OF the officers loved Randy, and it was obvious that they were committed to the endearing friendships they had developed with him, but I could see that they were beginning to grow weary of attending the many events. Besides the fact that several of the events were heart wrenching, with details that constantly reminded them of that terrible night, it also made them confront the dangers they faced head-on every day. I would look at their faces during these events, which usually started with smiles, as we ate and conversed around the banquet table, but they often ended in frowns as we relived video clippings of Randy, alive and talking, laughing and training. It was also sad for them to see his widow and his now fatherless children accept awards on his behalf. I knew it was difficult, but I felt that the request to honor him was a minimal sacrifice worthy of making. I continued to push through and accept his awards with honor and humility.

Ultimately, I became more selective about which events my kids attended, as they were constantly being pulled out of school, and their grades were suffering. In addition, I could see that some of the events were ripping them apart, thus puncturing an already deep wound. Sooner rather than later, I myself had to start using discernment and discretion in deciding what events to attend. I simply had come to the realization that physically I couldn't participate in every one.

There were the times when I felt somewhat bewildered about what I was experiencing. On the one hand, I was close to LAPD, and I couldn't say enough about their support, but on the other hand, I felt a sense of distance and isolation when it came to the investigation and matters surrounding Randy's death.

I heard rumors that the formal investigation pertaining to Welby Way was completed and a hearing scheduled. Eagerly, I called James Hart and asked him about the hearing. I felt I was at their mercy since the preliminary report was vague, and a trial wasn't going to take place since Edwin Rivera was killed. In addition, the report showed several corrections, and I didn't know if that meant it had been modified or revised again. I figured that by now all the officers would have been interviewed and the details of the incident would surely be accurate. James said he would look into it and get back to me right away.

The following week, James came to see me to deliver another gift, as people were still sending beautiful mementos, awards, and gifts to me through him. He also had something else he wanted to deliver, and it wasn't something I wanted to receive. He had a message for me from the investigation committee, informing me that my request to attend the formal hearing of the shooting on Welby Way had been denied. He stated that the committee said it was an internal hearing, and only those in the Los Angeles Police Department could attend. I could see the stress on James's face, as he knew I was extremely disappointed. I looked at James with my mouth wide open, and I believe I said something like the following: "I'm not invited to any part? I can't hear any of it?" I was choked up with tears.

"It's internal, Lisa," he replied sympathetically.

Naturally, I was upset because I couldn't understand why it was a closed hearing. I also felt that someone in charge could have made provisions for me or set up another meeting to go over the details if I wasn't invited; however, that was the final answer and there was no further discussion. It may have just been my imagination, but I felt that my inquisitive mind was becoming a nuisance to them, almost like a pesky fly that would not go away. The denial also gave me the sense that although I was Randy's widow, I had no rights to the details about what happened that night. Apparently, I was supposed to be satisfied with just the knowledge that Edwin Rivera shot Randy in a SWAT call-up while Randy attempted to rescue hostages ... period. But I was not satisfied, and I wanted to know more. I had already started developing some new ideas and was going to try plan B.

"I want to talk to Johnny Verman," I said sternly to James.

My initial purpose for wanting to meet and talk with Johnny privately was simply to get a feel for how he was doing. I heard that he was having a hard time with what happened. He was devastated by Randy's death, and his fellow SWAT brothers were seriously concerned about his physical and mental state. I had seen him out on several occasions and spoken to him briefly, but our conversations were hypersensitive, and they never went beyond a *Hello, how are you and the kids?*

It was obvious that Johnny wanted to avoid seeing me altogether, for whenever I saw him, he always had someone close by his side, almost like a body guard, safeguarding our brief conversation. He would then respectfully but subtly divert his attention away from me. I was usually with one of my escorts—James, Steve, or Floyd—during those brief conversations, and I tried to figure out what was going on by reading the demeanor of my escorts. I thought that perhaps it was just me feeling the awkwardness. The others would justify Johnny's behavior, attributing it to his having a hard time with what occurred. Consequently, I decided for the time being to leave Johnny alone. I wasn't going to be the one to push him over the edge.

After a great deal of time had passed, I began to pursue Johnny again. Of course, I wanted to make sure he was doing okay, but also I needed Johnny to talk to me. I wanted him to map out the call-up so that I could visually see it. Different officers, including some who were there and some who weren't, gave me their versions about what happened. The stories were somewhat similar, but the details were not the same. I knew for sure that Johnny had firsthand knowledge of what happened that night, and I wanted his version, especially since he was the team leader on the call-up. More important, he was right there next to Randy when he was shot. The more he avoided talking to me, the more eager I became about getting his side of the story. Since my attending the hearing was declined, Johnny was now my last resort.

James Hart and several of the other officers got word to Johnny that I wanted to talk with him, but it was to no avail. On a fluke, I saw him at a SWAT dinner and asked him if we could get together and just have lunch and talk. Immediately, his disposition changed, as he went from being pleasant to being somewhat anxious about my invitation. He respectfully declined and said something indicating that he was still working through what happened. He wasn't ready to discuss anything. I was left with an uneasy thought that I might have to file this one away as unresolved.

To maintain a positive attitude, I chose to mentally separate the investigation from the honors that LAPD was bestowing on Randy and my friendship with the SWAT officers. I kept reminding myself about the old saying "It's nothing personal ... it's just business," since that was how this tragic incident was playing out. For LAPD, the investigation component was business, but for me everything pertaining to Randy was personal. Nonetheless, it was imperative that I separate the two so that I could move forward while at the same time continuing to honor Randy's memory.

It was interesting, to say the least, that whenever I met with higher-up officials in LAPD at different events, nothing was ever said pertaining to my denial at being able to participate in the investigation hearing. It made me wonder if they were even aware of my inquiries. All conversations focused strictly on Randy and his heroism, so I humbly conformed to the mood of the event and did my best to carry on.

In May of 2009, I was invited to attend the California Peace Officers' Memorial Ceremony in Sacramento, California, at the state capitol. Governor Arnold Schwarzenegger was presenting awards to the families of officers who were killed in the line of duty. It was a sad but beautiful event.

Thereafter, my family, relatives, and a few of my close friends attended National Police Week in Washington, DC. National Police Week is a huge event that usually occurs in the month of May the following year after an officer dies. It recognizes all United States law enforcement officers who were killed in the line of duty. The invitation had initially been extended to me in 2008, so the kids and I had to wait over a year before attending this important event. But we were excited about going, so it was worth the wait, as we'd heard so much about the different activities that went on throughout the week for surviving family members. We were also told that there was a good chance we were going to meet the president, for he usually attended these types of events. I couldn't help but think about what an honor that would be, especially for my children. They once had an opportunity to visit the White House for a weeklong school field trip to Washington, DC, but if they had the opportunity to meet the president, it was going to be the icing on the cake. How awesome it would be for them to meet President Obama while attending a memorial in honor of their father. I knew it would bring them so much joy, offsetting the sadness that usually comes when attending these events. And believe me—my children had their share of tears attending countless memorials for their dad.

As it turned out, the experience was awesome, as the Los Angeles Police Department represented LAPD and Randy in an extraordinary way. When my family and I landed in Washington, DC and departed the plane, the SWAT team and other officers were there to greet us in their sharp blue uniforms, saluting us as if we were high-level national dignitaries. I appreciated their presence at the airport and for their giving us such an esteemed greeting.

As we exited the airport, the LAPD motorcycle division was also there on their bikes, complete with sirens and flashing lights. Each motorcyclist had a unique sticker on his helmet, which touched my heart. The sticker had Randy's SWAT code, "41D," attached, so as they rode by, we knew exactly whom they were representing. It was unlike any event I had ever been to or experienced in my life.

As wonderful as it was to honor Randy, we were not there just to honor him but also to honor all the men and women who paid the ultimate sacrifice and put their lives on the line to protect and serve. There were busloads and busloads of families who shared a common interest with our family. Having lost people near and dear to our hearts, every person there was paying homage to loved ones. There were also police officers from every part of the United States representing their cities or states and all dressed in their sharpest uniforms. Some were escorting families; some participated in the motorcade; and others were in the hundreds of police cars that helped direct and stop traffic on the freeways. It was unbelievable, and the recognition was well deserved. I know that if there are windows in heaven, all the officers in heaven were giving their city and departments two thumbs up for such an amazing weeklong event.

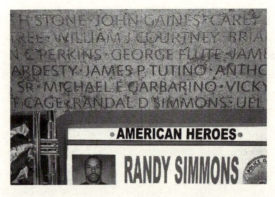

Randy's name is now etched in a National Memorial Monument for fallen officers during National Police Week in Washington DC.

Programs, badges, cards, placeholders in honor of our fallen hero who has now risen to a place we call our eternal home.

Officers salute surviving family members from all across the nation at National Police Week in Washington DC.

One of the highlights of the week was seeing Randy's name etched in the memorial monument along with thousands of other law enforcement officers who'd died in the line of duty, dating all the way back to the 1700s. We were able to take home a copy of the memorial by placing a piece of paper directly on Randy's name and rubbing it with a pencil until his name appeared visible on the paper. Another highlight was seeing the Los Angeles Police Protective League Unity Tour Cyclists ride in, coming all the way from Southern California in an attempt to bring awareness to the memorial that represented their fallen officers.

Then there was the candlelight vigil where each officer's name was read and a candle was lit in memory of that fallen officer. They also offered seminars to help grieving spouses, children, and other family members come to terms with the deaths of their loved ones. This was put on by Concerns of Police Survivors, Inc., also known as COPS.

Lastly there was a memorial ceremony where US Attorney General Eric Holder was the guest speaker. He honored officers for their great sacrifice and acknowledged the surviving families. After Eric Holder gave a heartfelt speech, singer and Grammy Award winner Patti Labelle did what she does best, and that was to sing her heart out with the touching song "Wind Beneath My Wings." I'd heard the lyrics so many times before, but on that day, they deeply resonated within my soul.

Following her spectacular performance was the Officers' Roll Call. As each officer's name was called, the immediate family went up to the podium with an escort. In our case, it was James Hart, at which time I pulled a flower from the beautiful red, white, and blue commemorative wreath. Hearing Randy's name called out over the speakers at this national event sent a wave of chills throughout my body. It was a somber yet exhilarating feeling, and we were so proud to take part in such an awesome and spectacular memorial.

President Obama was unable to attend the memorial ceremony due to other commitments, which was why Attorney General Holder stood in for him, expressing his utmost respect for the law enforcement profession. However, a day prior to our arrival in Washington, DC, my family and I learned that the Los Angeles Police Department SWAT team and some of their family members attended a private ceremony with the president. At the ceremony, he honored and recognized the SWAT team for their valor and service and for the incident that occurred on Welby Way. Ironically and unfortunately, this was the only ceremony that my children and I missed.

Various police officers told me that when LAPD booked our plane reservations, they didn't know that particular event was set to take place. I only wish I had been informed, as I would have happily paid for flight changes and rearranged our schedules so my kids and I could have met President Obama at a memorial that represented their father's sacrifice. My kids were puzzled and so disappointed, and they couldn't believe that of all the hundreds of events we attended in their father's honor, we missed one so special merely because of a "scheduling conflict."

I didn't want it to put a damper on the experience of being there, so I tried to lift the kids' spirits by reminding them as well as myself why we were in Washington, DC. It was to honor Randy and the other heroic officers.

Nevertheless, in an attempt to alleviate the disappointment my kids were feeling, SWAT officers Steve Scallon and R. J. Cottle scheduled two honorable events for the kids and me to attend. One was a tour of the White House, which Officer Steve Scallon was able to coordinate on our behalf. And Officer R.J. Cottle, also a Sergeant Major of the United States Marine Corps, arranged the other honorable event. It was monumental in that Matthew and Gabrielle had the opportunity to lay a wreath at the Tomb of the Unknown Soldiers at Arlington National Cemetery. I was unable to witness this honorable activity because I was at a seminar for grieving widows. However, later I explained to the kids the significance of such a sacred and respected honor. I reinforced the discussion that Steve and R. J. had with them earlier while participating in the wreath-laying ceremony, again explaining to them that this section of the cemetery was the burial grounds of soldiers who died fighting for the freedom of our country and whose remains are yet unknown. Thus they are laid to rest in Arlington National Cemetery. I further explained that we remember their sacrifice by paying homage and laying a wreath in their honor.

Matthew and Gabrielle were in awe of the patriotic opportunity that R. J. and Steve allowed them to experience. Sadly, the experience became of greater significance to them when we learned that SWAT Officer and Sergeant Major Robert "R. J." James Cottle was killed during combat operations on March 24, 2010, by a roadside bomb in Helmand

Province, Afghanistan. At forty-five, R. J. was younger than Randy was when he passed. The same officer who brought my kids to this sacred place where they honored our great soldiers had now joined the others who paid the ultimate sacrifice in defending our nation. Ironically, Randy and R. J. were on the same team in SWAT, and they both died doing something heroic.

We enjoyed our stay in Washington, DC, and every memorial brought about an array of emotions ranging from tears to laughter. However, we didn't let the sad emotions weigh us down; instead, we embraced and clung to the knowledge that we had the opportunity to honor the bravest and most courageous men and women of our nation in a phenomenal way.

After returning home, I was really missing Randy, so I tried to do things that made me feel close to him. My mother-in-law and I started talking on the phone more and paying visits to each other regularly. She and my sister-in-law Gina were attending events with us in addition to having Sunday dinners with the kids and me at the restaurant. I also took time out to visit with the Glory Kids. They all missed Randy so much and made claims that things just didn't seem the same without him. I knew how they felt because Matt, Gabby, and I felt the same way.

Then one day while I was sitting in my office staring at a picture of Randy, Matt, Gabby, and me, which I believe had been taken after a night service at church, I noticed in Randy's hand a black leather binder. I remembered browsing through his binder, which contained all the different activities that Randy wanted to carry out with the Glory Kids. Truthfully speaking, some of the activities were based on a wing and a prayer, as it would have been costly for the church to participate in the listed activities in Randy's book. Our church had a budget for every auxiliary, but Randy, having faith and hope, knew there was nothing too big for God to make happen. I smiled just thinking about all the times Randy and I robbed Peter to pay Paul so that we could help the Glory Kids. We had many intense dialogues over his continuous outpouring of love, but in the end, he always suckered me into coming to a total agreement in giving.

Honestly, before I knew Randy, I was a big giver, but he took giving to another level, and I was trying to play catch up. I guess subconsciously the thought of giving stayed on my mind because when I went to sleep that night, I tossed and turned, thinking about creating a foundation. My conscious state said, "No, no, no ... You're way too busy," but God was saying something else to me, and He was making it plain enough so that I could see the plan.

While I slept that night, the Holy Spirit was dealing with my heart on this issue, to the point of God showing me an image of the logo that would represent his foundation. It was a red heart divided by the cross in gold, giving the heart four quadrants. At the top of the heart, our wedding rings symbolized our oneness in the things of God. Each quadrant represented the things that Randy wanted to reach out and improve for these children: quality of life, education, health and wellness, and global outreach.

I jumped out of bed at about 5:00 a.m., opening the drapes of the picture window in my bedroom, trying to forget the thought that was laboring in my mind as well as the image I had just seen in my sleep. It was just before dawn, and the blue lights of the Long Beach Bridge were still shining brightly. The normally unpleasant view of the oil rigs that stood out in the day now lit up the city of Long Beach, giving it a beautiful heavenly image. As tears flowed from my eyes like a faucet, I sat there thinking about Randy and all he had given to this life. My inner being could hear Randy's voice asking me not to ignore what God had placed on my heart but instead to be obedient to what would first seem like a task but would ultimately become a joy. It was no longer just Randy's purpose to do outreach and to help people like the Glory Kids; it had now become mine, along with a committee of others that God saw fit to help see this mission through to fruition.

That same morning, I called my attorney friend Denise Beaudoin and asked her to put things in motion for a foundation in Randy's name. It would be called the Randal D. Simmons Outreach Foundation. I wanted the Glory Kids to know that although Randy was gone, his legacy would live on through his foundation and, more importantly, through God's grace.

By creating the foundation, other foundations reached out to help lend their support of the Glory Kids. One of the foundations that stands out in my mind is the Good News Foundation, with news anchorwoman Wendy Burch, Pat Harvey, Dorothy Lucey, Ana Garcia, Christine, Devine and Marc Brown, to name a few. They had a wonderful fund-raiser for Randy's foundation held in Santa Monica and donated money as well as a minivan to transport the Glory Kids on various field trips. They were very supportive before and after Randy's death.

Another organization that stands out for more reasons than one is the Water Buffalo Club. The Water Buffalo Club donated a nice amount and was kind enough to extend a fun field trip for the Glory Kids to the Santa Monica Pier.

While attending the Water Buffalo Club ceremony in Brentwood, California, I had an experience that I truly believe was led by divine intervention. Prior to the ceremony starting, I was in the lobby with my escort, James Hart. We were eating hors d'oeuvres and drinking a beverage when a woman walked up to me and introduced herself. Her name was Carmen Taylor-Jones.

"Ms. Simmons, I want to first say how sorry I am for your loss. I know you don't know who I am, but my daughter was the young lady who was killed in Long Beach at a party a month before your husband passed away."

I put one hand over my month and grabbed her hand with the other. I then gave her a big hug. In a flash, I remembered the day her daughter was killed as if it were yesterday. I was preparing food for a big Sunday dinner I was having the next day. Randy came in from work, running up the stairs and then rushing and yelling from upstairs that he had to go back out. He came down the stairs holding his Bible. I recall him giving me a kiss good-bye and telling me that he wouldn't be home for dinner because of a tragedy that happened with some teenagers in Long Beach.

Some teens were having a party when some uninvited gangbangers came in and started shooting like crazy. The teens were devastated and therefore required some counseling and prayer. I rushed him off so he could go see about the kids, and I prayed that no one was seriously injured. Later that night, when he returned home, he was clearly shaken by the events surrounding the party in Long Beach. He told me that two innocent young teens had been killed while just having fun at a party. He was sad and angry, and so was I.

This woman standing before me at the Buffalo Club fund-raiser was the mother to one of the victims. Sadly, her daughter died. She died on Carmen's birthday while she was out of town. Her daughter, Breon

Taylor, was fifteen years old. The other young victim, Dennis Moses Jr., was seventeen years old. They weren't targets, just teens hit by random gunfire.

Carmen continued to express how Randy counseled and prayed with the teens. She said that his presence and spiritual guidance did more than he could ever imagine in helping those devastated teens that night. Because of Randy's guidance, the teens formed a Bible study group that still meets to this day.

After we connected, I asked her if she knew I was going to be at the Water Buffalo Club fund-raiser. She informed me that she was invited by a friend and had no idea she was going to be attending an event honoring Randy's foundation until she got to the affair in Brentwood, California. To this day, in some miraculous and spiritual way, she and I are still divinely connected.

Hearing her story just reaffirmed the concept about why community outreach is so important. I thought about how someone's child was buried and another person's child was now serving a sentence in jail. I then thought about how mentors could have intervened in that young man's life and turned him away from a life of violence and crime. Perhaps Breon and Dennis would still be here today.

That was exactly what Randy was trying to do when he fought hard to get community leaders, churches, schools, and citizens in the community to understand. He wanted people to come together and mentor inner-city youth, especially the troubled youth, for he wanted to bring about a positive change. Ideally, core values begin at home, but when that isn't available, and a child does not receive the help needed from the parents, there should be a mentor available or a place in the community where the child can go to obtain the help that nurtures those values. These types of programs once existed, but they have fallen away. The activities that once were in the school system, such as the creative arts—i.e., music, dance, singing—and technical trade classes—such as automotive mechanics, electronics, carpentry, and home economics—no longer exist. Unfortunately, many of them have been eliminated because of budget cuts.

Randy felt that our teens needed positive role models and activities as a way of diverting their attention away from negative elements they were attracted to like magnets. He felt that we had done the teens a great disservice and injustice by taking away meaningful things that once cultivated and added value to their lives, starting with prayer and the Pledge of Allegiance in schools. Based on that belief, my board members and I have made a personal commitment to reach out and support mentor groups like the Randal D. Simmons Metropolitan Explorer Post #114, under the leadership of Officer Nicole "Nikki" Evans and Officer Willie Fajardo.

It's amazing how just a few loyal and dedicated people can change the lives of many kids simply by providing positive reinforcement. I have observed Nikki and Willie around the teen Explorers, some of whom are Glory Kids. I have watched them develop the kids into fine young men and women who walk with confidence and have respect for authority. Because of their mentorship, these teens have developed structure, critical thinking, and life skills that will stay with them through life's journey.

## CHAPTER 28

# A Twist in the Maze

ONE AFTERNOON, I WAS INVITED to support one of the LAPD cadet programs at Reseda High School. While there, a Latino student of about thirteen years of age, walking with a middle-aged Caucasian woman who appeared to be a teacher, approached me.

I was taken aback when I saw the student, as he was crying hysterically. I thought, *What the heck is wrong with this kid?* The woman accompanying him, the one I thought was a teacher, introduced herself to me, telling me she was a counselor. She also introduced the student, but his name escapes me, as I was distracted by his emotional behavior. My motherly instincts surfaced immediately, and I recall touching his face, trying to comfort him by giving him a hug and attempting to calm him down. The counselor and I waited patiently for him to settle down so that he could speak, at which time he began to cry again.

"Mrs. Simmons, I am so sorry. That guy that killed Officer Simmons was my cousin."

He continued to cry even more as I hugged him and listened intently to the words he was trying to get out of his mouth. "I was there that day. I had just left the house when my uncle and cousins were killed. I miss them. They were good guys, but Edwin had problems."

He paused for a moment and then looked me straight in the face. Speaking clearly, he said, "I made five crosses over at the house and put them on the grass. Four were for my family and one was for Officer Simmons. I put his name on the cross."

After talking with the young man, I gave him another big hug and told him how thankful I was that he thought of Officer Simmons—and how pleased I was that he'd made him a cross. Holding back tears, I thanked the counselor as well for allowing him to share his story with me. I then walked away, slowly glancing back at them as they left.

When they were no longer in sight, I made a mad dash to my car. I was in the city of Reseda, a few miles away from the city of Winnetka, and I had been contemplating whether I should go to the lot and see where the incident took place. This meeting with the young boy was reason enough for me to listen to my curiosity and eliminate any reluctance. I was going to go and see the cross that this young man made for my husband.

My car was parked on a busy street, so I had to wait for traffic to stop before getting in. I was so anxious and nervous that I dropped my keys in the street, along with a program booklet I had in my hand. I got in my car and started it up, sitting there with my hands on the wheel. A thought came to me that was frustrating. "Dang it!" I said, talking aloud to myself while hitting the steering wheel. "I don't know the address."

The only thing I knew was that it was on Welby Way. Not allowing that to stop me, I entered the street and city into the navigational system in my car and hit ENTER. I knew the navigational system would at least get me to the right street. The rest I would have to figure out through some deductive reasoning and a process of elimination. I remembered the detectives who came to my house telling me that the house was burned down because of the fire, that it was demolished. All I had to do was look for an empty lot with five crosses on it.

As luck would have it, Welby Way was a peculiar street that had lots of dead ends and twists and turns. Being unfamiliar with the area, I found myself getting lost and going into other parts of the city. But I was too close to give up. I was determined to see the lot and the crosses, so I knew I wasn't about to turn around and go home. I guess in the back of my mind I wanted to see the place where my dear husband lost his life and made his departure. I knew the records stated that Randy died at the hospital, but the notes in the records and what Officer Tony Samuelson told me when he rescued him indicated that Randy was making his journey to heaven at the site on Welby Way.

I decided to call my now-BFF (best friend forever), James Hart, to ask him for the address. I hesitated, though, because I knew I would first have to go through an interrogation to obtain it. James was always concerned about my mental and physical health, and if I called him, I would have to explain why I wanted the address. James was already worried because The Reseda High School Police Academy Magnet program was one of the first events he hadn't escorted me to since Randy's death. He felt bad about not being able to attend due to personal time off, and I didn't want to call and worry him on his day off. But I had no choice. I was comfortable enough with James to know that if I asked him for the address, he wouldn't think I was losing my mind or going crazy. I pulled my car over to the curb and called him on my cell. I had it planned out exactly as to how I was going to ask him. I was going to act as though I were in a rush so there would be no chitchat and no long dialogue. This would prompt him to hurry up and give me an address before he could really think about why I was asking.

When he picked up the call, the conversation went something like this: "Hey, James. Listen, I'm sorry to bother you, but I just have a quick question. What's the address on Welby Way?" I asked, talking fast.

"What?" James replied

"Address on Welby Way ... What is it?" I repeated this with urgency and in a rushed tone.

"Wait ... wait ... wait, *Lisa*. Push the pause button!" he said.

That was James's favorite phrase, "Push the pause button." He would say it and make a hand motion by drawing up his forearm with his fist balled signaling me to stop. Just as I thought, he was going to give me the third degree and take me through a series of questions before giving me the address of the house on Welby Way. After explaining to James the episode that took place with the Rivera cousin at Reseda High School and the handmade crosses he made, James said just what I thought he would say.

"Wait for me, Lisa. I'll go with you."

Randy and James were always clowning around. I can see why Randy liked James so much. He is a very caring and respectable man who has a heart of gold.

That was typical of my BFF, as he was always there to assist or support me, no matter what was going on. I'm going to "push the pause button" here because I want to share a few details about how kind Officer Hart has been to my family and me.

Prior to Randy's death, I knew Officer James Hart, but not as I know him now. From time to time, he would visit our church with Randy or join Randy at a family barbecue during a holiday if they were working together and on duty. But during that time, that was the extent of our acquaintance. After Randy died, it seemed as if James made it his mission to be sure the kids and I were okay. He was my primary escort to the countless ceremonies that we attended in Randy's name, supporting us through the darkest days of our lives. He too was grieving, so I guess in a sense, being close to the family gave him a sense of feeling closer to Randy.

It's no coincidence that he and Randy were good friends and partners. I believe that God brings certain people into our lives for a reason, for God knows our beginnings and our ends. He knew that a tragic day like February 7, 2008, would happen, and that Randy would need someone who was loyal, compassionate, consistent, patient, kind, and respectful to see after his family. He knew it would take a special man like Officer James Hart to take on this difficult yet honorable responsibility.

We would drive to various events sharing Randy stories, sometimes the same ones repeatedly, as if we were hearing them for the first time, laughing and even crying together. Without a doubt, James had a sincere loyalty to his partner, which was evident by the consistent commitments he made to the entire family. James wholeheartedly covered his partner by protecting and being there for his wife and kids during a tragic time. Because of his faithfulness to his partner, Randy, he, and I developed a true friendship, and I will always be eternally grateful for his thoughtfulness.

Over time, James and I got to know each other very well, and our conversations at times were like those of a brother and sister, with me of course being the difficult one and James frustrated and scolding me about my high-maintenance behavior. Needless to say, going to Welby Way perturbed him, as he didn't think that it was a good idea from an emotional standpoint. He saw that I was making progress emotionally and knew that time was slowly healing my broken heart, and James felt strongly that this could possible render a setback.

After talking to James for about five minutes and listening to his line of questioning and his insisting that I wait for him to go with me the next week, I somewhat agreed to his request. But only so I could get off the phone and complete my mission. However, I still asked him for the address. He hesitated but reluctantly gave it to me. I thanked James, hung up the phone, and then made a mad dash over to 17277 Welby Way. I felt bad for telling James that little white lie, but I had to do what I had to do to get the address.

I have to admit that at times I drove James crazy. He had the patience of Job dealing not just with me but also my sisters, Gina, Gabby, my nieces, and the two mothers, not to mention my group of friends. He was always surrounded by dozens of cackling women, so he was frequently asking us to "push the pause button."

Oh, I know without a doubt that when he gets to heaven, he's going to have a mouthful to give Randy about his early departure and the responsibility he left for him. Contrary to it all, I believe James enjoyed and loved the fact that we needed him to be there for us. However, going to Welby Way was a task I wanted to pursue alone.

When I turned onto the street of Welby Way, my heart started to palpitate. I imagined I was going to be nervous, but I didn't expect to feel my heart pounding instantly the way it did. I drove down the street, slowly looking at addresses. There was no need to watch for a street number, though, because I could see from a distance an approximately eight-foot-high chain-link fence with flowers all over it, complete with old ribbon and debris that looked like broken glass candleholders, cards, and posters. Strangely, within the gate, I saw a house. It was a dilapidated house whose windows were boarded up. Naturally, I was confused because the detectives told me that because of the fire, the house was completely torn down. I started shaking like a leaf. I didn't think I would react the way I did, but I couldn't help it. My body would not stop shaking, mostly from feeling puzzled and afraid. I didn't know what to think. Seeing that the house existed put me in a paranoid state of mind. As the adrenalin coursed through my body, I began to look around, using both my side view and rearview mirrors, but I didn't know who or what I was looking for. I couldn't believe how small the house was and that it was still standing. It looked so much bigger on television. I also couldn't believe how close the windows were to the front door, nor could I believe that based on the size of the house, Randy and the other officers decided to enter in the way they did. By no stretch of the imagination am I an expert, but at some point, logic as it pertains to safety has to kick in over procedures. As far as I was concerned, nothing was adding up. My perplexed reaction had nothing to do with being an emotional widow, but now I was stepping out as a friend who was concerned about the safety of the rest of the officers I had come to know and love.

Someone had a lot of explaining to do about this so-called hostage rescue procedure. I needed to understand the logic in entering through the front door of a small, dark house with no knowledge of the suspect's whereabouts. An array of emotions washed over me, ranging from anger to sadness. I needed some answers.

I took a couple of deep breaths and slowly stepped out of my car. I walked up to the fence and looked at the makeshift memorial with all the cards, decayed ribbon, and old artificial flowers that were barely attached to the fence. A lot of the writing on the notes was old, as it had been months since the incident, and the weathered elements had taken their toll on the memorial. My eyes were directed to the only picture that seemed to still be visible. It was a picture of Edwin Rivera, his father, and his brothers. They looked as if they were at a wedding or some formal event, as they were all dressed in tuxedos. Interesting enough, they were all hugging and smiling, appearing to be having a good time, except for Edwin Rivera. Honestly, there was no expression on his face that indicated or gave a sign that there was a soul in his body. He looked like someone who was angry at the world and had lost his soul.

Unlike his father and brothers, you could not see any expression of laughter or any sort of contentment. Instead, his face showed the opposite, although he was in the group hugging with them. I stood there and thought, *Wow, how could anyone commit such a heinous crime against his family members?* This was truly a crime committed by a sick man. Edwin Rivera should never have been released from a 5150 hold, which means that if there was a reason and probable cause to believe that Edwin Rivera was a danger to himself or to others, he would have been put on a seventy-two-hour hold. After the hold, he would be evaluated and a decision would be made on whether he should be released. This is common practice with people who have some sort of mental disorder.

The house on Welby Way still stands after four years.

The house is considered an eye sore to the neighbors and a constant reminder of the horrific incident. Photo taken June- 2012.

After looking at the makeshift memorial and feeling shocked at seeing the house, I had almost forgotten why I had come to the location in the first place. So I walked up and down the sidewalk, trying to find a clear spot on the fence to position my body so I could peek through the fence and see the crosses. I found an opening and located the five crosses that were placed in the ground in the front yard of the house. Just the thought of this young man taking the time to make not only his uncle and cousins a cross but Randy as well made me cry. I thanked God for this young man and thanked Him for sparing his young life. As he stated, he was there in the house right before Edwin snapped and started the shooting rampage. He was still in counseling, trying to work through this horrific ordeal.

Just as I was getting ready to turn around and head to my car, a neighbor walked up to me. She was a short Latino woman who appeared to be walking home from the store. She took notice of me based on my tears and then recognized my face since I had been on the news. She expressed her condolences with a heavy Latin accent and tried to console me. It was from her that I learned of the information she received from her sons, who used to play with the Rivera boys.

She said that the Rivera boys were typical teens and at times a little mischievous, but nothing out of the ordinary. As she continued to ramble on, a repairman who was unlocking the gate that surrounded the Rivera house interrupted us. While she was still talking about the characteristics of the boys, my attention was directed toward the repairman, who had keys to get inside the fence. I politely excused myself from the woman and said my good-byes as I walked over to the repairman.

I dried my tears and tried not to show any emotion. The repairman had opened the fence and closed it, but he left it unlocked. As he was walking toward the door, I quickly opened the fence and walked in behind him, following him to the door of the house. He heard my footsteps, turned around, and politely said with a puzzled look, "Ma'am, you have to go back. No one is allowed in here."

I didn't know what to say, so I had to use my sales skills quickly to say something convincing. I responded by saying, "Please, sir, I just want to see what it looks like inside. I have a client that is interested in purchasing the house."

"I can't, ma'am. I can get in trouble for letting you come this far on the property site. You're actually trespassing."

Getting emotional, I looked him directly in the eye, pointed to Randy's cross, and said, "Do you see that cross over there? My husband's name is on it. I just want to see where his spirit left. Where he possibly fell to his death ... Please ... just for a minute."

Stunned and suddenly realizing who I was, he said, "I know exactly who you are." He seemed a little moved by my comment. "I don't see you," he said as he walked into the house and straight to the back.

I waited until he was clearly out of sight and walked in slowly, but not before seeing the wall where the initial flash bang hit, which I was told caused it to malfunction. I walked around it slowly and saw a ramshackle house. It was trashed, and all over were belongings customary to most homes, including a comb, sunglasses, towels, a cup, and some papers that looked like bills. I looked on the floor and saw what appeared to be blood droppings. That sight paralyzed my body, and I couldn't take another step. I just looked straight ahead, where right before me was a hallway. It was the hallway where Edwin Rivera was hiding when he shot Randy and Johnny Verman. I stood there discombobulated, looking all around in disbelief. The inside of the house reflected the outside—small with extremely tight quarters. While standing there in a state of shock, I heard a voice loudly call out my name.

"Lisa! What are you doing in here? I knew you were coming here. I told you to wait!"

It was James Hart. By now, he knew my personality and had a hunch that contrary to his request for me to wait, I was going to the Rivera house.

"James, I had to see. I'm just trying to figure this thing out," I replied. "Look at it; this place is so small. What were they thinking?" I knew I was looking at him with an expression of perplexity.

James looked around, clearly amazed, and agreed with me about the small size of the house. Then abruptly he refocused and insisted on us getting out of the house. This was a sight he didn't want me to see, let alone be in. James and I walked off the property and stood by our cars, where we continued to converse about the house and the misinformation the detectives had given me. James was right there when they told us that the house no longer existed. I trusted that the little information they had given me was true. I was disappointed and frustrated. I felt deceived. I was angry and fed up with being left out of knowing exactly what measures had been taken to prevent my husband's death. No one that I needed to talk to was willing to talk to me. Johnny Verman was still having his issues, and for the life of me, I couldn't understand why no one on the investigation committee would sit down and share with me the final findings.

Unfortunately for James, he was my sounding board. He was going to hear my mouth as he had on so many other occasions, and he always listened with compassion and concern. But little did I know that today James was going to deliver some tough love. I started in on my ranting.

"James, they told me that the house was completely demolished!"

"I think they just didn't know, Lisa. They saw the house on fire and assumed it was demolished."

"What about the autopsy report that was finally delivered to me?"

"What about it?" James asked.

"There are errors in it, and I'm missing several pages."

"Lisa, you can order your own report."

"I tried to call and order a report just recently. Five staff members told me that Randy Simmons or the number that was provided did not exist. His name and case number are not even in the system. What the heck is going on?"

"What?" James said, surprised by this newfound information.

"I finally talked with a supervisor who informed me that the report stayed with the examiner's office because of security reasons. I want my husband's complete report! I shouldn't have to go through all these changes!" I was yelling, breaking down.

Trying to think rationally, James, in an effort to calm me down, said, "I'm sure there's an explanation for all of this."

"That's my point!" I exclaimed. "Why is it so hard for you all to give it to me? The investigation report that was given to me is inaccurate. Why can't I get a formal investigation committee to simply explain all the bizarre stuff that's going on? Why is it so hard to obtain actual facts about my husband's death? And I still don't know to this day who the heck Stephanie Pears is!" I shouted.

"Who?" James asked.

"That's the fictitious name on Randy's medical records," I replied.

By this time, James had had enough. He wasn't perturbed by my inquisitive behavior but was now concerned about my mental state of mind. He saw that I was becoming obsessed and emotionally overwhelmed by not knowing all the things surrounding Randy's death. He could tell it was getting to me and perhaps to him as well. I'm sure at times he felt as though he was in the middle and helpless.

In a compassionate but stern voice, James gave it to me straight. He told me something he had said before, but this time he ended it with a profound twist. He said that it was obvious that things didn't go the way SWAT had planned or Randy would be still alive today. He further said that it is because of the tragic outcome that so many of the officers are still affected today. He agreed that some of the facts were still not as clear as they should be, but all the information that I received from other officers and people was, for the most part, what actually happened. For James and the others, it was hard to believe that SWAT lost its first SWAT member, which happened to be one of their best ... Randy.

He concluded by saying, "Lisa, the bottom line is this. You know as well as I that Randy would have done anything to save those people's lives if he could, even if that meant risking his own. That was the type of man he was. You know that."

James had said what he had to say, leaving me speechless. He gave me a hug, kissed my forehead, and got in his vehicle, taking off and leaving me with a few things to think about. My BFF had spoken. What I liked most about James was that he wasn't going to make any excuses about the call-up, nor was he going to disregard the fact that I had a difficult time because I was not getting information accurately and formally. He spoke the truth, and one thing that I had to agree with was the fact that Randy would have laid down his life to save anyone in need. He was 41 D, a man of valor. I had to accept that fact and move on.

## CHAPTER 29

# Honors and Dedications

THE MEDAL OF VALOR IS a prestigious award and the highest honor given by the Los Angeles Police Department. It is given to those officers who have shown extraordinary bravery above and beyond police service. Matthew, Gabrielle, and I were at the event to proudly receive this highly regarded award on Randy's behalf. The new chief of police, Charlie Beck, had the honor of handing over the Medal of Valor to Matthew, hanging it around his neck as Gabrielle and I looked on.

Someone once said that the eyes are the windows to the soul. Whether you believe that or not, there's something about looking into the eyes of a person, as it often gives you a hint into his or her character. And although I don't profess to know Chief Beck, something about the sincerity in his eyes and his passion for his officers made me feel his genuineness.

I had the opportunity of hearing him speak on several occasions and each time he did, I was left with a lump in my throat. Although extremely articulate, he doesn't use large, meaningless words, nor does he say things because they sounded politically correct. He speaks from the heart, which is what I most appreciate about him.

On the day he gave us the Medal of Valor award he expressed with sincere passion his admiration and respect for the valor his police officers demonstrate as they go out into the streets, fighting the war on crime every day. Perhaps his own experience of losing a partner allows him to truly identify with the ultimate sacrifice that men and women like Randy courageously make in an effort to keep our streets safer. Whatever the reason, I truly like his genuine disposition, as it radiates from behind his badge and all through his blues.

Among all the award ceremonies, I think one of the most touching ceremonies I attended was the recent inaugural of the Purple Heart award. Unfortunately, Matthew was away at college and Gabrielle had tests that day, so it was just my mom, sisters, Gina, and I attending. I regretted that Gabby and Matt missed it because it was such a special ceremony. It was held at the JW Marriott in downtown Los Angeles and was sponsored by the Los Angeles Police Foundation. The Purple Heart ceremony honored eighty-two LAPD officers who died in the line of duty as early as the 1900s. These officers were recognized for their acts of heroism, thus sacrificing their lives to keep us safe. Many received awards for serious injuries, and others, like Randy, received awards for fatal injuries.

What was most interesting about this award ceremony was that many of the recipients accepting awards were either mature children or young children of officers. There was a son and a grandson, both well over sixty-five years of age, accepting an award. They'd lost their dad and grandfather, respectively, an LAPD officer, in the early 1900s. Then two little boys no older than five years of age accepted an award for their dad's heroism, a man who passed away in the line of duty. It saddened me to think that as years pass, they might have a hard time remembering their father.

A son walked up to honor his mother, Tina Kerbrat, who died in 1991, the first female officer in LAPD's history to be killed in the line of duty. Her son was now a young man, which meant he was just a little boy when she died because she stopped two men to question them about drinking in public. It was a senseless crime and a senseless death. I so wished Matthew and Gabrielle could have been there to witness this special ceremony where others walked in their shoes.

After the ceremony, a man in his mid-thirties approached me and introduced himself. He'd heard a lot about Randy and wanted to meet me. He shared with me that when his father died, he was about seven years old. He was remembering that his father had just been scolded by his mother for buying him a skateboard that she thought was too dangerous. His father, knowing that his son wanted a skateboard so much, was willing to take the scolding from his wife in stride. Hours later, his father was killed in the line of duty. Although his father's death occurred approximately twenty-five years earlier, he told the story as if it happened yesterday. It was almost as if some part of him had been captured in time and he still lived in that moment.

I can see the same thing taking place with Matt, Gabby, and myself. Our memories allow us to live in a given moment even when it's just for a matter of seconds. Not only does it console our hearts, but it helps us when we can feel, see, touch, and hear our loved one. Life for others moves on much faster in comparison to life for the brokenhearted family. Our memories of Randy will always be fresh, just like the young man whose father bought him the skateboard.

In addition to the formal honors, the officers of LAPD had their own special way of honoring Randy. A few days ago, I was looking at some pictures of the Randy Simmons 5K run fund-raiser. A woman named Alicia Alcantar, along with the entire Metropolitan Division, had spearheaded the fund-raiser. Alicia, like Randy, has a passion for helping children in underserved areas, so she works tirelessly along with other officers to assure that the 5K is a successful event. Thinking about her efforts made me contemplate the awesome legacy Randy left behind.

It was clear that Randy had touched so many lives by what he achieved. And because of the role he played in making a difference, it rubbed off on others, including me. It inspired so many people to see what one person could achieve and how those achievements could make such a tremendous impact on the lives of others.

Because of what they saw, a number of people began to step up and extend themselves in acts of service, while other volunteer leaders took their acts and good deeds to the next level, creating and organizing charitable events. The Randal Simmons 5K run is one of those events.

During the 5K, the city of Los Angeles joins LAPD, with men, women, boys, and girls of all ages, and comes together in full workout gear to honor not just Randy but the things he stood for, such as love, hope, and faith, especially to those in underserved areas. The 5K usually ends with the teens from the Randal D. Simmons Metropolitan Explorer Post #114, the LAPD Cadets, and other LAPD teams or divisions competing in a fitness challenge. Afterwards, I have the pleasure of passing out awards.

Then there is the Los Angeles Police Department West Valley Police Division, who sponsors the annual motorcycle ride, spearheaded by Officer Lyle Michelson. This is such an awesome event, with bikers riding in from different cities and counties all over the state of California. Even bikers from across the country and out of the country, from as far away as China, have participated in this spectacular event. It occurs every summer in August, with hundreds of bikes lined up to ride along our beautiful coast. It's amazing to see freeways and streets closed to allow the bikers safe access along the routes from West Valley to Malibu, from Malibu to Hollywood, and usually ending at Paramount Studios. More than twenty vendors are available, delicious foods are catered, and a live band completes the event.

This monumental fund-raiser usually benefits several worthy causes in addition to the Randal D. Simmons Foundation, including the Los Angeles Police Memorial Foundation, led by Executive Director Alan Atkins. It is an amazing event, and it gets larger and larger every year.

Then there are the beautiful dedication ceremonies from various cities, where Randy has a pedestrian walking bridge, a recreational park, and a freshman high school building named after him in his honor. Rancho Palos Verdes was the first city to honor Randy's memory with a pedestrian bridge; called the Officer Randal Simmons Memorial Bridge, it is located at Marilyn Ryan Sunset Point Park. It's in a breathtaking location that overlooks the ocean and Donald Trump's National Golf Club.

As I think back, I recall passing this bridge with Randy while it was being built. We were on our way to celebrate our anniversary dinner at Donald Trump's restaurant, and little did I know that it was going to become his special bridge ... or that it was going to be our last anniversary dinner together.

Rancho Palos Verdes also had a fabulous ceremony on the park lawn, with canopies and catered food, to celebrate the dedication of Randy's bridge. I will never forget that touching affair.

Another astonishing dedication was the LAPD SWAT Officer Randal Simmons Park, located in the city of Reseda. Councilman Dennis Zine, once a police officer for LAPD, with twenty-eight years on duty and a friend of Randy's, was instrumental in making sure the park was named after Randy. A huge memorial dedication plaque with a thank-you to Randy for his service sits on a beautiful rock near the children's play area. The park is so beautiful, and it defines the vitality of Randy's spirit and embodies the things he loved, such as the outdoors, nature, and most of all, a safe place where kids can play and run free. The Randal D. Simmons Foundation celebrated the dedication of Randy's park by busing over four hundred Glory Kids to partake in a big picnic with food, games, and rides. Each of the Glory Kids received a T-shirt with Randy's face imprinted on it, along with a quote referring to the scripture verse reaffirming God's promise: *God had a purpose and a plan for my life* (Jeremiah 29:11) They also received a picture to take home so they would never forget their mentor and his teachings. I bet our angel was among us that day.

The most recent dedication actually surprised me. It was a dedication that Councilman Mike Gipson labored to see come to fruition. It started when I was invited to a meeting in the city of Carson to discuss and vote on whether a new high school in Carson would be named after Randy. A number of people were there giving their thoughts and opinions about the recommendation of Randy's name for the school. The city council of Carson voted, and it was unanimous. The school was going to be named after Randy.

I went home and shared the news with the kids, family members, and friends, as it was truly an exciting achievement. I was very proud of what Randy had accomplished in his life—and extremely proud that he was given this high honor in his death.

Two and a half months later, sadly, I received a call from Councilman Mike Gipson, telling me that they wanted to rescind Randy's name. I later learned that the reasoning behind the change of vote was because they didn't feel that they had considered the concerns of the local residents, who some say wanted the school named after the farm workers union leader Cesar Chavez.

I recall a council member making a speech on the goodness of Randy during the community council meeting. He stated that his regret was that he didn't get a chance to know him. I remember his comments as if they were yesterday because I thought they were so heartfelt. I regret that others in the city of Carson who changed their votes didn't know Randy in the same way, for if they knew him, they would have known that he was all about the heart.

His love for children and their families wasn't predicated on their skin color but rather on their need. Thus Randy diligently served Carson for years, never seeking recognition. Why did he do it? Because he saw a community that had a need, and he extended himself to that community in an effort to make it a better place to live, not just for one particular nationality or ethnicity but for all. A good man is a good man, regardless of his race.

Naturally, I was disappointed that the city of Carson made the decision to rescind Randy's name from the school. However, much to my surprise, a year later I received another call from Councilman Mike Gipson, letting me know the good news. He stated that Randy's name had been selected as part of the Rancho Dominguez High School freshman building in Carson. It would be called the Randal Simmons Freshman Success Academy School.

I applaud Mike Gipson's efforts, for he admired Randy's humanitarian spirit and was adamant that a school or a building should be named in his memory. He relentlessly tried to get his recommendation approved, and he did.

I immediately contacted our church, Glory Christian Fellowship, located in Carson, the church that supported Mike Gipson in his recommendation. I informed them of the latest decision and the news of confirmation that the city of Carson had agreed to name a building in the high school after Randy. Walter Clark, a representative from the church, as well as the SWAT team, and the Randal D. Simmons Outreach board members were present, acknowledging once again an exceptional honor in Randy's name. I look forward to many other monumental dedications honoring this man of valor.

# CHAPTER 30

# My New Normal

THE YEARS PASSED, AND IT seemed as though the days were getting shorter and the nights were getting longer. Matthew was preparing to leave for college, having received a football scholarship from Randy's alma mater, Washington State, and Gabrielle was enjoying her last year in high school and preparing for college. We were all trying to adjust and find our new normal.

The ceremonies had started to slow down quite a bit, which gave me more time to engage in activities with my kids, work with the Glory Kids through Randy's foundation, and participate with the teens in the Randal Simmons Explorer Post. I enjoyed being around all the young people, as they kept me feeling energetic and young, especially while on field trips: snowboarding, swimming, picnicking, or daring me to go on the sky-high roller coasters at amusement parks. However, at the end of the day, I would come home to an empty, quiet house, where I would look forward to reading my mail and getting a card from the wonderful women of the LAPD Family Support Group; they would send cards and newsletters throughout the year, letting me know that I was loved and not forgotten. Their thoughtfulness always lifted my spirits. After reading my mail, I would then retreat to my room and take a shower, turn on the news, and call my mother, mother-in-law, or sisters. But every night would usually end the same, with me clinging to Randy's pillow and crying myself to sleep. I was really missing my bed buddy.

Although attending the ceremonies had slowed down, the invitations kept coming, but I became very selective about which of them I would accept. Some events that were highly significant weren't optional, and although it felt as if I had been to hundreds of them, each time I attended another event, it still pierced my heart, reminding me of Randy's vivacious life that no longer existed.

Since Randy died, people have said all sorts of things to me about my grief. With good intentions, some have said, "Lisa, you have to let him go and move on." Others have said, "You're grieving too long." Still others have said, "You're becoming obsessed with him, and you're idolizing him." They would say all sorts of things, but they could not understand that it was not their loved one who had died. My response to those comments is that everyone has to work through grief in their own way and in their own time. Under the circumstances, I think my children and I have done very well, as we continue to forge ahead regardless of the circumstances.

I would be remiss if I didn't admit that it's definitely more difficult to heal and to adjust to a new life when you're constantly reminded of what was once there. But regardless, I believed that in due time, God would help us find our new normal. He usually blesses us with something special when we least expect it or deserve it.

On another night, while attending a fabulous formal affair at USC, sponsored by the National Organization of Black Law Enforcement Executives (also known as NOBLE), an array of mixed emotions were stirred up. At this particular event, the organization was honoring Deputy Chief Kenny Gardner and Police Officer Randy Simmons. Kenny was the friend of Randy's who took sick at Randy's funeral. Sadly, Kenny passed away due to a heart attack at age fifty-three. It now became obvious that he was possibly having health challenges at Randy's funeral, thus causing him to pass out twice.

When it came time to honor Randy, a moving video of his life was played. I had seen bits and pieces of the video at other functions; however, this time very little music was played. Instead, it displayed Randy in action, training and talking, as if he were right there with us. I wanted to reach up to the video screen and just touch him. It was so surreal that it sent my emotions spinning out of control. But as always, I kept my composure, manning up and only showing evidence of tears as I accepted the award on his behalf. I looked at my sister Cookie and my friend Simone, whose emotions also got the best of them. There we were, the three of us, trying to look pretty as we floated around in evening gowns, but we were looking a mess, for our waterproof mascara failed to do all that it had promised.

Soon after the event was over, we headed to the restaurant, where things were still in full force. We had a huge birthday party going on, and Melinda had stayed behind to manage it. She was blowing up our cell phones, wanting us to get to the restaurant as soon as possible to help out. She was upset that I had booked a large birthday party and understaffed our servers for the night. She was expecting Cookie and me to come in and help work the party, even though we were in our evening attire. Needless to say, she wasn't interested in hearing the complaint of a torn ligament in my knee and the fact that I was limping. She had no sympathy for me.

When we arrived at the restaurant, Simone was concerned about my state of mind after feeling so emotional at the lovely but sad event. I was reconsidering going into the restaurant, as it was packed with people. I was so afraid that people would notice that my eyes were red from crying, so as a result, Simone and I sat in her car for a minute while I freshened up my makeup and waited for Cookie, who was driving behind us. When Cookie arrived, we all walked in together, and I guess we really did look nice, for we caught the eyes of many looking at us as if we had just come from the prom.

My precious mother was doing what she does best, and that's chitchatting with the guests. I could see her mouth going a mile a minute as she was talking to two gentlemen. They seemed to be enjoying her conversation, but we had asked our mother not to converse too long with the guests, as it kept them from eating their food. However, my mother was feisty. She wasn't going to let us give her instructions or tell her what to do. She loved us dearly, but she didn't hesitate to let us know who was in charge.

From my peripheral vision, I could see her looking at me and pointing to Randy's picture on the wall. My first thought was, *Please, Mama, not tonight. I don't feel like being introduced as the sad widow.* No sooner had I had the thought than I heard her call out.

"Cookie, Lisa, Simone, come here. I want you to meet somebody."

We walked over, and I turned on my smile. My mother went right into her story as the gentlemen stood up from the table to greet us.

"Remember my old boyfriend in New Orleans, the one I told you about, the one who lived down the street from me when I was a teenager?" my mother asked Cookie and me excitedly. "Well, this is William, his great-nephew, and this is William's cousin Raymond."

Simone, Cookie, and I greeted them with smiles and handshakes. We were happy to meet them, as we knew a few of their family members that lived on my grandmother's street in New Orleans.

My mother continued. "This is my daughter Lisa, who we were talking about. It was her husband that was killed," she said, turning her cheerful voice into a somber tone.

The gentlemen expressed their sincere condolences, with William looking really shocked. It was obvious that he was unfamiliar with the tragic news of Randy's death. It was then that his cousin Raymond spoke.

"She's the widow of the officer who had the big funeral I was telling you about."

William again expressed his condolences, but this time I could hear his quick New Orleans accent, the one that dozens of family members who live in New Orleans possess. Shortly thereafter, it was confirmed when Raymond shared that his cousin had just arrived from New Orleans, taking on a work assignment, which is why he knew nothing about Randy's death.

Simone and I walked back to a table far away from our newly acquainted guests, where I could sit down and rest my knee. Cookie gave me a pass on playing waitress because she knew I needed to heal from my knee injury. While my sisters hustled back and forth, waiting on the large party, Melinda kept giving me the evil eye for understaffing that night. I ignored her as Simone and I ordered champagne, laughed, and had fun girl talk.

It had been a hard, grueling night for me, and I was going to drink a glass of champagne with my dear friend and rest my nerves as I took in the ambience of the birthday party. I felt as if I deserved it. I was going to turn this night around and pull myself out of the depressed mood I had let myself fall into. My kids were with their cousin Amia, and I was spending the night at my mother's house, so I gave myself permission to have fun.

I chatted with another friend from high school, Troy Green. He had come into the restaurant and joined Simone and me at our table. He was there mostly to ask for donations to support his charity, and he was trying to make sure that I was going to participate this year. Sadly, Troy was a young widower too, as he'd lost his beautiful young wife to colon cancer a few years earlier. In her honor, Troy supports the American Cancer Society and promotes the Jog-a-Thon Relay for Life race.

Elevating my right leg and placing it on a chair for better circulation, I took a sip of my cold almond champagne and explained to him that it wasn't going to happen this year due to my injury. I told Troy that I would definitely make a donation, so he excused me, but he insisted that I be there next year. We sat and talked for a while longer.

I poured a glass of champagne for each of my sisters, who were hard at work and exhausted from running back and forth, with Melinda still giving me the evil eye. I was trying to put them in a better mood, or I knew I was going to hear about my inability to staff the restaurant correctly. I was feeling better and having fun with Simone and Troy, and I didn't want them to rain on my parade.

As soon as the restaurant closed, Melinda let me have it while downing her glass of champagne. I had to hear her verbal abuse for almost a minute or two before she sat down and talked with Simone and me almost as if nothing had happened, which is how my sisters and I operate. My parents taught us never to stay mad, and although we might get angry at each other, we say what's on our minds, get it straight, and then we let it go.

Randy and I also operated under that same biblical principal of forgiveness. I had people ask me the craziest questions because we had such a good marriage, like, "Did you guys ever argue?" My response was yes, and that's how we stayed married for over seventeen years. We had some intense fellowship, but the key to our successful marriage was always getting it right. Randy and I would stay up all night, until sunrise the next morning, to resolve an issue and get things right. The Good Book says, *Wisdom is the principal thing; therefore get wisdom. And in all your getting, get understanding* (Proverbs 4:7). Effective communication, understanding, and agreement are the keys to a good marriage. The Bible was our counselor, psychologist, teacher, advisor, and all the other things couples need to stay married. We also learned through losing others that life is too short to stay mad. And now I had learned through losing Randy that staying angry is absurd and foolish. Forgiveness is easy and good for the soul.

We all sat there talking, waiting for some of the stragglers to leave. William and his cousin Raymond were the only customers remaining in the restaurant, but it was okay. On the weekends, we always stayed afterward, cleaning up, closing, and balancing the cash register while having our own little private party. Raymond was chatting with Cookie, and they discovered that they knew many of the same people from New Orleans, which is actually common, since in New Orleans everyone knows everyone. We've learned that if you keep asking questions, you might find that you're related.

It wasn't long before Raymond's cousin William walked over and tried to get Raymond to be quiet long enough to tell him it was time to go. Raymond, who was quite a talker, wasn't planning to leave, so he ignored William. He was having too much fun chatting with the family and identifying the who's who in New Orleans.

Simone, Melinda, and I signaled for William to join us for a glass of champagne. We told him that he might as well have a seat because Raymond seemed ready to go on for at least another hour. William, being polite and aware that we were trying to close, refused to sit down but instead stood there and talked to Simone, Troy, and me for a while. Melinda had to count money, so she excused herself, taking her champagne with her.

William and I started discussing the fact that it was amazing how fate would have it that he would come to a birthday party as a guest of his cousin and meet his great-uncle's old high school girlfriend as well as his grandparents' neighbor. Before long, he and I were doing the same thing as Raymond and Cookie, talking about everyone we knew on Andry Street. We found ourselves getting excited about knowing some of the same people, and we forgot that others were at our table.

Eventually, feeling like a third wheel, Troy said goodnight. I felt bad for excluding him, but I made sure to extend an apology. My girlfriend Simone, who is naturally sociable, was vacillating back and forth between everyone's conversations.

William who had now been standing for almost twenty minutes, started to talk about how much he loved California. Our conversation was fun and different. I found myself talking about things other than subjects pertaining to the death of Randy. We talked and laughed for almost an hour. How ironic that just hours earlier, my heart felt weighed down with sadness, and now a complete stranger had lifted it up.

The next day was Sunday, and by afternoon, the entire family was back at the restaurant to celebrate my mother-in-law's birthday. My kids were present, along with Gina and her family, my mother, my sisters and their kids, and Simone. It was a special birthday party for a special woman. My mother-in-law had been through the fires and the storm and had handled all of life's obstacles with such great courage and grace. She was a strong woman and a believer in the word of God. She was certainly worthy of being honored for this birthday, and if the good Lord says the same … many birthdays to come.

We had a grand time at her celebration. Following the party, the teens left to hang out, and Gina, who'd accompanied my mother-in-law, was getting ready to leave. As usual, we were notorious for letting a party linger with long conversations. Although we had lost Randy, as a family we were still able to laugh and enjoy each other's company. Joy was still in our hearts, and for that we had to credit the good Lord.

In the midst of our laughter, one of our servers came over to the table and whispered to me that I had a telephone call. A Mr. Jones was on hold. I was baffled at first, not recognizing the name. Then I remembered that my friend Simone had told William, whose last name is Jones, that we were going to be in the restaurant the next day. For some reason, I became extremely nervous. Because I didn't really want to talk to him, I told the employee to tell him I was in a meeting. I had a slight suspicion that he had an attraction toward me, and although it was fun talking with him, I didn't want to entertain him in that way.

Within thirty minutes, a great-looking man walked into our restaurant, wearing glasses, a white shirt, black slacks, and a gray tweed jacket. It was Mr. Jones, accompanied by Raymond. I thought to myself, *Oh my God, he's back.* I tried to act as if I didn't see him, but Simone kept gesturing to me to look over in his direction as a server was escorting the two men to a table. Melinda kept whispering in my ear that William was handsome, and that I should go and say hello.

I wasn't surprised at Melinda's encouragement that I look at another man. Let there be no confusion—she loved Randy, and he was like a brother to her. But she didn't want me to live a life of loneliness. A beauty queen who had been single for a long time, she had just recently married for the first time at age forty. In fact, Randy had blessed her and Dwayne's marriage with a beautiful prayer. However, based on her own experience, she knew how hard it was to find a decent man, and she could tell by William's disposition and intelligent conversation that he could possibly be a good dating candidate.

I nudged her to be quiet, as I didn't want other family members to hear what she was whispering. I also didn't want anyone to think for one minute that I had an interest in William, because truthfully, I didn't. He was simply fun to talk with, a nice guy, and I have to admit that I thought he was handsome. But that's the extent of it. I wasn't ready to get into a relationship. It had been over a year since Randy's death, and I was still wearing my wedding rings.

In any case, I waved to him and his cousin from our table and added a smile. He and Raymond waved back. It was awkward because it was evident that William wanted to have some form of communication with me. Then I thought to myself that I should at least get up and say hello since he had called to try to talk to me.

With my injured knee, I limped over to their table and said hello. William gestured for me to sit and chat with them for a minute, so I did. Raymond moved over in the booth so I could sit directly across from William. I was nervous, but I felt that he was nervous too. I noticed that he had been eating our delicious crab cakes, but the moment I sat down, he stopped eating altogether. I apologized to him for not coming to the phone earlier, making an excuse that I was busy in a meeting. William seemed to accept my excuse without question. I then shared with him some fun things he could do in California, but I'm not sure if he was listening, for he abruptly interrupted me.

"Maybe you and I could go out sometime ... maybe to a movie or out to dinner."

"Well, I'm not sure. I'm really busy with the restaurant, and I'm trying to help my son get ready for college ... but we'll see," I said, rambling and stuttering like crazy.

"Can I have your number so I can call you?" he said.

"Sure," I replied, handing both him and Raymond a New Orleans Vieux Carré business card. I didn't want him to think I was interested in participating in his possibly flirty gestures. However, his attraction for me was confirmed when his cousin emphasized that it was William who wanted my contact information; Raymond gave me back my card. Realizing it was only the number to the restaurant, William took the bull by the horns and asked me for my personal cell number. I nervously wrote my cell number on the back of the card and gave it to William. He took it, smiled, and told me he would call me that night. He then informed me that he and his cousin were leaving, as they were late for evening services at a church located in Los Angeles.

"What church?" I asked.

"West Angeles Church of God in Christ, Bishop Blake's Church," he replied.

A Christian man, nice-looking, and employed. This could be the start of a "new normal." William called me that night, and we laughed and talked until four the next morning. We went out to dinner the following day and had a great time. It felt strange to have him ask me about the things I loved and cherished, for I had almost forgotten me. I was so busy running around and honoring Randy and the things that he had loved that I had suppressed or ignored everything I once enjoyed or deemed important. It felt weird, and I almost felt guilty for once again enjoying a life of normalcy, especially with another man.

Within a short period, William and I developed an ideal friendship, as we had a lot in common. He had a death to deal with—the death of a marriage—while I had the tragic death of Randy, a death I was still working through. We sought comfort and solace in each other's friendship, and before long, we were feeling things that could not be denied. I remember William saying to me, "Lisa, I know I am not Randy, but I am a living, breathing soul right in front of you. I just want to make you happy again."

Those words combined with his compassion were so heartfelt. I knew I had found a special friendship in William.

# CHAPTER 31

# Grace for a New Season

As of this writing, it has been four years since Randy's death, and our family has gone through many different seasons, literally and figuratively. We've had our sunny days and our winter storms, with additional struggles that were difficult to endure. Our second big storm hit us nearly two years after Randy's passing, when, in December 2009, we lost one of the matriarchs of our family, Mrs. Constance Simmons. Ms. Simmons lost her battle to cancer, and although she is greatly missed, it's good to know she has a home in heaven waiting for her. I take comfort in knowing that she has joined her son, Randy, and that together they are rejoicing in the glorious wonders of heaven.

Connie's funeral was beautiful, with everyone speaking so highly of her, and as always, the SWAT team was there with us, saluting and paying respects to this awesome woman of God.

A week after Ms. Simmons passed away, Randy's father, Mr. Dallas Simmons, took his rest. Mr. Simmons's burial was private, with his new family making all the funeral arrangements. To this day, the family knows nothing about the whereabouts of his remains. Interestingly, even in his death, it seems that Dallas Simmons is missing in action again. However, I am happy that he was able to make amends with his family prior to his death.

After almost thirty years, Connie and Dallas are able to unite and honor their son at the first annual Legacy of Love event sponsored by the Randal D. Simmons Outreach Foundation at Trump National Golf Club.

I'm also glad that Randy's mother and father were able to attend and witness a couple of the honors that were bestowed on their son prior to each of them passing. The light that shined on Randy was also reflected on them as parents, for it was their love, influence, good parenting skills, and biblical teachings that cultivated his character. Truthfully, their wisdom made him the rock-solid hero who is still honored today.

As the honors for Randy continued, I began making some crucial decisions in my attempt to reestablish a new direction for my life. After attending Glory Christian Fellowship for fifteen years, I decided it was time to leave the church. I felt ready for newness, but I also felt that my children needed a fresh start as well. That was later confirmed when both Matthew and Gabrielle confessed that being at Glory church was at times difficult for them. We all felt the same way, but we had never expressed it with each other. In truth, it was hard for us to sit in the church without envisioning Randy roaming through the church building. He had been a major figure there, so being at the church kept our hearts heavy and diverted our attention from the Sunday sermon. Thus it was a new season in our lives, and it was time to find another word-based church.

One Sunday morning while I was changing television channels attempting to find Pastor Joel Osteen, of Lakewood Church, I came across Pastor Joseph Prince speaking, and although he had a strong Singaporean accent, I could tell by his sermon that he was of the Christian faith. However, his accent was so strong that at first I couldn't understand what he was saying, and I had to listen really intently to grasp his sermon. I started to change the channel, but for some odd reason, my hand would not let me touch the remote. Maybe it was because Pastor Prince was preaching so well and with so much passion that I had to stop and listen to the word he was delivering.

As I listened, I soon developed an ear for his accent, and I eventually understood every word that came out of his mouth. He was preaching on "unmerited favor" and explaining how God gives us things that we do not deserve, but because of His unconditional love and grace, He freely extends His goodness to us regardless of our deservedness. I was so moved by his sermon that I went and purchased his book *Unmerited Favor*.

The book sat on the nightstand of my guest bedroom for about a month. I would peruse it every so often, slowly reading different chapters.

One evening when I picked it up, I studied the cover, which featured Pastor Prince's face. Then suddenly, without knowing why, Johnny Verman's face flashed across my mind. Perhaps it was because they were both from the Asian culture and looking at Pastor Prince reminded me of Johnny. A thought then occurred to me that if I ever saw Johnny again, Pastor Prince's book would be a good book to give him. I didn't feel that way because of his ethnic background but because of the powerful message that was written inside the book. I thought Johnny might find it useful.

In the following weeks, Johnny stayed heavily on my heart. He kept crossing my mind, and I remember wondering if he had ever come to an acceptance about the things that transpired. Several officers informed me that he was missing in action, as he was no longer with LAPD and had pretty much vanished from the face of the earth. Only a few officers occasionally heard from him, and one of them was my good buddy Officer Todd Rheingold, now retired from LAPD SWAT. I was genuinely concerned about Johnny since I was told the incident had left him deeply scarred. The last time I saw Johnny, I asked him if we could go to lunch, and he respectfully declined. I will never forget what he said to me as he stared in another direction, making sure he made no eye contact with me.

"I'm not ready yet, Lisa," he said. "I'm in a dark place right now."

One can only assume that Johnny was torturing himself about the events that went on at the house on Welby Way. My assumption came about because information received from several sources led me to believe that Johnny was in a painful place, and although I wanted so much to talk to him, I knew he was beyond any help I could give. I felt that his dark place was far from a place that anyone in the earthly realm would have been capable of reaching. He needed God's healing hands.

I couldn't help but feel as though Randy would have wanted me to give him a word from God to help him out of a life of darkness and to heal. Perhaps he needed to forgive himself or ask for forgiveness for things that were warranted or unwarranted. Possibly, whatever was hurting him was causing him to stay in a self-destructive mode. Maybe he needed to be relieved of any anguish or guilt he was feeling. I didn't know what it was, but what I did know for sure was that Randy would have wanted Johnny *saved*, in every sense of the word.

As fate would have it, Officer Todd, who was always in my corner and always understanding toward me, located Johnny. I was shocked to learn that he had received permission from Johnny to share his phone number with me. As you might well imagine, I couldn't believe that he was finally willing to talk with me and possibly even meet with me after almost four years.

I called him immediately, and Johnny answered the phone. It was weird hearing his voice, and both of us were a little nervous. We talked about the incident in general for a while and then agreed to meet in person at Starbucks in Torrance, California, the following week.

We had scheduled to meet at 11:00 a.m., I believe it was a Thursday morning, and as I prepared to meet him, my mind was racing with a million thoughts. I wanted to make sure I conveyed all the things I needed to say to him, and although I was eager to see him, for some reason, I wasn't really nervous. Perhaps it was because I was embracing my new normal, and I didn't feel as anxious about things as I had in the past. Possibly a healing was taking place, which was becoming apparent based on my attitude and behavior about things that happened on Welby Way. It might have been that I was coming to the end of the grieving stages that so many books talk about. I don't really know what made the difference, but I knew that I was excited about seeing Johnny. I was also excited about giving him Pastor Joseph Prince's book and some pamphlets I'd picked up from Pastor Bayless Conley's Cottonwood Church, located in Los Alamitos, California, where my family and I had visited a few times. My hope was that these materials as well as my words would somehow encourage him so that he could be free of any shame, condemnation, or guilt.

Just as I arrived at Starbucks and was about to walk in, I heard a voice call out my name.

Startled, I turned around and saw that it was Johnny. I hadn't recognized him from the back, but he was occupying one of the two chairs and a table on the patio of Starbucks. I had seen a man sitting there, medium in stature, with hair down to the middle of his back, but it hadn't crossed my mind that that man could be Johnny.

If I remember correctly, he had on a nice spring shirt with shorts and sandals. He reminded me of a California tourist sitting there basking in the sun on a hot, bright sunny day. It looked as if Johnny had lost some weight in addition to letting his hair grow long. It was obvious by the movement of his mouth that he was still undergoing treatment on his jaw because of the shooting. But overall, Johnny looked good as well as relaxed. I, on the other hand, looked the complete opposite: a conservative, stuffy businesswoman in need of some rest and relaxation. Nevertheless, we were happy to see each other and greeted each other with a hug.

I had Johnny's books and pamphlets in a gift bag and presented them to him. I told him that I thought they were good books that he could read and enjoy. He thanked me, and then we casually caught up on what was going on in each other's lives, as a lot had transpired since our last encounter. We were both headed in new directions, and we each had a new perspective regarding how we viewed the world and people.

After having an interesting conversation about the events in our lives, somehow the conversation was redirected to the events of Welby Way. Surprisingly, right up front, and without any prodding from me, Johnny let me know that if given the chance to do it over, the tactics they used that night would have been handled in the exact same way. Johnny stated "I do not believe anything went wrong, sometimes the outcomes of noble and well intended actions are not the ones that one would hope for." I didn't comment because Johnny had a story to tell and I needed to listen.

He then emotionally gave me a systematic account of every action that took place that night. He explained that "The core of SWAT tactics requires that although there may be an initial plan; the ability to be flexible and adjust on the fly is a much sought after component of superior movement." Johnny went on to say that "once a plan is (much like that night on Welby Way) put into motion the order of personnel becomes a secondary issue." In his opinion, the mix up or jumbled configuration of the stick order, when the officers enter in on Welby Way, is a moot point as it pertains to the outcome of the call up.

I could tell by the expression on his face that it was a painfully deep wound that had yet to heal. However, Johnny emphasized that the grief and sadness over an unfavorable outcome is not necessarily a reflection of doubt or regret.

To my understanding, Johnny was an outstanding SWAT officer. I was told that he was a great shooter and confident about his shooting accuracies and tactical abilities. In the past, I heard the guys mimic a statement Johnny made when joking around during training as he scored high on a shooting test: "I was born with a .45 in my hand," Johnny once said, referring to a gun and his bull's-eye preciseness.

I never heard anyone dispute his exceptional tactical skills. In fact, I heard that he was good at his craft and somewhat of a perfectionist. Maybe that could account for part of the depression that was weighing so heavily on him. Perhaps being a perfectionist and the team leader on call that night, Johnny felt that somehow he had failed the mission. Yet he said he wouldn't change anything that was done that night. I don't really know if that's the case, but what I do know is that Johnny didn't show up at two of the major award ceremonies, the Medal of Valor and the Purple Heart ceremonies, to be honored for heroism. I wanted to ask him about it to see why he was a no-show, but I decided not to ask. I considered that possibly it was because he didn't feel worthy of such an honor, which is very hard for me to say. Regardless, I didn't want to ask any questions; rather, I thought it best to let Johnny talk and express himself so that he could relinquish everything.

There were a few times that he got extremely emotional while we talked, so I tried to assure him that everything was going to be okay. I attempted to get off the subject, as seeing him still agonizing over what had happened four years ago really got to me. But then he said something that I had to question. He talked about how he and Randy went back and forth over the shock lock tactic. He told me that Randy wanted to shock lock the door and be one of the first to enter that night. Johnny, being the team leader, denied Randy's request. He said that he was adamant, and that he didn't want Randy in that position because it was time for Randy to take a backseat. Johnny said he was trying to minimize Randy's exposure by putting him toward the end of the stick. He felt that Randy, getting ready to retire in a few years, had paid his dues as far as SWAT call-ups, and that it was time for the newer SWAT guys to step up. I really didn't want to ask, but based on the conversation, it appeared that this was the only thing they disagreed about that night.

With the exception of this newfound information, Johnny's story was pretty much in line with a report I'd received from an undisclosed source and the tactics that were disclosed earlier. The report stated that Randy was supposed to enter in the fifth position and wind up in third position while making entry, and Johnny was supposed to enter third in the stick formation and end up entering second. Johnny stated that he didn't know where Randy came from or how he wound up being third in the stick. Because of this new information, I was left to wonder how and why the stick formation changed. What made Randy freight train his way up to the front of the stick? I was no longer questioning whether something did go wrong; instead, I was questioning *what* went wrong. I guess I'll file away that question and wait until I get to heaven so that I can ask Randy.

Johnny said something else extremely profound. He stated something like the following, and I'm paraphrasing: "There are some things that everyone does not need to know."

He was speaking about tactical procedures that the police and military employ.

"Disclosing too much information can fail or compromise a mission or get others hurt," he said.

He then gave the example of the Navy SEALS helicopter that had been shot down in eastern Afghanistan. There was speculation that too much information was disclosed, possibly giving the insurgents notice of the US Navy SEAL's mission. In his opinion, the same concept applied to SWAT and the tactics they practice.

His comments were certainly food for thought for the media as well as all the others who were seeking detailed information on the operations of SWAT, and perhaps even for me.

I considered what he said, and there was no doubt that Johnny had a valid and good point. Whether it was with good or bad intentions, once information was out, it could cause a great deal of damage. Like a rumor, it spreads rapidly and usually ends up causing some kind of catastrophic destruction. How could SWAT effectively accomplish a mission if the suspects or criminals knew how they operated? How can the ones who govern our safety stay ahead of the game when our opposition knows exactly what cards they're going to play?

Johnny's entire disposition had changed when it came to talking about things relating to tactical procedures being disclosed. He was serious, and you could tell that he stood firm on the topic and no one was going to sway him from this line of thinking.

We talked for a few hours, skipping lunch. When our conversation was wrapping up, I knew that Johnny had already decided that he wasn't going to leave without telling me about Randy's courageous character. Emotionally speaking, with his eyes filling with tears, he candidly and sincerely gave reverence and respect to his fellow brother, the one who came on SWAT around the same time he did. He said with confidence and conviction that Randy was a man of valor and would have done anything he could to save those hostages. He went on to say that Randy took his oath seriously and was fearless when it came to performing his duties as a SWAT officer. He also stated that Randy was unique, different, and an exceptional man, one that stood out among his peers. I could see as he spoke that those comments clearly made him question his own existence after Welby Way. Based on his tone and the way he talked, I feel that perhaps Johnny was experiencing survivor's guilt.

After his last comment, I decided it was time to end our conversation by sharing my thoughts with him about how I felt ... and why I believed Johnny and the others were still here. Looking him in the eyes, I said something like the following: "Johnny, I never blamed you or any of the other SWAT officers. I have the utmost respect for your line of work and profession. I just wanted to know in detail what happened. It was just hard for me to fathom, based on the little information I was given, that you all walked into a situation without having knowledge of where the suspect was located."

Johnny, sometimes making direct eye contact with me but mostly staring into the sky, listened carefully as I continued.

"I know you were adhering to the hostage rescue procedures, but going into a situation blind, in my opinion, was absurd. It's like playing Russian roulette with your life. Tell me, what is the purpose of running in and saving a life if you haven't taken measures to preserve your own?"

Johnny stared and pondered that thought and then said, "I guess that's the X factor."

He continued by painting a visual that I could personally relate to, by having me think about a concept and answer a rhetorical question.

"If you or a family member were ever in a hostage situation, wouldn't you want someone to expeditiously make entry so that you or your loved ones were rescued safely?"

Johnny knew the answer to that question so he continued. "That's what we do. That's what your husband did."

His comment was interesting to me because Johnny, SWAT, and most of the police officers all maintain the same school of thought as it pertains to the hostage rescue procedure: "It's part of the job." As Chief Beck said at one of the ceremonies I attended, "While others are running away from danger, police officers are running toward danger for the safety of others." I guess that type of mind-set gives them the title of being men and women of valor.

Johnny and I left on a good note. I wished him well and emphasized that God loves him and has a purpose and plan for his life as well as all the officers who survived the ordeal on Welby Way. I explained to him that he had to figure out what that purpose and plan was and continue on his journey. I told him that he needed to seek peace by forgiving himself and others, and asking others for forgiveness as well. Then I assured him that Randy was in good hands with our Lord and Savior.

We hugged and said our good-byes, and Johnny admitted that had he known our meeting was going to be that easy, he would have talked to me a long time ago. When he made that statement, all I could do was laugh and shake my head in disbelief.

All the way home, I thought about my conversation with Johnny. I can't say that talking to Johnny gave me complete closure, but at least I had congruent information, confirmation, and a better sense of what happened. I also realize that as a widow of a police officer, I may never see eye to eye with Johnny and the others about the hostage rescue deployment on Welby Way. However, Johnny gave me something to think about from a victim's standpoint, and I gave him something to think about from a widow's standpoint. I can definitely see things from two points of view, but I think I will always remain baffled by the course of action.

I have since come to realize that so often we allow ourselves to be tormented by lack of knowledge, distorted perceptions, or a fear that doesn't even exist. Maybe now, after a long overdue conversation, Johnny and I both can finally get some much-needed mental rest. And possibly my subconscious mind will be satisfied with the knowledge of having received confirmation about some of the things that happened that tragic night. Perhaps this meeting with Johnny would give me hope that my nightmares would soon go away.

As far as how the investigation was handled, for what it's worth, at least I let my concerns be known. In addition, I didn't just accept a general incident report as the final answer to my husband's tragic ending, but I gathered my courage and did everything possible to find out more, even if that made others uncomfortable. I no longer have to wonder, as I now have some confirmed facts that lend more clarity. And essentially, that is all I ever really wanted.

As I think about this entire tragedy while evaluating my journey from beginning to end, there are no words to express my sincere gratitude to the men and women of the Los Angeles Police Department and to everyone who supported my family and me as we journeyed in and out of seasons. It is my hope that we take challenging and tragic times as an opportunity to gain knowledge that will better equip us for the next tragic storm, keeping in mind that understanding leads to clarity and ultimately a peace of mind.

As I press forward and forge ahead, I will continue to honor Randy's memory and seek peace, sweet sleep, and guidance from my Heavenly Father. Most of all, I will remember and cherish the legacy of this man of valor who sacrificed his life carrying out the duties of 41D.

Randal (Randy) David Simmons
41D, Man of Valor
07-22-1956 - 02-07-2008

# *Epilogue*

I had an amazing seventeen and a half years with Randy. Those years are etched in my heart forever, for they hold their own special place, tucked in securely and well protected. A day does not go by that I don't think about him, especially since I see him in the faces and the smiles of our children. My heart aches when I realize that my son will never again be able to sit and watch a football game with his dad, nor will my daughter ever know what it would be like to have her dad walk her down the aisle on her wedding day. And as for me, I will never know what it would have been like to share a golden anniversary with Randy. But these are the cards we are dealt, and in spite of it all, I can honestly say that God is good and His mercy endures forever! We are grateful that He has blessed our lives with a remarkable man that enriched our lives. I wouldn't trade a moment of my life with Randy for the world.

Our goal today is to live a righteous life so that someday when our journey is over, we can join him and all our loved ones in the heavenly kingdom. Until then, we will *live*, continue to trust God, and fulfill the purpose and plan that He has for our lives.

As I end this book, I would like to share with you a scripture verse that I love, one that I have read hundreds of times. It resonates with me now more than ever as I journey in and out of seasons.

Me, Gabrielle and Matthew still smiling after the storm.

Gone, but never forgotten.

## A Time for Everything

There is a time for everything, and a season for every activity under the heavens:

**a time to be born and a time to die,**
a time to plant and a time to uproot,
a time to kill and a time to heal,
a time to tear down and a time to build,
**a time to weep and a time to laugh,**
**a time to mourn and a time to dance,**
a time to scatter stones and a time to gather them
a time to embrace and a time to refrain from embracing,
**a time to search and a time to give up,**
a time to keep and a time to throw away,
a time to tear and a time to mend,
a time to be silent and a time to speak,
a time to love and a time to hate,
a time for war and a time for peace.

—Ecclesiastes 3:1–8 NIV

Made in the USA
Lexington, KY
10 December 2015